Triune Well-Being

Triune Well-Being

The Kenotic-Enrichment of the Eternal Trinity

Jacqueline Service

LEXINGTON BOOKS/FORTRESS ACADEMIC
Lanham • Boulder • New York • London

Published by Lexington Books/Fortress Academic
Lexington Books is an imprint of The Rowman & Littlefield Publishing Group, Inc.
4501 Forbes Boulevard, Suite 200, Lanham, Maryland 20706
www.rowman.com

86-90 Paul Street, London EC2A 4NE, United Kingdom

Copyright © 2024 by The Rowman & Littlefield Publishing Group, Inc.

All rights reserved. No part of this book may be reproduced in any form or by any electronic or mechanical means, including information storage and retrieval systems, without written permission from the publisher, except by a reviewer who may quote passages in a review.

British Library Cataloguing in Publication Information Available

Library of Congress Cataloging-in-Publication Data

Names: Service, Jacqueline, 1976– author.
Title: Triune well-being : the kenotic-enrichment of the eternal trinity / Jacqueline Service.
Description: Lanham : Lexington Books/Fortress Academic, [2024] | Includes bibliographical references and index. | Summary: "Synthesizing trajectories across Orthodox, Catholic, and Protestant theologies, Service explores the constitutive factors for an ontology of Triune well-being. Not merely of theoretical interest, the book presses a new trinitarian theology of 'kenotic-enrichment' as essential, not only for divine being, but for the well-being of humanity"—Provided by publisher.
Identifiers: LCCN 2024012950 (print) | LCCN 2024012951 (ebook) | ISBN 9781978715158 (cloth) | ISBN 9781978715165 (epub) Subjects: LCSH: Trinity. | Religions.
Classification: LCC BT111.3 .S47 2024 (print) | LCC BT111.3 (ebook) | DDC 231/.044—dc23/eng/20240520
LC record available at https://lccn.loc.gov/2024012950
LC ebook record available at https://lccn.loc.gov/2024012951

∞™ The paper used in this publication meets the minimum requirements of American National Standard for Information Sciences—Permanence of Paper for Printed Library Materials, ANSI/NISO Z39.48-1992.

Contents

Acknowledgments — vii

Introduction — ix

PART I: AN ONTOLOGY OF TRIUNE WELL-BEING — 1

Chapter 1: The Logic of Divine Self-Enrichment — 3

Chapter 2: Beyond Static Perfection: Divine Self-Enrichment and Classical Theism — 31

Chapter 3: Beyond Deficiency: Enrichment from Divine Fullness — 57

PART II: THE ECUMENICAL THREAD OF DIVINE SELF-ENRICHMENT — 73

Chapter 4: Divine Self-Enrichment in Sergeĭ Bulgakov — 75

Chapter 5: Divine Self-Enrichment in Wolfhart Pannenberg — 95

Chapter 6: Divine Self-Enrichment in Hans Urs von Balthasar — 117

Conclusion to Part II — 139

PART III: THE DIVINE "DANCE-STEPS" — 141

Chapter 7: Kenotic-Enrichment: Characteristics and Implications of Divine Self-Enrichment — 143

Chapter 8: Epilogue: The Doxological Posture of Enrichment — 169

Bibliography	175
Index	193
About the Author	201

Acknowledgments

To my most treasured loves—Elliot, Audrey and Spencer. This book has been long in the making but your encouragement kept me going. Thank you for your unending support and love and laughter throughout some very difficult years. My greatest desire is that you will always know Him who is able to keep you from falling and follow His ways of truth and life. May you be bold to relinquish yourselves always to His trusting hands, and, in the giving away, may you find the enriched welcome of the beauty of our triune God.

To my parents—all I can say is thank you for every robust theological discussion around the dinner table since I was small. Thank you for stretching my mind but also for pointing me to the gospel. You gave me the most precious gift.

To my sister—you have cried, laughed and been patient with me over many years! Thank you for being a rock, never wavering in your support and love.

To my colleagues and friends—your conversations, your lives and your commitment to truth and beauty have seeped their way into this work. Thank you to those who have walked with me on the journey of discovery, who have revised and commented on drafts, who challenged and inspired me. Most special thanks to Grant Buchanan, Andrew Cameron, Jonathan Cole, Amy Erickson and Stephen Pickard. And thanks to my most dear "Stiletto Theology" sojourner, Anna White-Atkins—for all the profundity and fecundity of our joyful musings.

Introduction

Throughout history and across cultures, an observable phenomenon unfolds—the persistent pursuit of human *well*-being. Never content with the status quo, humanity demonstrates an almost insatiable desire to enhance its condition. Across the world, ideals and actions are instituted to enrich the human context of being and life. This inclination manifests in a vast swathe of interests, industries, and professions—spirituality, education, economics, law and justice, aid and development, health and beauty—to name but a few. Herodotus' *Histories* documents criteria for a blessed or happy life.[1] As does Aristotle, who identifies "happiness" (*eudaimonia*) and "living well" (*eu zēn*) as the highest goods for humanity.[2] Among his categories for a well-lived life, Aristotle includes security, material prosperity, children, a good old age, health, beauty, and honor and virtue, asserting that "all people agree that happiness is pretty much one or more of these."[3] In the Christian tradition, Thomas Aquinas affirms a similar impetus governing human life, arguing that "each and every human act aims at some good as its end."[4] For Aquinas, even though humans could be mistaken as to what is good for them, each seeks the same ultimate outcome—a form of well-being—and acts accordingly.[5]

Today, the contemporary landscape is not dissimilar. Human well-being is conflated with a range of concepts including "quality of life, welfare, well-living, living standards, utility, life satisfaction, prosperity, needs fulfilment, development, empowerment, capability expansion."[6] Implicit in all these ideas is a norm capturing an ideal that forms a teleological assumption of a satisfactory goal or endpoint. And yet, never far from these criteria looms a disquieting question—such as posed by Russian theologian and philosopher, Sergeĭ Bulgakov—"Where . . . lies the evidence for the existence of ends, especially ends that are satisfying to human beings?"[7] Bulgakov's incisive question gives rise to related inquiries: On what basis do humans advance endpoints that prescribe human well-being? Do goals of well-being have substantive rationales and ontological discoverability, or are they merely a matter of human whim and construction at any given time in history—forms of pragmatism based on nothing more than a mythical mirage? And even if goals of well-being are discoverable, can we know the constitutive characteristics by which these goals might be achieved?

For modern secular philosopher John Gray, the answer is stark. A secular concept of human progress is no more than an illusion, a mere "antidote to nihilism,"[8] and an attempt to bring meaning beyond the fact that humans, as animals, "are born, seek mates, forage for food, and die."[9] Gray's position appears extreme. Yet, in the absence of an ontological norm, telos, or purpose for humanity, it reflects a philosophically honest appraisal.[10] In a Western worldview, increasingly expunged of the notion of objective truth or divine revelation, the determining narrative for what constitutes "human well-being" is, at best, opaque. Questions linger as to the basis of humanity's desire to improve their condition and pursue well-being, as well as the discernible characteristics that condition it. Bryant Meyers simplifies the ambit of such an inquiry: "what human well-being actually is and how one goes about increasing it."[11]

It is at this juncture that Christian theology, with its tradition of recognizing that God's nature is primary to both initiating and shaping concepts of human well-being, becomes uniquely placed to provide a "why" and a "how" to these questions. Certainly, Augustine, working from theological and metaphysical reasoning, traces the good in "both great and small, both celestial and terrestrial, both spiritual and corporeal" to the Christian triune God, "the highest Good," and concludes that "no good things whether great or small, through whatever gradations of things, can exist except from God."[12] Aquinas, attuned to a similar ontology of divine goodness, likewise resolves that humans attain "their last end by knowing and loving God."[13] Crucial for both Augustine and Aquinas is the presupposition that God's eternal being determines all created goodness. More specifically, we might say, that God's own all-blessed *well*-being determines the characteristics that condition the *well*-being of creation.[14]

While Christianity indeed affirms the all-blessedness of divinity, in the shadow of apophatic caution it is almost taboo to articulate *how* God actualizes such a state.[15] Such a consideration is potentially seen as speculative overreach, grasping at an ever-unknown transcendence. Yet, one would think that given the nexus between divine and created goodness, such a question is vital to a Christian comprehension of created well-being. At the outset, such a question assumes that divine life is *dynamic*, that the implied movement of the interrogative of "how" is relevant to apprehending divine being. Asking—*How* does God actualize well-being?—assumes that God's perfection is not static, a petrified edifice of all-blessedness. Such an assumption is not unremarkable. Since the Cappadocians, Christians have recognized triune life as a unified *movement* of mutuality between the triune persons.

Yet, notwithstanding theological affirmation of triune perichoresis—the "divine dance"[16]—an in-depth synthesis of the "dance-steps" has not been pressed. That is, the "how" of the divine dance has remained somewhat vague. More commonly, theologians have reduced the idea of the mutuality of the triune relations to Social Trinitarianism[17]—a theological archetype to develop analogous conclusions regarding anthropology in the areas of ecclesiology,[18] politics,[19] equality in society,[20] gender and sexuality,[21] human rights[22] and disability.[23] What remains largely uncharted is a theological and metaphysical exploration of the constitutive features attending the dynamics of triune well-being. It is to this end that this book is purposed. Specifically, it examines the nature and operation of God's life and action in terms of a dynamic "enrichment," defined as *Divine Self-Enrichment*; the concept that God's life is an enriching dynamism of the perfection and fullness of well-being.

While providing a new conceptual category for systematic theology, Divine Self-Enrichment is not merely restricted to theoretical or dogmatic interest. Neither is the concept simply speculative or abstract. This is important to emphasize, as an exploration of the ontological patterning of the triune God can regrettably unfurl the critique that one's theology exclusively lingers in the "odour of abstract and unpractical theological speculation," thus rendering it all but useless.[24] To this I would say—the considerations advanced in this work, while representing higher-level theological logic, arise from the events of God's work in the world, from temporal encounters recorded in Scripture. These encounters originate and sustain a theological logic that is not mere abstraction, unrelated to embodied earthly reality. Neither is extended attention on the constitutive logic of God's *own* well-being an abstracted foray into positing a closed-off God of introspection or divinity wrapped up in a shallow contentedness of self, detached from the vicissitudes of creaturely life. Rather, the extended logic of Divine Self-Enrichment locates triune life as the transcendentally-intimate ground of all life. Divine Self-Enrichment ultimately drives to the heart of a doctrine of God that impacts contested issues concerning the very possibility for human enrichment.[25] To this end, the work here develops in the wisdom of Thomas Torrance, who reminds us that, "All technical theological terms . . . are to be used like 'disclosure models,' as cognitive instruments . . . to help us work out the 'inner logic' . . . But once we see the connections more clearly in this way, they have to be translated back into 'the flesh and blood' of reality."[26]

In commencing an initial appreciation of the concept of Divine Self-Enrichment, comparison to antonyms proves helpful—diminishment, impairment, or impoverishment. The Christian tradition patently does not regard the Trinity as relations of diminishment. Instead, Trinitarian theology postulates that the Father, Son and Holy Spirit, the giver of life and love, permeate enrichment, blessing and gift *in se*, and in the economic works of God. It is important, though, to highlight that recognizing the life of the Trinity as a dynamic of enrichment is not to impute a prior deficiency within God that requires further fulfillment. Positing a potentiality of improvement to divine life would indeed eviscerate the very notion of the "perfection" of God. Perfection requires no improvement. Rather, the logic that unfolds in this work is that divine enrichment is an eternal movement that constitutes the triune God's all-blessed life—a perfecting of perfection, glorifying of glory, or blessing of the blessed. This God is the antecedent source of *all* enrichment, and the ontological context and content for why and how humans engage in actions toward well-being. It follows, then, that determinations regarding what constitutes creaturely enrichment, and the processes by which it might be attained, are not arrived at from mere autonomous human reasoning. Rather, resonating from the very being and initiative of God, we move necessarily into the territory of revelation, which, for the Christian tradition, locates us in the midst of Scripture.

Although the guardrails of apophatic theology remain a relevant caution for speech about the divine, Scripture undeniably places God in our epistemological midst, inviting positive reflection. On this point, Katherine Sonderegger's theological approach comes to mind, where she argues that "the negative Attributes of God must in the end and properly be *positive*. They must be, in Barth's fine phrase, *Perfections*."[27] At its heart, this book echoes Sonderegger's affirmation and assumes with her "that in a very particular, but decided sense . . . Holy Scripture is the Word of God; that God is its Author, and that in reflecting upon the Word we will learn something of what the Divine Voice says to us."[28] Yet, unlike Sonderegger (with her focus on divine unicity), the reflections here affirm that the "Divine Voice" has imprinted in the testimony of Scripture a triadic pattern of grammar that reveals divine identity.[29] Certainly, the scriptural witness of the Incarnation transgresses an inherited Judaic view of a mono-singularity of divinity and compels a transformed understanding toward divine tri-unity.[30] It is this triune grammar of divinity, markedly attested in the New Testament Scriptures, that provides fertile ground for expanding a theological metaphysic of triune being. In reading the New Testament, it is necessary to resist a monotheism that reduces divine being to a numerically singular metaphysic. Such a reading arguably imposes an interpretative framework foreign to the New Testament grammar of the Trinity that diminishes biblical and theological interpretations.[31] With these cautions in mind, this work attunes to the biblical theater of triune relationality to understand *how* God lives the life of absolute *well*-being.

Evident in the New Testament are various depictions of gifting and receiving between Father, Son and Holy Spirit. This biblical attestation of the economic activity *between* the divine persons provides narrative gestures to discern characteristics inherent to God's eternal life. That is to say, God demonstrates who and *how* God eternally is through revelatory activity in the world. Karl Barth distills the logic here, saying: "That this revelation happened and how it happened is no accident . . . He is completely himself in this That and How."[32] Bulgakov, likewise, perceives a congruence between divinity and creation based on God's "replication" of himself in created non-divine existence.[33] While Daniel Hardy views the correspondence between God's being and God's acts in the world as an "energetically consistent congruence with the world by which he [God] remains himself."[34] In a similar vein, and without reducing the immanent Trinity to the economic Trinity, conflating divine and creaturely ontologies, or advocating a form of pantheism, this work infers a divine ontology from the economy of intra-triune relating. In so doing, it recognizes a congruity between God's eternal being and God's acting in creation; where God's acts in the world are simultaneously a self-communication. Specifically, I develop inferences about divine being that arise from the economic expressions present in Scripture that depict interchanges of gift and receipt between the triune persons.

Intratrinitarian gifting and receiving, as it unfolds throughout Scripture, may be identified in several ways. Wolfhart Pannenberg, for instance, identifies such a concept in the scriptural references of the Father "handing over" (gift) the kingdom to the Son (receipt) and the Son "handing back" (gift) the consummated kingdom to the Father (receipt).[35] Further, the New Testament Scriptures depict dynamic interactions between the Father, Son and Holy Spirit in the form of mutual praise and thanksgiving (Mt 11:25; Jn 11:41; Rev 19:5), gift (Mt 11:27; Lk 4:1), prayer and request (Lk 6:12; Mt 14:23; Heb 5:7), intimate knowing and belonging (Mk 14:36; Rom 8:26–27; Mt 11:27; Jn 10:15), glorification (Jn 12:28; Jn 16:14–15; Jn 17:24; 2 Pt 1:16–17), blessing and honor (Jn 14:28; Jn 8:49; Rev 3:21), mutual love through affirmative speech (Mk 1:11; Mt 17:5) and action (Is 11:2; Acts 10:38). The triune persons display enriching characteristics through encouraging, upholding and sustaining each other. Concordant with Trinitarian orthodoxy, these movements not only characterize activity distinct to each divine person but also constitute the dynamics of God's unified life. These movements reveal, in the words of Klaus Hemmerle, "*agape* itself . . . the rhythm of Being . . . the rhythm of giving that gives itself."[36]

Consider the account of the baptism of Jesus (Mk 1:9–11; Mt 3:13–17) that reveals a glimpse into the inner life of the Trinity that evidences the exchange of gift and receipt between the Father and Son in the Spirit.[37] Here, in this vignette, the continuity of the life of the triune God in the temporal world is heard and seen.[38] While slight variances in the synoptic gospel accounts exist, the key elements remain: the Holy Spirit physically descends on Jesus and a voice from heaven affirms the Son's worth through speech—"You are my Son, whom I love, with you I am well pleased" (Mk 1:10–11). Within this revelatory cameo is a glimpse of the eternal mutuality of the triune God, where the Father and the Spirit affirm the Son in love. Perceptively, David Bentley Hart identifies that the relational interactions in the baptism theophany not only reveal "God as *perichoresis*" but "also shows him to be the God whose life of reciprocal 'giving away' and 'containing' (χωρειν) is also a kind of 'dancing' (χορεύειν), and the God who is τερψιχόρη, delighting in the dance."[39] The God of the baptism is revealed as a God who "addresses and responds," who is, in the very inner life of divine being (*ad intra*), "the openness of *shared* regard."[40] Similarly, the account of the Cross illustrates the Son's unwavering trust in the Father's loving faithfulness, culminating in the final breath of surrendered words of "gift"—"Father, into your hands I commit my spirit" (Lk 23:46). The resurrection likewise serves as a powerful testament to the gifted sustenance of the Son by the Spirit (Rom 8:11; 1:4). While the prayers of Jesus in the Gospel of John also underscore the glorification of the Father by the Son (Jn 17:4) and glory received by the Son from the Father and the Spirit (Jn 17:5).

Although the multi-directional nature of giving and receiving between the divine persons is not the conventional locus for a theology of divine life (more often than not a prior commitment to the sole one-way relations of origin restricts such an interpretation of the biblical narrative), it is not unusual for theologians to infer that triune life is constituted through a mutuality akin to gift and receipt. Oliver Davies identifies that the "*dispossessive mutuality of self and other* is . . . a *trinitarian rhythm* of universal and personal love which was communicated first in the historical narrative of Father, Son and Spirit."[41] Lutheran theologian Christoph Schwöbel observes that it "is the actuality of *divine self-giving and receiving* that constitutes the life of the triune God of love, the primordial generosity anchored in the very being of the triune God."[42] Schwöbel's intuition regarding the gift and receipt inherent to the life of God compels a further logical question that, as we will see, becomes highly pertinent to the present work. Schwöbel asks—"Is there a *kenosis* in the eternal Trinity?"[43] What is interesting here, and to be borne out in part 2 of this book, is that influential theologians across the three major traditions of Christianity (Protestant, Catholic and Orthodox) all similarly identify, from the economic demonstrations attested to in Scripture, that triune gifting and receiving is *constitutive* for the divine life of absolute well-being. This conclusion compels two intriguing questions: (1) Do the triune economic demonstrations contain discernible features intrinsic to the actualisation of God's own well-being? And (2) do these features resonate in the ontology of the created order? By the conclusion of this book, these two inquiries are answered in the affirmative.

At this point, some may wonder whether such a project amounts to mere speculation or a tenuous handling of perichoresis to merely project anthropocentric views on God. Here, Karen Kilby's concern comes to mind: "Projection, then, is particularly problematic in at least some social theories of the Trinity because what is projected onto God is immediately reflected back onto the world."[44] Central to Kilby's criticism is a concern that analogies drawn from Trinitarian perichoresis are largely based on conjecture, amounting to little more than circular projectionism. While I agree with Kilby that scholarship in this area has often failed to utilize Scripture as a normative tool for understanding the nature of divine perichoresis, I do think it is possible to trace the revelation of God and attempt to provide an authentic, albeit provisional, understanding of what we may find. By examining biblical and theological material that address the relational activity of the triune persons it is possible to expand an understanding of the nature of God in a way that does not amount to mere projection. In my view, with Scripture and theological and analytical reasoning at our side, we can approach a deeper apprehension (not replete comprehension) of the patterning inherent to the nature of divine well-being.

None of this can side-step, however, the potential for problematic conclusions that can arise from interpreting the relations of the Trinity in Scripture.[45] There is a certain history contained with the Christian tradition where narrow readings of selectively chosen Scriptures culminate in warped theology and ecclesial praxis. The fourth century disputes surrounding Arius' interpretation of the relationship of Father and Son immediately comes to mind. More recent controversies exist within Evangelical circles regarding the interpretation of Scriptural accounts of the economic Trinity to draw ontological implications for the immanent Trinity. Bruce Ware and Wayne Grudem are two such theologians who impute eternal and ontic relations of hierarchy and subordination in the immanent Trinity from the economic.[46] Both theologians have faced substantial criticism, in particular by Scott Harrower, who defines Ware's method as an "ontological approach" with a "selective strict realist reading" of Scripture.[47] That is, based on selective biblical texts an "unqualified identification" is drawn "between the immanent and economic trinity" to assert "that God acts and relates as Father, Son and Spirit in the economy of salvation in exactly the same way that he eternally relates within himself."[48] Through this "ontological approach," Ware interprets the Son's relationship with the Father in terms of *subordination*, leading him to conclude that the eternal Trinity is likewise constituted by a subordination of the Son to the Father. Such a view, however, in stark contradiction to the consubstantial co-equality of the divine persons affirmed at Nicaea, cannot but amount to a position considered anathema by the early church.

In contesting Ware's problematic "ontological approach,"[49] Harrower advocates a preference for a "loose realist reading" of Scripture with a corresponding "epistemological" approach.[50] This "epistemological" approach restricts drawing ontological implications for divinity from Scripture by recognizing that the interpretation of the triune relations are "limited by both the nature of revelation and our possibilities for comprehending God."[51] Harrower is not alone in attempting to avert an eternal ontology of triune subordinationism by restricting ontic implications. Millard Erickson is another notable critic who uses a similar strategy.[52] Yet, as I will discuss with more precision in chapter 1, Harrower's and Erickson's strategies here are perhaps not the optimum path to take when it comes to interpreting the relations of the economic Trinity. Although Ware's reading strategy that leads to the imputation of hierarchy and subordination in the immanent Trinity carries significant negative theological consequences, so too does eliminating ontological inferences arising from the biblical depictions of triune relating. Certainly, formulating coherent ontological implications for the nature of the Trinity from Scripture requires more than Ware's reductive and "selective strict realist reading" approach. However, reading the Scriptural depictions of the triune relations bereft of ontic implication risks devolving into mere nominalism or Trinitarian agnosticism. What is required is that triune ontology be considered in light of the broader witness of Scripture, the testimony and wisdom of the church, and the theological consequences of various assumptions and conclusions.[53]

Mindful of the potential drawbacks associated with adopting either an "ontological" or "epistemological" approach, this book's constructive theology recognizes *both* ontological implications and epistemological constraints involved in interpreting the biblical narratives of triune relationality. Instead, this project is committed to the feasibility of discerning a *pattern* embedded in the triune narratives that is biblically and systematically coherent, ontologically demonstrative, *and* simultaneously open to epistemological mystery and apophatic qualification.[54] It develops the possibility of understanding the nature of the triune God by tracking the "true" without asserting the exhaustive and complete. Such a cautiously-certain epistemology is not at odds with the Apostle Paul's conclusion, "For now we see indistinctly, as in a mirror, but then face to face. Now I know in part, but then I will know fully, as I am fully known" (1 Cor 13:12).[55] Volf aptly summarizes a similar cautiously-certain path when he likewise concludes that the economic narratives of the Father, Son and Holy Spirit speaking to "each other and to humans," implies "there must be something in them before the creation of the world that allows such dialogue and interaction, *even if we stutter when we try to express what that something might be.*"[56] It has always struck me that a similarly hesitant interpretation of God emerges from Christological narratives as with Trinitarian ones. What is intriguing, however, is the heightened reluctance to infer eternal and ontic significance from Scripture for the Trinity than for Jesus Christ. Undoubtedly, hermeneutical caution is required, but it seems to me that no greater hesitation arises for what we might say of the Trinity than for Christology. Both have significant implications for the nature of God and downstream implications for ecclesiology and temporal life.

Attentive then to the New Testament relational patterning between the Father, Son and Holy Spirit, the chapters that follow engage the wisdom of Scripture, Trinitarian theology, Christian metaphysics and broader systematic thought to clarify the logic of an overarching theological concept I call Divine Self-Enrichment, axiomatically defined as—*God enriching God in the perfection and fullness of God*. Integral to the coherent logic of this definition, and to avoid various unintended theological and metaphysical snares, three key propositions are sustained throughout this exploration. These are:

1. "*God*" enriching "*God*": Divine Self-Enrichment affirms that through the distinct hypostatic activity of the triune persons, giving and receiving occur within Godself. This affirmation is consistent with a theology of divine self-positing. However, to guard against the inference of tritheism, this Trinitarian interaction is located in harmony with the well-established theology of perichoresis—the understanding that the Trinitarian relations are themselves the unity and essence of God. In this way, the free agency of the Father, Son and Holy Spirit, as they give and receive one to the other, is joined to a theology of "inseparable operation."[57] Thus, the interrelation of the divine persons, as they give and receive enrichment, is considered the *desideratum* of triune unity.
2. God "*enriching*" God: this dimension of the axiomatic definition seeks to clarify the characteristics of enrichment. It considers the defining hallmarks by which God enriches God. Simply put, it considers how enrichment occurs within the Godhead. The contention here is that the Scriptural attestation of a movement of gift and receipt between the divine persons evidences not only the relational structure of perichoresis, but crucially demonstrates its content. It follows that such identifiable relational content is constitutive for perceiving God's nature. Through tracing the dynamic contours of divine relationality, what becomes clear is that the unifying impetus of divine enrichment is personal self-giving; a kenosis.[58] In the simple being of Trinity, enrichment and kenosis are symbiotically unified. Such an integral dynamic,

constitutive for divine life, is aptly captured as "enriching-kenosis" or "kenotic-enrichment."
3. God enriching God in the *"perfection and fullness of God"*: Christian classical theistic understandings of the perfections of God, most notably, the perfections of simplicity and aseity, and the associated principles of impassibility and immutability, underlie Divine Self-Enrichment. Divine Self-Enrichment is not established through a contemporary Hegelian turn, positing divine enrichment from an understanding of a deficiency within God that requires fulfillment from the creation. Divine Self-Enrichment is, instead, the enrichment of the antecedently rich life of eternal divinity. Such a concept, however, does not exclude God's reception of enrichment from the creation—it merely precludes that God is made replete by it. Hardy recognizes this as the notion that creation's "praise perfects perfection."[59]

These three foundational suppositions regarding the inner logic of Divine Self-Enrichment signify that the fullness of God's eternal life is commensurate with the intratrinitarian "movements" of gift and receipt. Central to the dynamic life of divinity is an "enriching-kenosis." The kenotically enriching life of God is consequently revealed to humanity through God's actions in the world, first and foremost through the Incarnation and is that toward which all things move eschatologically.[60] It is important to emphasize here that God's essence, fullness or unity is not separate from the triune persons but subsistent with them and, as such, enrichment is not derived from God as a separate concept; it *is* the content of triune life. To clarify, enrichment is the omega of God stemming from the alpha of God; enrichment is that to which all things converge in God. As Augustine states concisely, "to whom it is not one thing to live, another to live blessedly, since thou art thyself thine own blessedness."[61] We might say, in the paucity of human language, that the glory of divine well-being is the founding principle, the process and the goal of divine life. It follows therefore that the foundational theological logic of divine well-being informs the ontological context for, and contours of, created well-being because, returning to Augustine, "no good thing . . . can exist except from God."[62]

Before setting out the broad contours of the argument of this book, it is necessary to clarify two key conclusions that arise from the logic of Divine Self-Enrichment that impact a more traditional concept of kenosis. First, the inherent nature of kenosis, vividly expressed in Christ, originates in the being of the triune God. Second, enrichment, not diminution, is central to the definitional substance of kenosis. These conclusions deviate somewhat from more common and popular understandings of kenosis. The reason for this deviation lies in the fact that the starting point and primary focus of this work is *Trinitarian* theology. This approach, commencing with the constitutive elements of triune well-being, contrasts with typical works on kenosis, that commonly commence with a Christological lens, emphasizing a renunciation or limitation of divine potentiality and power arising in the particularities of the Incarnation.[63]

This distinction in approach is worth clarifying, especially for those who might anticipate a particular engagement with conventional kenotic theologies. While many excellent works are dedicated to elucidating the nuances of kenotic-Christologies,[64] this present work takes a different route. Unlike more popular kenotic theologies, the considerations and conclusions developed here are not generated by a myopic Christological starting point. Instead, this project locates the kenotic expressions found in Christ within their ontic origin and destination—that is, the very nature of the triune God. Kenotic-Christology is, in my opinion, a derivative theology. Our understanding of the kenosis of Christ, though arising noetically from the economy of divine acting, fundamentally stems from the ontic precedence of the unified essence of the triune God. Such a perspective is recognized in the kenotic theology of Karl Theodor Albert Liebner (1806–1871). In his work, *Die christliche Dogmatik aus dem christologischen Princip dargestellt* ("Christian Dogmatics Portrayed on the Basis of the Christological Principle"), Liebner situates the ontic origination of the Son's temporal kenosis in the life of the Trinity.[65] According to Liebner, the kenosis of the Incarnation is preceded by an "eternal kenosis" located in the Trinity. In this eternal kenosis, the Son and Father, in the love of a mutual dependency, give themselves to each other as the primacy of self-communication.[66] Donald MacKinnon, likewise, emphasizes that the Trinity is the ontological ground for Christ's kenosis. He says of the Son's Incarnation "the very ground of its possibility is only approached if we dare to ask: *Quomodo Deus homo*. And asking that question, we are made to see that the seeking after that ground thrusts us towards the very arcana of the deity itself."[67] Donald Baillie, critical of conventional kenotic theories, also espouses an epistemologically "convergent" connection between Christology and Trinitarian theology.[68] In this cadence, he issues a reminder with contemporary relevance: "Do we not seem to have forgotten that the peculiarly Christian view of God is to be found in the doctrine of the Trinity? And if that is the case, ought not the Trinitarian conception be our starting-point in Christology?"[69] Ultimately, he argues, that Christology needs to be "crystalized" into Trinitarian conceptions, and Trinitarian theology needs to "absorb" Christological conceptions.[70]

Baillie's reasoning necessarily compels his fragmentary, yet pertinent, contention—that the nature of the triune God revealed in Christ's Incarnation "this outgoing love of God, *His self-giving*, is not new nor occasional nor transient, but 'as it was in the beginning, is now, and ever shall be, world without end."[71] For Baillie, Trinity clearly implicates Christology. And yet, if we accept Baillie's assertion that Trinitarian theology must also "absorb" Christological conceptions, we are left to consider how the embodied expressions of Christ's kenosis impact our notions of the Trinity. An immediate issue arises: whether traditional views of kenosis problematically ascribe a property pertaining solely to the Son (either economically or immanently) in a manner that undermines the unified essence and attributes of the triune God. If such a restricted attribution exists then it seems that a significant characteristic of divinity, that is kenosis, is functionally and ontically unrecognizable in the Father and the Holy Spirit. Such a position is perhaps the very type of issue Baillie's insight challenges—that Trinitarian theology seems resistant to "absorb" Christological concepts.

Part of a corresponding issue here is how we are to conceive the substance of kenosis. While kenotic theories commonly emphasize a renunciation or limitation of divinity associated with Christ's Incarnation, there are some theological adumbrations that do not narrow kenosis toward mere self-surrender or diminution of divine being. Resonating with my concept of kenotic-enrichment, some Christologically-focused kenotic theologies, in fact, regard Christ's kenosis as the *actualization* of divine being, not its diminution. In the Catholic tradition, Hans Küng associates divine fullness (πλήρωμα; pleroma) with kenosis, saying: "The 'Godhead' was manifested 'bodily' in the depths of the flesh and not in a God who dwells in a spurious sublimity; and the πλήρωμα, the fullness of the Godhead, was revealed in the emptying of his κένωσις."[72] In the Protestant tradition, P.T. Forsyth initiates considerations along a similar vein, speaking of an accompanying "plerosis" to Christ's kenosis. With soteriology as the backdrop, Forsyth understands Christ's kenosis not as loss of divinity but as the actualization of it. The deeper Christ's descent into kenotic Incarnation ("Every step he victoriously took into the dark and hostile land") the greater his Godhead is realized ("was an ascending movement also of the Godhead which was its base").[73] A similar contemporary perspective is present in Michael Gorman's kenotic Christology, where he interprets Christ's kenosis not as "emptying himself of his divinity (or of anything else)" but rather as Christ "*exercising* his divinity."[74] Gorman, assumes, from the revelation of Christ's Cross, an inseparable "kenotic character" of divinity, concluding that God "is essentially kenotic."[75] While Küng, Forsyth and Gorman, along with others recognize divine actualization, not diminution, as inherent to Christological kenosis,[76] and Liebner and Baillie locate Trinitarian ontology as the ground for incarnational kenosis, what is not undertaken, but now commenced in this work, is a robust exploration of the *logic* for such conclusions.

CONTOURS OF THE ARGUMENT

This book is divided into three parts. The first three chapters of part I expound the theological and metaphysical presuppositions and logic supporting Divine Self-Enrichment. Chapter 1 underscores foundational Trinitarian principles, including a discussion, inter alia, regarding the distinctions and unity of the triune persons to explore how God enriches God without collapsing into tritheism. Additionally, as Divine Self-Enrichment assumes the consideration of God's perfect being, not merely evidenced in the outer works of God (*ad extra*), but as an eternal movement of Godself (*ad intra*), the chapter canvasses the contemporary debate concerning the relationship of the immanent and economic Trinity. These deliberations necessitate further reflection on the nature of revelation to understand and construe the perfections of God and to apprehend God's relationship with the creation.

Chapter 2 considers the implications of the attributes of God for establishing Divine Self-Enrichment. In essence, Divine Self-Enrichment implies a dynamism within God. Yet, how should this dynamism be understood? What are the attributes or characteristics of God that regulate such dynamism? Modern theology is inclined to argue that the dynamism envisaged by Divine Self-Enrichment would require divine attributes antithetical to classical theism. The argument that is generally advanced claims that a dynamic divinity, constituted through intra-relatedness, is incompatible with divine simplicity (and its correlates). Against such reticence toward classical theism, chapter 2 demonstrates how Divine Self-Enrichment is not only consistent with but also secured by a Christian interpretation of the classical attributes. Divine simplicity, as it undergoes a radical development via the doctrine of the Incarnation, is specifically considered. In the process of this argument, a fundamental premise for those who reject classical theistic conceptions—the alleged capitulation of Christian thought to Hellenistic philosophy—is interrogated and shown to be a "straw-man" argument rather than robust engagement with early church thought. It was the Incarnation, and not an alleged static singular ontology inherited from Greek metaphysics, that initiated a radical reinterpretation of metaphysics that shaped the Christian tradition's interpretation of classical theism. In congruence with this tradition, the chapter demonstrates why the concept of Divine Self-Enrichment requires the theological guardrail of divine simplicity. Without divine simplicity, two key issues will result for a theology of Divine Self-Enrichment. First, a concept of a dynamically inter-related Trinity will collapse into tritheism. Second, the concept of a divine ontology distinguished and identifiable from the creation, that is, the concept of a *Divine-Self* (enrichment) will evaporate. The chapter, therefore, offers a way to move past the prevalent dialectic that views the dynamism of God's being as mutually exclusive from classical theistic concepts.

Chapter 3 continues to affirm Divine Self-Enrichment in consonance with classical Christian theism by addressing objections to the concept of "God *enriching* God" arising due to a preconception that this amounts to an admission of deficiency within God. Divine Self-Enrichment is not commensurable with a human understanding of enrichment—that of enrichment from deficiency. God's enriching life derives from God's fullness and self-sufficiency (divine aseity). Human enrichment, in contrast, acknowledges the absence of "fullness" and attempts to remedy such a state. Chapter 3 provides the foundational arguments for God's "perfection" and "fullness" that undergirds the axiom of Divine Self-Enrichment. The chapter argues that maintaining an ontological distinction between God and the world, consistent with divine aseity, does not, as popular theology suggests, undermine God's intense relationality with the world nor posit a narcissistic, isolated God. Instead, upholding divine self-sufficiency actually secures both the active relationality of God with creation and the stability of divine ontology (divine faithfulness). Aseity safeguards the logic that divine relationality with creation is founded on a fullness of well-being that is gifted *freely* to creation as love, not as a necessity for divine actualization. In other words, God does not need creation to be the fullness of divinity. The chapter concludes by considering the relationship between creation and a self-sufficient God. In particular, how the concept of the fullness of divine aseity allows creation to both receive enrichment from a stable source and gift enrichment back to God. Such a notion envisages creation's worship of God as a participative act that joins the divine life in eternally perfecting perfection.[77]

Following the establishment of key principles by which Divine Self-Enrichment is established, part II affirms and integrates these theological foundations through an analysis of Trinitarian theologies across ecumenical lines. Part II interrogates Trinitarian scholarship from Orthodox theologian Sergeĭ Bulgakov (chapter 4), Lutheran theologian Wolfhart Pannenberg (chapter 5), and Catholic theologian Hans Urs von Balthasar (chapter 6) to demonstrate that, despite their distinct views, all three theologians tacitly identify the conceptual parameters of Divine Self-Enrichment. Significantly, all three theologians (with some nuances) regard the guardrails of the tradition's interpretation of classical theism as necessary for construing the dynamism of triune life.

Part III synthesizes the considerations of the preceding chapters concluding that God's abundant well-being is actualized through the triune relationality of Father, Son and Holy Spirit *giving* and *receiving* each to the other in unifying oneness. The constitutive dynamic of this divine enrichment is concentrated in self-giving (kenosis). Simply put, divine life is constituted through intratrinitarian self-giving; exemplified as "enriching-kenosis" or "kenotic-enrichment." Importantly, the mutual kenosis identified between the triune hypostases is both gift *and* receipt, where receipt is also understood as a category of self-giving; a giving way, a relinquishment complementary to receiving. Understanding such a concept is very different—indeed quite alien—from notions of deficiency, or mere passive agency, associated with the divine hypostases. Furthermore, it allows us to distinguish kenotic-enrichment from (a) egoistic-enrichment (self-enhancement devoid of self-giving) and from (b) theological interpretations that reduce the concept of kenosis to a truncated-kenosis[78] (a self-giving severed from enrichment)[79]—the kind that feminists rightfully critique as too easily distorted to justify abuse.[80]

Attending to the "flesh and blood" implications for Divine Self-Enrichment takes place in chapter 7, whereby nascent features of kenotic-enrichment are identified and implications of this ontological *grundnorm* for human well-being are considered. Significantly, the analogous implications for humanity culminate on the horizon of worship—that sacred space where theological lucidity collides in the uncertain-certainty of communing with God. Far from exhorting a mere moral exemplar for a Pelagian-type human imitation, the concluding epilogue of chapter 8 frames the implications for humanity through the lens of worship—as creaturely communion in the patterning of God's own well-being. The pattern of God's being is, not surprisingly, the deep patterning for human life and the created order—entered into and actualized with increasing glory by worship that recognizes and orientates to the divine ways. A theology of triune well-being therefore holds central significance for not only apprehending the beauty of the triune God but for the situating the rationale and pragmatics of a thoroughly *Christian* response to the divine initiative for created well-being.

Finally, it is not lost on me that the journey of insights I am taking my readers on may challenge deeply held assumptions regarding the nature of perfection (that by common definition cannot admit of ongoing change and enrichment), commitments to an exclusive one-way relations of origin, or more familiar definitions of kenosis associated with divine diminution, limitation, or loss. Familiar conventions may indeed assist in "faith seeking understanding" (*fides quaerens intellectum*) but can equally operate as intellectual resistance, the kind that Thomas Torrance calls a "penultimate belief" that, at times, requires reconfiguration to accommodate the expansion of new insights.[81] It is my contention that the kenotic shape of triune well-being is not only scripturally, theologically and ecumenically compelling, but ultimately authenticated as the ground of all well-being in the *a posteriori* realm of creaturely worship.

NOTES

1. Brent A. Strawn, "The Bible and . . . Happiness?" in *The Bible and the Pursuit of Happiness: What the Old and New Testaments Teach Us about the Good Life*, ed. Brent A. Strawn (Oxford: Oxford University Press, 2012), 11.

2. Aristotle, *Nicomachean Ethics*, in *Aristotle's Nicomachean Ethics: A New Translation*, trans. Robert C. Bartlett and Susan D. Collins (Chicago, IL: University of Chicago Press, 2011), 1095a.

3. Aristotle, *Rhetoric*, in *Aristotle: On Rhetoric: A Theory of Civic Discourse* 2nd edn, trans. George A. Kennedy (New York: Oxford University Press, 2007), 56.

4. Ralph McInerny, "Ethics," in The Cambridge Companion to Aquinas, eds. Norman Kretzmann and Eleonore Stump (Cambridge: Cambridge University Press, 1993), 198.

5. McInerny, "Ethics," 201.

6. Matthew Clarke and Mark McGillivray, "Human Well-Being: Concepts and Measures," in *Understanding Human Well-Being*, eds. Matthew Clarke and Mark McGillivray (New York: United Nations University Press, 2006), 3.

7. Sergeï Bulgakov, "Osnovnye problem teorii progressa," Problemy idealizma: sbornik statei, ed. P. I. Novgorodtsev (Moscow: Moskovskoe Psikhologicheskoe Obshchestvo, 1902), 1–47. Cited in Paul Valliere, *Modern Russian Theology: Bukharev, Soloviev, Bulgakov: Orthodox Theology in New Key* (Grand Rapids, MI: Eerdmans, 2000), 233.

8. John Gray, *Straw Dogs: Thoughts on Humans and Other Animals* (London: Granta Books, 2002), 29.

9. Gray, *Straw Dogs*, 38.

10. Craig argues that in the absence of a divine good establishing a moral ontology, there "is no foundation . . . for objective values, duties and accountability." See William Lane Craig, "The Kurtz/Craig Debate: Is Goodness without God Good Enough?" in *Is Goodness without God Good Enough? A Debate on Faith, Secularism and Ethics*, ed. Robert K. Garcia and Nathan L. King (Lanham, MD: Rowman & Littlefield Publishers, 2009), 36.

11. Bryant Meyers, *Walking with the Poor: Principles and Practices of Transformational Development* (New York: Orbis Books, 2011), 31.

12. Augustine, *Concerning the Nature of Good: Against the Manicheans*. NPNF 1/4: 351.

13. Thomas Aquinas, *Summa Theologiae* IaIIae 1.8, trans. Fathers of the English Dominican Province (Westminster: Christian Classics, 1981), www.corpusthomisticum.org/sth0000.html.

14. Here, Daniel Hardy's concept of "attraction" comes to mind, described as "the direction of creatures toward their creator . . . creatures are not created 'moving away' from the creator but moving toward him. God creates things toward him, not away from him." Daniel W. Hardy et al., *Wording a Radiance: Parting Conversation on God and the Church* (London: SCM Press, 2010), 46.

15. Ellen Charry and Elaine Padilla have independently constructed theologies of divine happiness and divine enjoyment. Both theological constructions, however,

reject divine aseity, a position that I believe holds negative consequences for understanding divine being. See Ellen T. Charry, *God and the Art of Happiness* (Grand Rapids, MI: Eerdmans, 2010); Elaine Padilla, *Divine Enjoyment: A Theology of Passion and Exuberance* (Bronx, NY: Fordham University Press, 2014).

16. Catherine Mowry LaCugna, *God for Us: The Trinity and Christian Life* (San Francisco: HarperSanFrancisco, 1991), 271. Paul Fiddes identifies that the metaphor of the divine dance was first used in the Middle Ages as an image of perichoresis. Paul S. Fiddes, *Participating in God: A Pastoral Doctrine of the Trinity* (London: Darton, Longman & Todd, 2000), 72.

17. For more on social Trinitarianism see Richard Swinburne, "The Social Theory of the Trinity," *Religious Studies* (2018): 1–19; Cornelius Plantinga, "Social Trinity and Tritheism," in *Trinity, Incarnation and Atonement*, eds. R. J. Feenstra and C. Plantinga (Notre Dame: University of Notre Dame, 1989): 21–47; William Hasker, "Objections to Social Trinitarianism," *Religious Studies* 46, no.1 (2010): 421–39.

18. Miroslav Volf, *After Our Likeness: The Church as the Image of the Trinity* (Grand Rapids, MI: Eerdmans, 1998). See also C. Gunton and C. Schwöbel, *Persons, Divine and Human: King's College Essays in Theological Anthropology* (Edinburgh: T&T Clark, 1991); Colin Gunton, *The Promise of Trinitarian Theology* (Edinburgh: T&T Clark, 1991); Daniel L. Migliore, "The Communion of the Triune God: Towards a Trinitarian Ecclesiology in Reformed Perspective," in *Reformed Theology: Identity and Ecumenicity*, eds. Wallace. M. Alston, Jr. and Michael Welker (Grand Rapids, MI: Eerdmans, 2003): 140–54.

19. Leonardo Boff, *Trinity and Society* (Tunbridge Wells: Burns & Oates, 1988).

20. Jürgen Moltmann, *The Trinity and the Kingdom of God: The Doctrine of God*, trans. Margaret Kohl (Minneapolis: Fortress Press, 1993) originally published as *Trinität und Reich Gottes.* Munich: Chr. Kaiser Verlag, 1980; Jürgen Moltmann, "The Reconciling Power of the Trinity in the Life of the Church and the World," *Triune God: Love, Justice, Peace,* ed. K. M. Tharakan (Mavelikkara: Youth Movement of Indian Orthodox Church, 1989), 32.

21. Elizabeth Johnson, *She Who Is: The Mystery of God in Feminist Theological Discourse* (New York: Crossroad Publishing Company, 1993); Eugene F. Rogers, *Sexuality and the Christian Body: Their Way into the Triune God* (Malden, MA: Blackwell, 1999); Margaret Farley, "New Patterns of Relationships: Beginning of a Moral Revolution," *Theological Studies* 36, no.4 (1975): 645.

22. Michael J. Himes and Kenneth R. Himes, *Fullness of Faith: The Public Significance of Theology* (New York: Paulist Press, 1993).

23. Myroslaw Tataryn and Maria Truchan-Tataryn, *Discovering Trinity in Disability: A Theology for Embracing Difference* (Maryknoll, NY: Orbis Books, 2013); Nancy Eiesland, *The Disabled God: Toward a Liberatory Theology of Disability* (Nashville, TN: Abingdon Press, 1994); and regarding a critique of Trinity and disability see Jacqueline Clark [Service], "'A Disabled Trinity:' Help or Hindrance to Disability Theology?" *St Mark's Review*, 232 (2015): 50–64.

24. Jürgen Moltmann, *A Broad Place: An Autobiography* (Minneapolis: Fortress Press, 2008), 231.

25. For further thinking in relation to implications of Divine Self-Enrichment for Christian engagement in the sphere of International Aid and Development, see Jacqueline Service, "*Divine Self-Enrichment and Human Well-Being: A Systematic Theological Inquiry, with Special Reference to Development and Humanitarian Aid*" (PhD diss., Charles Sturt University, Australia, 2018).

26. Thomas. F. Torrance, *Incarnation: The Person and Life of Christ*, ed. Robert T. Walker (Downers Grove, IL: IVP Academic, 2008), 233.

27. Katherine Sonderegger, "The God We Worship; the Worship We Owe God," *St Mark's Review*, no. 250 (2019): 18. Original italics.

28. Sonderegger, "The God We Worship," 18.

29. Katherine Sonderegger, "The Perfection of Divine Love," in *Systematic Theology: The Doctrine of God, volume 1* (Minneapolis: Fortress Press, 2015), 481.

30. Various scholars affirm a triadic pattern of divinity in the New Testament. See C. Kavin Rowe, "The Trinity in the Letters of St Paul and Hebrews," in *The Oxford Handbook of the Trinity*, eds. Gilles Emery and Matthew Levering (Oxford University Press: Oxford, 2011), 41–54; Wainwright, *The Trinity in the New Testament (London: SPCK, 1975)*; Wesley Hill, *Paul and the Trinity: Persons, Relations and the Pauline Letters* (Grand Rapids, MI: Eerdmans, 2015); Craig A. Blaising, "Creedal Formulation as Hermeneutical Development: A Re-examination of Nicea," *Pro Ecclesia* 19, no. 4 (2010): 371–88; Lewis Ayres "A Christological Epistemology," in *Augustine and the Trinity* (Cambridge: Cambridge University Press, 2010), 142–70; and Matthew Bates in his book, *The Birth of the Trinity: Jesus, God, and Spirit in New Testament and Early Christian Interpretations of the Old Testament* (Oxford: Oxford University Press, 2015) advocates an exegetical strategy based on the biblical relationality between the divine persons (*prosópon*) called "prosopological exegesis."

31. Wesley Hill presents such a case, arguing that the suspicion of biblical critics toward Trinitarian hermeneutics is, at times, born from a "view of reason's priority in the process of biblical interpretation" which results in monotheistically interpreted scriptural passages (such as 1 Cor 8:6) being favored over, what may be considered as the "manifestly illogical notion of a plurality of persons subsisting in a numerically one God." See Hill, *Paul and the Trinity*, 21. Dahl also highlights that a lack continuity between New Testament theology and scriptural interpretation has contributed to the diminished use of Trinitarian exegetical strategies. Nils Alstrup Dahl, "Trinitarian Baptismal Creeds and New Testament Christology," in *Jesus the Christ: The Historical Origins of Christological Doctrine,* ed. Donald H. Juel (Minneapolis: Fortress Press, 1991), 167. Rowe is critical of those who reject employing a Trinitarian framework to interpret Scripture on the basis that it imposes an "artificial schema upon the New Testament." Rowe, "The Trinity in the Letters of St Paul and Hebrews," 44.

32. Karl Barth, *Church Dogmatics: The Doctrine of the Word of God. Part 1*, vol. 1, eds. G. W. Bromiley and T. F. Torrance (Edinburgh: T&T Clark, 1975), 297. Herein *CD I/1*.

33. Sergeï Bulgakov, *The Lamb of God*, trans. Boris Jakim (Grand Rapids, MI: Eerdmans, 2002), 149.

34. Daniel Hardy, *God's Ways with the World*: *Thinking and Practising Christian Faith* (Edinburgh: T&T Clark, 1996), 81.

35. Wolfhart Pannenberg, *Systematic Theology, volume 1*, trans. Geoffrey W. Bromiley (Grand Rapids, MI: Eerdmans, 1991), 313.

36. Klaus Hemmerle, *Theses towards a Trinitarian Ontology*, trans. Stephen Churchyard (Brooklyn, NY: Angelico Press, 2020), 35.

37. Thomas G. Weinandy, *The Father's Spirit of Sonship: Reconceiving the Trinity* (Edinburgh: T. & T. Clark, 1995), 27–29. See also Hart, *The Beauty of the Infinite*, 169, where he opines that if "the economic Trinity is God in himself, graciously extending the everlasting 'dance' of his love to embrace creation in its motion, then one dare not exclude from one's understanding of the trinity the idea, however mysterious, of *a reciprocal Thou*." My italics.

38. Arthur. W. Wainwright, *The Trinity in the New Testament* (London: SPCK, 1975), 251. Wainwright identifies the triadic structure of the baptism saying that "the event itself is one which has a threefold pattern . . . in which the triad is prominent."

39. David Bentley Hart, *Beauty of the Infinite: The Aesthetics of Christian Truth* (Grand Rapids, MI: Eerdmans, 2003), 175.

40. Hart, *Beauty of the Infinite*, 168–69. My italics.

41. Oliver Davies, *A Theology of Compassion* (London: SCM Press, 2001), 220.

42. Christoph Schwöbel, "The Generosity of the Triune God and the Humility of the Son," in *Kenosis: The Self-Emptying of Christ in Scripture and Theology*, eds. Paul T. Nimmo, and Keith L. Johnson (Chicago: Wm. B. Eerdmans Publishing Co., 2022), 223.

43. Christoph Schwöbel, "'Taking the Form of a Servant': Kenosis and Divine Self-Giving in Thomas Aquinas and Martin Luther," *Angelicum* 98, no. 1 (2021), 55.

44. Karen Kilby, "Perichoresis and Projection: Problems with Social Doctrines of the Trinity," *New Blackfriars* 81, no. 957 (2000): 442.

45. Timothy Wiarda outlines scholarly objections to drawing ontological inferences from the biblical conversations between the Father and Son in "Theological Exegesis and Internal Trinitarian Relations," *Scottish Journal of Theology* 76, no. 2 (2023): 101. See for example, Stephen R. Holmes, "Classical Trinity: Evangelical Perspective," in *Two Views on the Doctrine of the Trinity,* ed. Jason S. Sexton (Grand Rapid, MI: Zondervan Academic, 2014), 44.

46. Bruce A. Ware, "How Shall We Think about the Trinity?" in *God under Fire*, eds. Douglas S. Huffman and Eric L. Johnson (Grand Rapids, MI: Zondervan, 2002); Bruce A. Ware, *Father, Son and Holy Spirit: Relationships, Roles and Relevance* (Wheaton. IL: Crossway, 2005); Wayne Grudem, *Systematic Theology: An Introduction to Biblical Doctrine* (Grand Rapids, MI: Zondervan, 1994); Wayne Grudem, *Biblical Foundation for Manhood and Womanhood* (Wheaton, IL: Crossway, 2002).

47. Scott Harrower, "Bruce Ware's Trinitarian Methodology," in *Trinity without Hierarchy: Reclaiming Nicene Orthodoxy in Evangelical Theology,* eds. Michael F. Bird and Scott D. Harrower (Grand Rapids, MI: Kregel Academic, 2019), 311. See also Kevin Giles, *Jesus and the Father: Modern Evangelical Reinvent the Doctrine of the Trinity* (Grand Rapids, MI: Zondervan, 2006).

48. Harrower, "Bruce Ware's Trinitarian Methodology," 312.

49. Harrower outlines a number of problems faced by a "strict realist reading" in Scott Harrower, *Trinitarian Self and Salvation: An Evangelical Engagement with Rahner's Rule* (Eugene, OR: Pickwick, 2012), 23–24.

50. Harrower, "Bruce Ware's Trinitarian Methodology," 313.

51. Harrower, "Bruce Ware's Trinitarian Methodology," 313.

52. Robert Letham and Kevin Giles, "Is the Son Eternally Submissive to the Father? An Egalitarian/Complementarian Debate" (Christian Research Institute, 2009), 14; Kevin Giles, *Jesus and the Father: Modern Evangelicals Reinvent the Doctrine of the Trinity* (Grand Rapids, MI: Zondervan, 2006), 39; Erickson, Millard J. *Who Is Tampering with the Trinity? An Assessment of the Subordination Debate.* Grand Rapids, MI: Kregel, 2009.

53. See for various views of scriptural and Trinitarian exegetical considerations Kevin J. Vanhoozer and Daniel J. Treier, *Theology and the Mirror of Scripture: A Mere Evangelical Account* (Downers Grove, IL: IVP, 2015); Fred Sanders, *The Image of the Immanent Trinity: Rahner's Rule and the Theological Interpretation of Scripture. Issues in Systematic Theology* 12 (New York: Peter Lang, 2005); Miroslav Volf, "Apophatic Social Trinitarianism: Why I Continue to Espouse 'a Kind of' Social Trinitarianism," *Political Theology: The Journal of Christian Socialism* 22, no. 5 (2021): 407–22; Wiarda, "Theological Exegesis," *Scottish Journal of Theology* 76, no. 2 (2023): 99–111.

54. For possible apophatic qualifiers see Karen Kilby, *God, Evil and the Limits of Theology* (London: T&T Clark Bloomsbury, 2020).

55. Holman translation.

56. Miroslav Volf, *Exclusion and Embrace, Revised and Updated: A Theological Exploration of Identity, Otherness, and Reconciliation* (Nashville, TN: Abingdon Press, 2019), 258. My italics.

57. For more information see R. P. C. Hanson, *The Search for the Christian Doctrine of God: The Arian Controversy 318–381 AD* (Edinburgh: T&T Clark, 1988), 694–99, 734–37.

58. Davies notes a similar enriching movement accompanying kenosis, as "self-emptying on behalf of another" or "self-displacement . . . [*that is*] *enriched existence.*" Davies ultimately traces this definition to the nature of God and the foundation for the Christian life, saying the "iconic beauty of the authentic Christian life is itself founded on the prior movement of a divine kenosis." Davies does not, however, expound a further Trinitarian logic. Davies, *A Theology of Compassion*, 220, 275.

59. Daniel W. Hardy, *Jubilate: Theology in Praise*, ed. David Ford (London: Darton, Longman & Todd, 1984), 6.

60. Based on the premise that Jesus Christ embodies the exact representation of divinity (Heb 1:1), a preliminary application of the kenotic-enrichment of divine being could infuse new significance into the Incarnation of Philippians 2:5–11. Is it possible that the depiction of Christ's Incarnation in the *Carmen Christi* elucidates a deep patterning of the nature of the triune God? Where divinity in the triune life is not grasped in agonism ("did not consider equality with God something to be grasped" v6), but rather divinity is lived in self-emptying ("emptied himself" v7), vulnerability and humility ("he humbled himself" v8), that results in gifted exaltation

("Therefore God exalted him" v9) and other-centered praise for the "enrichment" of God ("every tongue confess that Jesus Christ is Lord, to the glory of God the Father" v11). Approaching this passage through a hermeneutic of triune kenotic-enrichment, reveals the potential for the pericope to unveil a symbiotic unity of kenosis and enrichment. Where, not only Christ's descent into kenosis (κενόω) in verse 7 is demonstrative of the eternal ontology of divine being, but so the resulting enriching exaltation (ὑπερυψόω) described in verse 9.

61. Augustine, "The Confessions of Saint Augustine," in *A Select Library of Nicene and Post-Nicene Fathers of the Christian Church: 1886–1889*, 28 vols. in 2 series, eds. Philip Schaff and H. Wace (Reprinted Grand Rapids, MI: Eerdmans, 1956), 191. (Herein *NPNF*).

62. Augustine, *Concerning the Nature of Good: Against the Manicheans*. *NPNF* 1/4: 351.

63. David Law summarizes the fundamental question agitating early kenotic theologians as "How can the divine, pre-existent Logos become a human being and live a genuine human life without undermining his divine nature?" David R. Law, "Kenotic Christology," in *Blackwell Companion to Nineteenth Century Theology*, ed. David Fergusson (Oxford: Wiley-Blackwell, 2010), 254. Niels Henrik Gregersen, considering divine kenosis in both Incarnation and Creation, identifies four main categories of kenotic models that range from "voluntarily abdicating," "radical metamorphosis or historization," "kenotically refrains from the exercise of detailed predetermination in order to give room for creaturely self-development," to "God neither withdraws from the world nor gives up divine power, but actualizes divine love in the history with God's beloved creatures." Niels Henrik Gregersen, "Deep Incarnation and Kenosis: In, With, Under, and As: A Response to Ted Peters," *Dialog: A Journal of Theology* 52, no. 3 (2013): 256–57.

64. Modern kenotic theories proliferated in Germany in the mid-nineteenth century followed by movements in Britain and Scotland. For general canvassing of historical and theological kenotic theories see David Brown, *Divine Humanity: Kenosis Explored and Defended* (London: SCM, 2011) and Law, "Kenotic Christology," 251–79. For contemporary considerations see John Polkinghorne, ed., *The Work of Love: Creation as Kenosis* (Grand Rapids, MI: Eerdmans Publishing Co, 2001); Stephen C. Evans, ed., *Exploring Kenotic Christology: The Self-Emptying of God* (Oxford UK: Oxford University Press, 2006); Paul T. Nimmo and Keith L. Johnson, *Kenosis: The Self-Emptying of Christ in Scripture and Theology* (Chicago: Wm. B. Eerdmans Publishing Co, 2022); and Samuel Youngs, *Making Christ Real: The Peril and Promise of Kenosis* (Eugene, OR: Pickwick Publishing, 2022).

65. K. T. A. Liebner, *Die christliche Dogmatik aus dem christologischen Princip dargestellt*, vol. I/1: *Christologie oder die christologische Einheit des dogmatischen Systems* (Göttingen: Vandenhoeck und Ruprecht, 1849). Law states that Liebner regards this eternal kenosis as mutual, consisting of "the Son's self-emptying in relation to the Father, and the Father's eternal self-surrender to the Son. Father and Son exist in a relationship of reciprocity in which they mutually subordinate themselves to each other." Law, "Kenotic Christology," 259.

66. Liebner, *Die christliche Dogmatik*, 330; 129–30.

67. Donald MacKinnon, "Reflections on Donald Baillie's Treatment of the Atonement," in *Christ, Church and Society: Essays on John Baillie and Donald Baillie,* ed. David Fergusson (Edinburgh: T&T Clark, 1993), 121. See also Timothy G. Connor, *The Kenotic Trajectory of the Church in Donald MacKinnon's Theology: From Galilee to Jerusalem to Galilee* (London: T&T Clark, 2013), chapter 5.

68. D. M. Baillie, *God Was In Christ* (London: Faber and Faber Ltd, 1955), 144.

69. Baillie, *God was in Christ*, 122.

70. Baillie, *God was in Christ*, 144.

71. Baillie, *God was in Christ*, 123. My italics.

72. H. Küng, *The Incarnation of God: An Introduction to Hegel's Theological Thought as Prolegomena to a Future Christology* (Edinburgh: T. & T. Clark, 1987), 451.

73. P. T. Forsyth, *The Person and Place of Jesus Christ* (London: Independent Press, 1948), 349.

74. Michael J. Gorman *Inhabiting the Cruciform God: Kenosis, Justification, and Theosis in Paul's Narrative Soteriology* (Grand Rapids, MI: William B. Eerdmans Publishing, 2009), 28.

75. Gorman, *Inhabiting the Cruciform God*, 28 and footnote 67.

76. Timothy Herbert highlights that Moltmann likewise considers divine kenosis, not as diminution, but as "the power of . . . God's potentiality . . . not in death or loss but in resurrection and renaming." T. D. Herbert, *Kenosis and Priesthood: Towards a Protestant Re-evaluation of the Ordained Ministry* (Carlisle, UK: Paternoster, 2009). Samuel Youngs provides a further useful discussion in "Rehabilitating Kenotic Christology: A Critically Constructive Examination and Strategic Systematization of Jürgen Moltmann's Doctrine of Christ," (PhD diss., King's College London, 2017), 255ff.

77. Hardy, *Jubilate*, 6.

78. As will be argued, the theological guardrails of simplicity and aseity are necessary to guard against a logic that results in God being imputed with deficiency. Without such a philosophically framed theology of divine being, the symptoms of truncated-kenosis or egoistic-enrichment emerge. For example, if God is not self-sufficiently simple, in other words, God is contingent on creation for being, God is perceived to derive enrichment from creation to compensate for a self-deficiency. From this, a logical conclusion could be that God is selfishly using the creation for divine satisfaction and divine fulfillment. Such a theological framework would, I think, necessarily result in the charge of divine egoistic-enrichment. Similarly, if God's self-giving is merely a contingent response to the creation (where evil is the necessary impetus for God's self-giving goodness, thus, God's being requires evil to be good, thus, suffering must be metaphysically necessary to God's being) a view of divine truncated-kenosis may logically form; whereby self-giving cannot be symbiotic with divine *life*. Divine kenosis under this theological construct will struggle to avoid a view of God's self-giving as little more than divine symbolic solidarity with human suffering, yet unable to alleviate it.

79. P. T. Forsyth's Christological kenotic theory likewise recognizes a two-fold movement of both kenosis and plerosis to protect against kenosis becoming merely "a one-sided idea." Forsyth, *The Person and Place of Jesus Christ*, 349.

80. Coakley states, "there has been a long-standing critique by feminist theologians of 'kenotic' Christology on the grounds that it may make normative for women forms of 'self-sacrifice' and 'self-abasement' that keep them in subordinate roles and can even lead to the condoning of abuse." Coakley, *Powers and Submissions*, 207.

81. For more on "ultimate" and "penultimate" beliefs, see Thomas F. Torrance, *Transformation and Convergence in the Frame of Knowledge* (Grand Rapids, MI: Wm. B. Eerdmans Publishing Company, 1984), 199–203; Thomas F. Torrance, *Belief in Science and in Christian Life: The Relevance of Michael Polanyi's Thought for Christian Faith and Life* (Edinburgh: The Handsel Press, 1980), 10–12.

PART I

An Ontology of Triune Well-Being

Chapter 1

The Logic of Divine Self-Enrichment

That God enjoys a state of well-being and dwells in unmatched glory is largely uncontested in the Christian tradition. The biblical witness attests to the perfection of God, encompassing moral blamelessness as well as mature completeness. God is without blemish. Psalm 18:30 declares, "This God—his way is perfect."[1] Jesus directed his disciples to "Be perfect . . . as your heavenly Father is perfect" (Mt 5:48).[2] Moreover, God is considered the original source of all creaturely goodness—"*Every good thing* given and every perfect gift is from above, coming down from the Father of lights" (Jas 1:17). Statements concerning divine all-blessedness seem ubiquitously obvious; however, beneath these lie reservoirs of under-analyzed logic that give rise to the parameters of Divine Self-Enrichment: *God enriching God in the perfection and fullness of God*. Specifically, three theological propositions are necessary for the initial logic of an ontology of triune well-being. These are:

Proposition 1—God is unified in hypostatic distinction;
Proposition 2—God is ontologically distinct in freedom from creation; and
Proposition 3—Divine acting in the economy is a reliable *self*-revelation of the eternal nature of God.

The first presupposition undergirds the concept of "*God* enriching *God*" by demonstrating that God is not only unified as the One God (thus tritheism is excluded—this is not "God*s* enriching God*s*") but also that God is replete with relational distinction through which tri-hypostatic giving and receiving (acts of enrichment) occur. Divine Self-Enrichment requires both predicating "unimpaired unity" and "unimpaired differentiation" to triune identity.[3] As we will see, the related concepts of perichoresis ("unimpaired unity") and divine self-positing ("unimpaired differentiation") provide the necessary theological coordinates. Perichoresis provides the theological structure congruent with the relational *unity* of God. While divine "self-positing"[4] (derived from Sergeĭ Bulgakov), or its conceptual equivalent "Divine Self-Distinctions"[5] (derived from Wolfhart Pannenberg), provides the apparatus to advocate enrichment *between* the distinct divine persons.

The second presupposition required to construe Divine Self-Enrichment is that God is ontologically distinct in freedom from creation. In the absence of this theological condition, positing a divine "otherness" or a divine "self" relatable to creation is difficult to sustain. If God is considered, theologically and metaphysically, undifferentiated from creation, or contingent on creation for being, it becomes problematic (if not impossible) to logically posit characteristics specific to *divinity*. Establishing the ontological differentiation of God from creation necessarily moves our exploration into considering the relation between the immanent (*ad intra*) and economic (*ad extra*) Trinity. Contra theologians who advocate the conflation of the immanent and economic Trinity, a strict distinction is sustained here as a theological necessity. Without distinction between the economic and immanent Trinity, one may be able to posit a process of divine-enrichment derived from creation, but not a Divine *Self*-Enrichment.

Finally, the third proposition necessary to delineate Divine Self-Enrichment is that the self-revelation of God in the world (economic Trinity) is a reliable demonstration of who and *how* God is in Godself (immanent Trinity). Such a proposition is necessary to interpret the relational depictions of Father, Son and Holy Spirit, recorded in Scripture, as evidential signposts of divine ontology. While this divine self-revelation is not exhaustive, it is a genuine and reliable self-revelation of divine being.

PROPOSITION 1: GOD IS UNIFIED IN HYPOSTATIC DISTINCTION

> WE BELIEVE in one God,
> the Father, the Almighty,
> maker of heaven and earth,
> of all that is, seen and unseen.
> We believe in one Lord, Jesus Christ,
> the only Son of God,
> eternally begotten of the Father,
> God from God, Light from Light,
> true God from true God,
> begotten, not made,
> of one Being with the Father . . .
> We believe in the Holy Spirit, the Lord, the giver of life,
> who proceeds from the Father and the Son.
> With the Father and the Son he is worshipped and glorified.[6]

The confession of the Trinity, articulated in the Nicene-Constantinopolitan Creed, expresses the indivisible nature of the One God while advocating the distinct appropriations of the hypostases of the Godhead. The creedal affirmation holds that the three distinct hypostases of the Trinity are co-equal, co-eternal and consubstantial. Each divine person[7] (hypostasis) of the Trinity is deity, of the one essence (*ousia*), with no hierarchy or subordination. Articulated through a doctrine of inseparable operations, orthodoxy also maintains that the act of a divine hypostasis of the Trinity is the act of the One triune God. Maintaining the simultaneous unity and distinctiveness of the divine persons has been vital for orthodox Christian faith to guard against modalism, subordinationism and tritheism.[8] This is what the classic doctrine of the Trinity, in part, sought to do.

Against Arius, the early church at the Council of Nicaea affirmed the Oneness of God and repudiated the concept that the Son is subordinate to the Father, a created being of the Father that serves as an agent of the ineffable God toward humanity.[9] Such an argument was later expanded at the First Council of Constantinople to affirm the co-equal deity of the Holy Spirit. While the co-equality and unity of the persons of the Trinity is a vital aspect of Trinitarian orthodoxy, such a position does not, however, blur hypostatic distinction. The Council of Nicaea clarified that the distinctions of the divine persons are real distinctions, not merely differing appearances of God's same[10] essence in different modes, as Sabellianism (modalism) proposes. Later the pro-Nicene filioque would uphold that God is Father, Son and Spirit but each are only distinct through relational opposition, that is, through what relation they do not contain as proper to their origin—*In Deo omnia sunt unum, ubi non obviat relationis oppositio* ("In God everything is one except where there is opposition of relation").[11] Against Patripassianism, the Son was incarnate, suffered and died, not the Father. Thus, God is "unimpaired differentiation."[12] Yet, guarding against tritheism, by which Father, Son and Holy Spirit are perceived as three separate deities in a collective, orthodoxy maintains that God is also "unimpaired unity."[13] The logic may be expressed helpfully like this—the Father is divine, but divinity is not the Father; the Son is divine, but divinity is not the Son; the Holy Spirit is divine, but the Holy Spirit is not divinity. Divinity requires the *unity* of Father, Son and Holy Spirit. Gregory of Nazianzus' wisdom expresses well the mysterious paradox of the One in Three and the Three in One that is simultaneously unity and distinction: "I cannot think of the one God without being quickly encircled by the splendour of the three; nor can I discern the three without being immediately led back to the one."[14]

Perichoresis

A vital component of the definition of Divine Self-Enrichment—"*God* enriching *God*," is premised on divinity having a relational structure that allows for the movement of giving and receiving while simultaneously upholding divine unity so as not to collapse into tritheism. The concept of perichoresis provides this theological premise.[15] As such, Divine Self-Enrichment adopts the basic meaning of perichoresis as a necessary theological construct. In contradistinction from an Augustinian-type substance-oriented divine ontology,[16] the Cappadocians used the term perichoresis (literally "rotation") to conceptualize the mutual reciprocal relations of the Trinity as constitutive for their Oneness.[17] Implicit in the Cappadocian concept was the metaphysic of divine simplicity; through which the relations between the divine persons are not "accidental to God's being; they simply *are* God's being."[18] As John Webster clarifies: "relations of Father, Son and Spirit are not some extended process in the course of which God acquires supplementary properties, behind which lies the unchanging divine essence."[19]

Perichoresis has acquired a family resemblance of definitions that aptly captures its semantic essence. Colin Gunton defines it as the "interrelation and interanimation" of the triune persons that expresses the "unity deriving from the dynamic plurality of [divine] Persons."[20] Jürgen Moltmann, whose work continues to exert considerable influence on the perichoretic understanding of the Trinity, argues that "the doctrine of *perichoresis* links together in a brilliant way the threeness and the unity, without reducing the threeness to the unity, or dissolving the unity in the threeness."[21] Cornelius Plantinga describes the perichoretic movement of the Trinity as "a zestful, wondrous community of divine light, love, joy, mutuality and verve," where there is "no isolation, no insulation, no secretiveness, no fear of being transparent to another."[22] The contemporary prominence of perichoresis, through Moltmann's *The Trinity and the Kingdom of God*[23] and John Zizioulas' *Being as Communion*,[24] is likewise invoked by theologians to describe the Trinity in relational or social terms. As a result, Trinitarian persons in reciprocal relationship has become the foundation of "Social Trinitarianism"[25]—a now familiar, yet contested, way by which theologians comprehend a variety of relational human issues made in the image of God's relational self. The concept of perichoresis, however, is not without its issues. As Karen Kilby explains,

> First, a concept, *perichoresis*, is used to name what is not understood, to name whatever it is that makes the three Persons one. Secondly, the concept is filled out rather suggestively with notions borrowed from our own experience of relationships and relatedness. And then, finally, it is presented as an exciting resource Christian theology has to offer the wider world.[26]

Kilby's analysis raises a legitimate concern. However, it also leaves open a possibility. What if the notion of perichoresis could be "filled out," not from mere human projection as Kilby suggests, but from interpreting the biblical depictions of the relating activity of the divine persons? Such an interpretive method is not inherently problematic. Kilby's remarks, while cautious and critical, compel us to consider underlying interpretative foundations. Is Trinitarian contemplation, like Kilby suggests, merely operating from a self-referential framework of autonomous and subjective human reasoning, or is there a notion of biblical revelation that may shape the content of analysis? Notable theologians, across ecumenical lines, have indeed discerned dynamic traits inherent to the triune relations *from Scripture* (discussed in part II). What is absent in contemporary Trinitarian scholarship, and addressed in this present work, is a synthesis of these Scriptural observations. Perichoresis posits a general concept of the "divine-dance." The concept of Divine Self-Enrichment, however, attempts to identify the divine "dance-*steps*" by considering the content of the dynamics among the three persons of the Trinity where, "[t]hose relationships [are] . . . economic events that image immanent states."[27] In other words, the characteristics pertaining to the reciprocal relations of Father, Son and Spirit evidenced in the Scriptural accounts are not superfluous to apprehending the ontological nature of God's being but are, in fact, an epistemic centerpiece.

Divine Self-Positing

Alongside perichoresis, the logic of Divine Self-Enrichment synchronously employs Pannenberg's "Divine Self-Distinctions"[28] and Bulgakov's concept of divine "self-positing"[29] to ascertain the purpose of gifting and receiving between the divine persons—that is, the constitution of divine life. Developing his concept from Hegel's idea of "self-distinction,"[30] Pannenberg formulates the concept of the "Reciprocal Self-Distinction of the Father, Son and Spirit,"[31] where he argues that "'person' is a relational, correlative term: one gains one's personality by giving oneself to one's counterpart; thus identity is gained in separation from, yet also in dependence on, the other."[32] Through reflection on the biblical materials pertinent to the economic Trinity, Pannenberg concludes that the intratrinitarian relations of active self-positing between the Father, Son and Spirit are constitutive for divine life. For example, he interprets the Scriptural articulation of the Father's handing over of the kingdom to the Son as both an act of distinct paternal agency as well as the rendering of the Father's kingship (paternal identity) dependent on the Son.[33] Thus, the Father's deity is actualized through the communal and active distinction of the Son. Pannenberg maintains that this mutual dependency is inherent to each divine person and is an essential feature of unified deity.[34]

Pannenberg's concept here strongly resonates with the insights of Bulgakov. Surmising that self-positing toward another actualizes human self-consciousness, Bulgakov regards God as "self-positing absolute subject."[35] Extrapolating from the actualization of human personhood (made in the image of God) he advances that God's being is likewise personal self-consciousness as self-positing to another.[36] Bulgakov thus concludes that the "others" in relation to the personal self-positing of God, in which this absolute subjectivity is completed, are themselves God.[37] The "others" of the Trinity are their "own person centres, together constituting the 'we' of the divine Trinity."[38] Bulgakov, therefore, deduces that "in the Divine Absolute subject . . . all altero-positing of I cannot be actualised outside of it, because of the absence of all 'outside,' but must be contained in itself, so that it itself is for itself simultaneously I, though he, and therefore we and you."[39] Bulgakov considers that the actualization of divine being, through triune self-positing, is akin to a triune self-revelation, which is, for Bulgakov, the essence of divine being. On this basis, he proposes that the patterning of divine being is, in fact, the ontological ground for God's self-revelation to the "other" of creation. Succinctly condensing this insight, he asserts that God is "free to commune with what is not God because *God's life is one of self-positing as self-revelation.*"[40] Simply put, the ontological priority of God's being as triune self-revelation precedes God's self-revelation toward the creation.

The insights of both Pannenberg and Bulgakov are valuable for framing the theological parameters of Divine Self-Enrichment. Their views offer a harmonized theological mechanism to support the claim that unified all-blessed divinity is constituted through tri-hypostatic acts of enrichment. In other words, as the Father, Son and Holy Spirit give and receive each to the other, or posit one to another in distinctive mutual unity, divine life is actualized.

The Implications for Divine Self-Enrichment

Let us now briefly take stock. Our discussion thus far has proposed that the related themes of perichoresis and "divine self-positing" are essential preconditions for the logic of Divine Self-Enrichment. The interdependence of these presuppositions is integral to establishing that God's life of well-being (enrichment) is derived from a divine mutuality of active—not static—self-distinction, which flows from, nurtures and actualizes (as *purus actus*) the one triune life of God. These two theological presuppositions are vital for guarding Divine Self-Enrichment against modalistic or tritheistic tendencies, where: (1) the activity of the divine persons could be misconstrued as serving a divine attribute posited prior to the hypostatic relationality; that of the goal of enrichment (modalism); or (2) it could appear as three deities enjoying one another from three separate centers (tritheism). Furthermore, upholding the self-positing divine relations of perichoresis protects the inference that God's self-enrichment—the hypostatic movement of gift and receipt one to the other—implies either a prior diminution or acts of self-interested hypostatic narcissism. Rather, these qualifiers conceptually frame God's abundantly ecstatic, ever-enriching, self-sufficient life. Without these a priori suppositions, Divine Self-Enrichment would fail to reflect the mutually contingent relational life of God *ad intra*, render God's unified being as asymmetrically construed, and hold obdurate consequences for a number of other theological doctrines including, inter alia, theological anthropology. It is with these concepts in place that further inquiry regarding the nature of God's all-blessedness life (*ad intra*) may be undertaken.

THE IMMANENT AND ECONOMIC TRINITY

In establishing two further presuppositions necessary for the logic of Divine Self-Enrichment—God's ontological distinctiveness from creation and the reliability of the self-revelation of God in the economic Trinity—we need to consider briefly some complexities associated with the immanent and economic Trinity. That is, we need to wade into conceptual categories used by theologians to comprehend the nature of God and God's relation to the world.[41] The "economic Trinity" (*ad extra*) denotes God's life and activity in the world. The "immanent Trinity" (*ad intra*) considers God's interior life, apart from the world. The epistemic and ontological aspects of these two categories have engendered extensive debate, not only due to the relevance for understanding divine being but for navigating divine and human relations. How we comprehend the immanent and economic Trinity is critical to defining the scope of Divine Self-Enrichment. If Divine Self-Enrichment is thought merely as an introspection on the immanent Trinity (of which humans have no direct and unmediated knowledge) any conclusions we might make immediately descend toward speculation. However, this charge can be circumvented if Divine Self-Enrichment is approached as a theological interpretation of the immanent Trinity revealed in the economy. But this also means that in order to ascertain characteristics inherent to a distinct *divine* enrichment there needs to be a distinction between the immanent and economic Trinity. We must be able to logically demarcate "God" from "not-God." The alternative proposition—to dilute the "sharp and shining barrier between Creator and creature"[42] by conflating the economic and immanent Trinity and perceiving God as only ever "God for us" (*pro nobis*)—yields an array of negative consequences for various interrelated theological propositions. As we will see, these positions counterintuitively undermine divine relationality with the creation, restrict divine and human freedom, deprive a logic of

God's being as ontological stability and trustworthiness, and fundamentally sabotage the notion of the perfection or fullness of divine well-being.

The Contemporary Debate

To assess the contemporary lines of debate regarding the immanent and economic Trinity, and its importance to the foundational presuppositions of Divine Self-Enrichment, this section engages primarily with the divergent views of Catherine Mowry LaCugna and Paul D. Molnar. LaCugna's *God for Us: The Trinity and Christian Life*[43] and Molnar's *Divine Freedom and the Doctrine of the Immanent Trinity*[44] epitomize the polar arguments of those who either conflate the economic and immanent Trinity (LaCugna) or uphold a distinction between the two (Molnar). Before assessing the divergences between these interlocuters, it is noteworthy that LaCugna and Molnar, in fact, agree on a fundamental principle governing God's self-communication. They both argue that Trinitarian theological pursuit that commences with self-transcendence (the immanent Trinity) and not God's self-communication in the economy is fundamentally flawed. LaCugna, affirming aspects of Karl Rahner's theology, states that: "the starting point and context for knowledge of the eternal mystery of God (*theologica*) is the economy of salvation (*oikonomia*)."[45] Molnar agrees, saying: "Unquestionably we all agree that we cannot leave the economy behind without disrupting the important connection between the Trinity and the life of faith."[46] While both agree that theology must start noetically with God's self-communication in the economy, they part ways concerning the impact God's acts in the world have on God's being. Broadly speaking, LaCugna makes three essential moves to arrive at her position.[47] First, she considers that the economic Trinity is not necessarily a commensurate revelation of who God is immanently (what I refer to as pseudo-revelation).[48] Second, evoking a Hegelian logic, God's being is understood as contingent on creation; a mutuality of conditioning between Creator and creation.[49] Here, LaCugna argues that God's acts in the world have a determinative and mutable impact on God's being. And third, based on these preceding points, she (necessarily) renders the classical theistic concepts regarding the divine perfections as inevitably incoherent. She rejects divine simplicity and aseity and embraces divine mutability and passibility. The pattern of these theological moves (either all three or a variety of points two and three) are likewise discerned in other theologians who similarly discard classical divine perfections.[50]

On the other hand, Molnar arrives at his position on quite different terms. First, he understands divine revelation as an absolute (yet not exhausted) self-communication; as God is *ad intra* so is God toward us in creation. Alternatively stated, God's acts in the world demonstrate God's being.

Second, God's being is conditioned only by God, in which case God is free in God's aseity; God does not need creation to make God who God is. This, however, does not infer that God is non-relational but rather highlights that God is ontologically distinct from creation. And finally, he perceives that the Christian tradition's interpretation of the divine perfections of simplicity, aseity, immutability and impassibility are consistent with a fully dynamic and relational God toward creation.

The importance of navigating these polar positions cannot be underestimated. At stake is the preservation of a logic by which to identify and construe the nature of God's enrichment or whether we can even posit an enrichment in the divine being that is distinctly divine. Here, our next two presuppositions that form the theological parameters of Divine Self-Enrichment press further into the consequences pertaining to the immanent and economic Trinity. These are: proposition 2—God is ontologically distinct in freedom from creation; and proposition 3—Divine acting in the economy is a reliable *self*-revelation of the eternal nature of God. Without these presuppositions, sustaining a logic that identifies characteristic movements of the enriched life of divinity is severely restricted. Why? Because if proposition 2 does not hold, then there is no epistemic divine "other" distinct from creation, in other words, no *Divine Self*-Enrichment. And, in the absence of proposition 3, information derived from the economy to apprehend divine ontology is reduced to mere speculation.

PROPOSITION 2: GOD IS ONTOLOGICALLY DISTINCT IN FREEDOM FROM CREATION

Theologians, such as Molnar, who contend for divine love, grace and freedom maintain that the ontological distinctness of God from creation is an essential precondition.[51] The argument broadly proceeds that if love, grace and freedom are necessitated rather than gifted, they cease to reflect their definitional essence. Love is not love if it is necessitated and not freely given. Thus, if God's being is made replete through relationality toward the creation, then creation becomes necessary for God to be who God is. Creation, under these terms, is no longer a freely gifted grace but a necessitated end. Hence, if one conflates the Creator and creation, the divine attributes of grace and love are rendered void, as freedom and voluntary givenness are inherent to the virtues of grace and love.

LaCugna's *God For Us*, however, carves out a different position as she views the doctrine of God as "inseparable from soteriology."[52] Although we might agree that this view holds true from the perspective that the economy of salvation provides epistemological insight about God's being, this is not what LaCugna means. LaCugna refers to an inseparability between God and God's acts—where the act *determines* God's ontology. Put differently, God's salvific acts in the world *condition* God's nature rather than *reveal* God's nature. LaCugna arrives at a notion of divine contingency on creation by adducing that the ontic content of God's relational being derives from God's relational engagement with creation. LaCugna proposes a causative relation; because of "God's outreach to the creature, God is said to be essentially relational, ecstatic."[53] Thus, God is relational because of creation, not because relationality is antecedently constitutive of God's immanent being. LaCugna, equates a strict distinction between the immanent and economic Trinity with an interpretation of divine aseity that gives rise to a non-relational God, and thus argues that her model of conflating the economic and immanent Trinity (unlike a distinction model) "does not banish the Trinity of Persons to an intra-divine sphere, unrelated to the creature."[54] LaCugna is adamant that "as soon as we begin to argue on the basis of such intra-divine distinctions, we leave the economy behind."[55]

Molnar, on the other hand, argues that a view, such as LaCugna's, reflects the faulty assumption "that if a theologian argues on the basis of the intra-divine distinctions, then the economy must be left behind."[56] Molar is adamant that upholding the freedom and distinction of the immanent Trinity does not undermine God's relationality toward creation. Rather, ontological divine distinction *from* creation is the theological basis to uphold God's profound relationality *with* creation. Instead of LaCugna asserting an excessively free, gracious and loving relationality of God toward humanity (through her rejection of divine aseity) she inadvertently sets up the conditions for a metaphysically obligatory relationality that impinges on the very logic of gifted love. LaCugna infers a relationship between creation and God that collapses to a necessity for divine being. Not only does this imperil the content of divine attributes but her conflation of the economic and immanent Trinity arguably morphs God's wholly distinct otherness into a contingency that dissolves the concept of the created "other." Such a move neglects the simple and profoundly important logic of the immanent Trinity that Molnar summarizes—"we cannot speak intelligibly about God's life with us unless the God of whom we speak is distinguishable from us."[57] In consonance with Molnar, Thomas Weinandy also asserts, "LaCugna is absolutely correct that the God who is must be God-for-us. There is no other . . . However, in order for there to be a God-for-us there must be '*a*' God."[58] LaCugna's view of the Christian God and God's relation to humanity is "fatally and disastrously flawed"[59] as it distorts the ontic conditions of love and freedom and encroaches on the substantiveness of the "otherness" of God and creation from which mutual relationality arises.

It is true that the biblical witness indelibly supports LaCugna's emphasis that the life of God is not God's alone but is shared with the created order. God is indeed Emmanuel (Mt 1:23). However, while we might affirm the dependency creatures have on God, it does not follow that God's life is correspondingly dependent on creation. God has "God's life" before God can share God's life "with us." LaCugna errs when she reduces God's freedom to a necessity to be in communion with the creature, making God's freedom not freely determined. Such a solecistic logic arguably ensues because this aspect of her doctrine of God commences with human analogy rather than revelation. LaCugna states "Divine freedom, *like human freedom*, is achieved in communion."[60] Here, LaCugna draws a straight analogous line to equate creaturely relations with triune relations. Rather than locating God's life in the self-sufficiency of the divine intra-relations (which she erroneously correlates with solitariness),[61] she locates God's fulfillment of God's relational being with the creature—not first within God and *then* with the creature. She argues, "Since the exercise of freedom requires a plurality of Persons, God's freedom cannot be located in solitariness. The Spirit is the freedom of God permeating, animating, quickening, incorporating, affiliating, engrafting, consummating *the creature* out of love."[62] LaCugna's statement here implies that the plurality of the persons of the Godhead are not sufficient to source and fulfil the essence of divine freedom. Rather, her conception of divine freedom appears to require the exercise of an additional movement toward the creation. The scope of LaCugna's overall logic compels an ironic conclusion—that God is not essentially free to be relationally for the creature but rather needs the creature in order to even be a "relational" or "free" God.

The assertion that God "is love" (1 Jn 4:8) holds intriguing implications when considering God's distinct self-sufficiency as the foundation for God's profound relationality in the economy. In order for God to create the creation *in* and *from* love, God must first *be* love prior to the act of creation. Certainly, God could not *be* eternally love if God's love is derived from the act of creation. Love is relational, but this is first and eternally expressed within the triune relations of God.[63] It is from the reality that "God is love" (1 Jn 4:8) that God extends loves toward creation. If though, as LaCugna suggests, God's being as love hinges on the creation for its actualization, the inference remaining is that prior to the creation of the world the fullness of divine love was un-actualized.[64] The conceptual fallacy in her logic is, however, addressed by upholding the distinction of the immanent Trinity. It is because God is eternally, actively and essentially loving within the self-sufficient enriching subsistent relations of God that we do not need to construe God's being as contingent on the creation for God to be God or for God's love to be actualized.[65] Rather, we need only to understand that the "*oikonomia* is the realm where God, in all his wholly otherness as God—ontologically distinct from the *oikonomia*—is present and acts" as love.[66]

Relevance for Divine Self-Enrichment?

The concept that the eternal enriching relations of the Godhead are a priori evidenced in, not determined by, God's works in the world is fundamental to a theology of Divine Self-Enrichment. This claim upholds the ontological antecedence of the immanent Trinity necessary to maintain a theological distinction between the Creator and the creation. Such a distinction is necessary to establish the theological basis for discerning and identifying a *divine-self* that is the subject of enrichment. In the absence of distinction between the divine and the created, conclusions regarding the characteristics of divine well-being would indeed be elusive. Furthermore, eliding distinction arguably erodes relationality between God and creation and makes voluntary human imitation of the "other" of the Creator challenging to sustain. Without distinctiveness of a divine ontology, it is difficult to draw reasonable implications from *divine* well-being for an understanding of the dimensions of *human* well-being. Moreover, while human well-being formed as the image of God (*imago dei*) in the presence of God (*coram deo*) derives its contours from the divine archetype, human well-being is actualized in a manner appropriate to human, not divine, ontology. Again, in the absence of recognizing the ontological difference between divinity and humanity, analogies drawn between the two concerning well-being may well amount to utopian myth, where a replete patterning of divine well-being may misleadingly be considered attainable by the creature this side of the eschaton.

PROPOSITION 3: RELIABLE *SELF*-REVELATION OF THE ETERNAL NATURE OF GOD

Part of the discussion to this point has inferred that knowledge of the nature of Divine Self-Enrichment is only identifiable in the economic acts of God; that God's acts in the world reveal the nature of God. Such a conclusion necessarily implies that the revelation of the triune God in creation and salvation history may be understood as a reliable self-revelation of the eternal triune God. It follows, then, if the economic Trinity, as depicted in Scripture, is relational and dynamic, then, as an act of divine *self-communication*, relationality and dynamism must exist within the immanent Trinity. On this basis, we can push a little further and interpret the specific manifestations of the life, love, blessing, words and actions of the triune God depicted in the biblical account as eternally existing within the immanent Trinity. Without this understanding, there is no possibility of viewing the biblical depictions of Father, Son and Holy Spirit as evidence of the nature of divine being. Furthermore, if the theological foundation for the logic of Divine Self-Enrichment does not commence with revelation, it runs the risk of attributing createdness to the Creator. Indeed, Barth considers that the idea of a "second root" for the doctrine of the Trinity, apart from revelation, gives rise to a creaturely created God.[67] He argues that if conceptions of the Trinity "may be just as well found in human consciousness or other created orders as in Holy Scriptures," God becomes conceived as "a supreme principle of the world and ultimately of man."[68] In a similar vein, Hans Urs von Balthasar argues that interpreting the nature of God, apart the reliability of divine self-revelation, inevitably leads to the invention of a mythic God. Referring critically to Moltmann's *Crucified God*, he opines, "wherever the internal divine process . . . is lumped together with the process of salvation history," God becomes "entangled in the world process and becomes a tragic, mythological God."[69] With these cautions in mind, let us now briefly consider the third theological presupposition supporting Divine Self-Enrichment—that the revelation of God in the economy is a reliable *self*-revelation of the life of God.

Considering the doctrine of the triune God in the context of his broader project to establish a doctrine of revelation, Barth's *Church Dogmatics* proposes that God (Revealer) is identical with his act (Revelation) and its effect (Revealedness).[70] For Barth, therefore, revelation is not an act separable from the being and nature of God. Justin Stratis neatly summarizes Barth's logic of revelation and its implications for the economic and immanent Trinity, stating:

> But how can Barth be so sure that God is true to himself in the event of revelation? . . . The logic runs like this: if in the event of revelation we have to do with a *divine* act (that is, we can designate the Subject of the action as God), then we must recognise this event as *entirely characterised* by its principal actor, namely, God, himself. If it were otherwise, then it would not be *God himself* who is revealed, but rather some sort of temporally conditioned modality of God. Consequently, the very *event*-ness of revelation is information of God's life in himself. What we have in revelation, therefore, is not a timeless, remote deity accommodating and therefore acting in opposition to himself by taking the form of our temporal punctiliarity. No, his being is *aptly* construed as event because God *himself* is, in some sense, event. In God's self-unveiling, then, eternity literally becomes time, which means, significantly, that the temporal is comprehended by the eternal, and not vice versa. The activity, or life, that God manifests in his movement toward man is therefore *his* activity and life.[71]

For Barth, the economic Trinity, revealed through Jesus Christ, is the reliable self-revelation of divinity. However, although a creaturely understanding of the Creator arises in the economy of revelation and revealedness, the "eternal Trinity has ontic priority."[72]

In LaCugna's understanding of revelation we might observe a level of congruence between her statements and Barth's premise that the economic Trinity is the noetic ground for the immanent Trinity. For instance, LaCugna says: "What is given in the economy of salvation . . . is the mystery of God which exists from all eternity as triune."[73] However, unlike Barth, due to LaCugna's conflation of the economic and immanent Trinity, her argument does not propose that the revelation in the economy is strictly contiguous with the immanent. Upholding Piet Schoonenberg's opinion,[74] LaCugna advances that "God's self-communication in history is *not exactly* identical with God's eternal self-communication because God's self-expression in Word and Spirit must be a genuinely new way in which God exists."[75] Although a generous reading of LaCugna's assertion could propose that she means that God's being is *translated* in a 'new way' into the temporal and created world,[76] or that there always remains an excess in the immanent Trinity, this is not what she intends. Her equivocation as to the reliability of divine self-communication is more evident when she claims that "the question of whether God would be Trinitarian apart from salvation history is purely speculative and cannot be answered on the basis of revelation."[77] Such "pseudo-revelation" is similarly expressed by Gordon Kaufman, whom LaCugna enlists in her argument. Kaufman considers the doctrine of the Trinity as a symbol constructed by human knowledge rather than as an actual revelation of who God is as the eternal God. Speaking of the immanent Trinity, he says: "this innermost essence we have no access in history or revelation; and anything said about it is pure speculation."[78] LaCugna maintains that "what God is remains ineffable, and not fully identical to God's economic self-expression."[79] And again, "there cannot be a strict identity, either epistemological or ontological, between God and God for us."[80] Even if one attempts to read these statements as cautions against univocal contemplations of God, or that God is equivalently ineffable in the economy as God is *ad intra*,[81] or that there always remains an incomprehensible excess to God's being, it remains that her argument is not intended to affirm God's ineffability as the wholly ontological "other." Rather, LaCugna conflates divine ineffability with humanity's epistemologically constrained comprehension of God. In other words, God is ineffable, not because of ontological distinctiveness from creation, but because of the inadequacy of the human perception of God.

Although humans do not have an exhaustive revelation of God, there must be a strict identity between "God" and "God for us" for there to be a notion of divine *self*-revelation. Weinandy is particularly critical of LaCugna's dissolution of God's ineffability as the wholly other God. He equates such an analysis as "ending up with either a finite God or a 'Christian' expression of atheism."[82] Weinandy concludes with such a forceful pronouncement because when one does not equate God's being in the economy with God's noumenal self, one ends up with a merely phenomenal God who "appears" to the observer potentially other than who and how God actually is. The Kantian overtone here is obvious.[83] Weinandy explains the consequences of LaCugna's flawed reasoning, saying, "While wanting to eliminate the gap between God and us, LaCugna has actually constructed a chasm between God and us that is now unbridgeable. We only come to experience and know the phenomenal God of the *oikonomia*, and never the noumenal God who actually exists in his wholly ontologically distinct otherness as God."[84] In other words, on LaCugna's logic, humanity only ever has a hunch about the true nature of God and is, at the end of the day, none the wiser in forming positive affirmations of universal significance. Molnar calls this ambivalence toward revelation "Theological Agnosticism."[85] Enlisting Barth as a fellow opponent to this trend, Molnar emphasizes how the question of whether God is Trinity apart from salvation history is integral, not only to our understanding of revelation, but to how we perceive God. Molnar highlights Barth's contention that if one maintains an "agnostic inability to perceive that the truth of revelation hinges on the fact that God is in revelation what he is in himself then one will succumb to subjectivism, pantheism, panentheism . . . or dualism."[86] Ultimately, none of these "isms" allow for clarity in perceiving attributes relevant to *divine* well-being.

The irony for LaCugna's theology, and others like it, is that while she cautions theologians to take care "not to use the economic Trinity as a synonym for God as God appears to us, and immanent Trinity as a synonym for God as God really is *in se*,"[87] she ignores her own caution in the manner by which she perceives revelation. As she conflates the economic and immanent Trinity, she appears to denote the economic Trinity "as a synonym for God as God *appears* to us," because elsewhere she concludes that one cannot say whether "God would be Trinitarian . . . on the basis of revelation."[88] LaCugna could only have reached this conclusion if God only "appeared" to creation in a manner different from who God is. The logical conclusion that stems from LaCugna's reasoning is that divine activity in salvation history cannot be considered a reliable self-revelation of God's being. The result of these theological moves is that divine being is primarily construed on the basis of autonomous human reasoning. Humanity decides which aspects of the divine "appearances" depict "God" as God is and which "appearances" do not. However, a theology that does not espouse that divine revelation in salvation history expresses God *ad intra* essentially removes the reliability or "self-fidelity" of God's economic self-communication and offers conjecture regarding the divine attributes.[89] Indeed, LaCugna's interpretation of the divine nature demonstrates such conjecture. For example, relying on Yves Congar, she advances the thesis that there is a "disparity between what God is *ad intra*, and what God is able to be *ad extra*"[90] because the mode of self-communication in the economy is kenosis, a mode according to Congar and LaCugna that "is not connatural with the being of divine Persons."[91] Yet, how do Congar and LaCugna conclude that kenosis is not "connatural" with God's being? Is this not mere speculation? Certainly, if we understand that God is toward us in the economy as God is immanently, would not then the kenosis of God, displayed in the economy, be the revelation that God is immanently kenotic?[92] As Weinandy concludes: "there is no ontological difference between what God is in himself and what God is for us."[93]

Interpreting Scripture for Ontic Significance

At this juncture, it is imperative to pause to consider qualifications regarding what the scriptural accounts of triune relationality might reasonably and coherently infer about the divine nature. Recent scholarly debate within Evangelical circles has brought attention to the need for some caution. Here, I refer to problematic ontic inferences that have arisen in the deductions made by complementarian theologians, Bruce Ware and Wayne Grudem. Ware and Grudem, pursuing a theological rationale to maintain male headship over women in Evangelical Churches, interpret a range of selective Scriptures of the Son's "deferential" behaviors to the Father (what Harrower calls a "selective strict realist reading")[94] to assert that authority and submission, hierarchy and obedience are eternally inherent to the nature of triune relationality.[95] Contra established orthodoxy of the co-equality of the divine persons and aligned more closely with Arian trajectories, Ware and Grudem deduce from Scripture an eternal and ontological functional subordination (EFS) of the Son to the Father. These divine relations are subsequently employed to justify analogous hierarchical relations between men and women in the Church, giving rise to disturbing real-world implications.[96] Much has been written on this subject not requiring a replete rehashing here but for those interested, Michael Bird and Scott Harrower's book *Trinity without Hierarchy* provides a thorough analysis.[97] What I wish to draw attention to here are a few issues relevant to the constructive theology of Divine Self-Enrichment that emerge from these debates.

Concerned about the introduction of hierarchy and subordination into the very nature of the Trinity, some Evangelical scholars have responded by advocating a restriction on attributing ontic significance to the Trinitarian narratives in Scripture. This strategy, however, is itself problematic. First, it uncritically adopts a similar conception present in the argument of those they oppose; conceding that the economic triune relating should be interpreted primarily as "subordination." This position then leads necessarily to the second problem—restricting the ontic implications for the nature of God arising from Scriptural interpretation. These moves of logic are evident in the work of Millard Erickson, a critic of EFS.[98] Erickson, not wanting to impute into the eternity of the immanent Trinity what he affirms as the Son's "functional subordination" to the Father in the economy, considers the relational depictions as *"temporary* . . . accepted for the performance of a particular task of redemption."[99] Erickson expresses a legitimate concern for safeguarding the immanent Trinity against perverse conclusions of ontic hierarchy, however, his assumption that the economy of triune relating should be interpreted in terms of "subordination" imposes an immediate constraint on the rationale of this "safeguarding." That is, faced with what is seen as only two choices (ontic or temporal *subordination of the Son* to the Father), the "lesser of two evils" is chosen—a reading of the economy removed of ontic consequence. Thus, the Son's alleged "subordination" to the Father is confined to the temporal economy of salvation. A problem of this strategy is that emptying the economic of ontic significance cannot but result in theological agnosticism or a shallow nominalism. A point, in fact, correctly made by proponents of EFS.[100] The strategy to restrain ontological inferences to prevent spurious conclusions of inner-Trinitarian subordination seems to be an unfortunate case of "throwing the baby out with the bathwater." Poor interpretation does not invalidate the self-revelation of God nor the possibility of provisional insights about divine ontology that arise from the economy.

Furthermore, the characterization of divine relating in "subordinationist" terms appears to align more with human distortions that often perceive relations in terms of dominance, authority and control, instead of the divinely-infused perspectives that define relational authority and power in consonance with giving and serving (Mt 20:26–28).[101] It is with these issues in mind that the theological patterning of kenotic-enrichment makes a significant contribution, recasting the relations of the Trinity beyond the confines and challenges associated with relations defined through narrow subordinationists categories. Alongside Fred Sanders' deduction from Gregory of Nazianzus' insights, one might say, that those in favor of EFS (and potentially even those who contest EFS but agree that the Son's economic relating to the Father should be narrowly interpreted as "subordination") are hemmed into "a narrowly literal approach to Scripture [that] is unable to detect all that Scripture teaches."[102] That is, scriptural readings that reduce the divine relations to "subordinations" become "dreadfully servile to the letter . . . following the syllables . . . [but letting] the realities go."[103] These interpretations, that either impute relational subordination ontically or restrict it to the economy, run the risk of de-emphasizing the broader cadences of the biblical witness. A biblical witness that expresses equal dynamics of tri-hypostatic relating and Being as mutual movements of gift and receipt.[104]

One final point to be pressed here is that guarding triune theology from heretical consequences of an unequal hierarchy is not the only issue being safeguarded by those proposing a restriction of the ontic implications arising from the economy of triune relating. An additional anxiety appears to be that the triune narratives in Scripture give rise to a multi-directional triune dynamic, potentially challenging the inherited view of the distinctions of the divine persons found in the (one-way) relations of origin. This is a live concern in Harrower's work where, in part, he questions possible ontic implications for the immanent Trinity on the basis that the Scriptural data, particularly Luke–Acts,

> produces inconsistent results in terms of the changing patterns of relationships between Father and the Son, and also the Son and the Spirit because of the dynamic and somewhat fluid nature of the trinitarian actors and actions . . . the successive reversed subordinations between God the Son and God the Spirit to each other.[105]

Harrower appears wary of drawing ontic implications from the triune narratives not only due to hierarchical problems, but also on account of his interpretation of the fluidity of the hypostatic relations as "reversed *subordinations*."[106] On this basis he opines—"one might expect that this pattern of relationships to be an analogues of eternal relationship" but concludes it is "hard to see" how certain aspects of relational fluidity "can be made to comport with this view."[107] Harrower, leverages evidence of these "fluid" Trinitarian dynamics in Scripture to argue against selective readings that impute an ontological and eternal Trinitarian hierarchy. He goes as far to assert, based on his robust exegetical study of Luke–Acts, that the Trinitarian taxis "are *not fixed* hierarchically."[108] Nevertheless, he stops short of affirming an ontic significance for divinity from his exegetical findings. Suggesting instead that the fluidity of the economic relations and "God's eternal taxis" require future research.[109]

It is into that suggested arena of required research that this book, in part, delves, contending that the biblical witness of the fluid and multi-directional patterns of triune relating compels a reconsideration of the conventional views of the relations of origin. As elaborated in part II, such a reconsideration is directly expressed by Pannenberg, and hinted at by both Bulgakov and Balthasar. This is not to suggest that the dynamics of Divine Self-Enrichment and the mutual directions of triune kenotic-enrichment are necessarily at odds with conventional views of the relations of origin. Nor am I proposing a zero-sum game, an "either-or" situation. I merely, like Pannenberg, express consternation as to whether the traditional view of the relations of origin can be "justified exegetically"[110] as the *sole* determining factor to account for the life of unity and distinction of the triune Persons.[111] Pannenberg never opposes the concept of the relations of origin. Instead, he opposes, based on the evidence of Scripture, "the *exclusive view* of the trinitarian relations in terms of relations of origin."[112] Like Pannenberg, I think it insufficient to merely treat the diverse catalysts of triune relationality, gleaned from the biblical witness, as not ontologically constitutive for the divine identity.[113]

CONCLUSION

Hopefully, what has become obvious in this short discussion is that the underlying propositions regarding the nature of revelation, the relationship between the economic and immanent Trinity, and the interpretation of Scripture wield a profound influence on the construal of a theology of Divine Self-Enrichment. The logic of God's truthfulness and faithfulness necessitate an ontological consistency in the divine movement toward creation. If this is not the case, an understanding of God becomes merely an edifice of human endeavor rather than a work of divine benediction. Upholding the reliability of divine self-revelation in the economy is key to conceptualizing the contours of Divine Self-Enrichment beyond mere abstraction or speculation. Divine Self-Enrichment is identified through the consideration of salvation history as the theater of God's revelation of who and *how* God is *ad intra*—the God who eternally lives from and in the delight of the enriching triune relations of Father, Son and Holy Spirit. The concept of Divine Self-Enrichment is established on a logic of revelation that recognizes that the immanent Trinity is the ontic ground for the economic Trinity, pre-eminently discerned and known through the Incarnation of the eternal divine Son, Jesus Christ. The acts of God in the economy are not contingent "appearances" assumed to merely accommodate finite creaturely understanding. As Barth contends: "It is equally important to understand that God in himself is not divested of His glory and perfections, that He does not assume them merely in connexion with his self-revelation to the world, but that they constitute His own eternal glory."[114]

With this logic in place, the foundation is set to appreciate that the reciprocal relations of the Trinity represent definitive content to identify inherent characteristics attending Divine Self-Enrichment. In particular, we will discover that the mode of triune-communication in the economy is quite divergent from Congar and LaCugna's denial that kenosis is "connatural" with the being of the divine persons. In fact, in the unfolding of this work, the concept of kenosis, interpreted from the reliable self-revealing events of God's acting in the economy reveals itself not only in the self-giving of the Son (Phil 2:7) but as connatural to each divine person and the unity of the divine nature. Such must be the case to avoid acute implications that undermine the unity of will, essence and nature of the One God.[115] The very core of *homoousios* is undermined, if not obliterated, if we fail to recognize kenosis as an essential, not accidental nor temporally functional property of the triune God.

NOTES

1. All biblical translations are from the NRSV updated version unless otherwise stated.

2. William F. Arndt, Frederick W. Danker, and Walter Bauer, *A Greek-English Lexicon of the New Testament and Other Early Christian Literature*, 3rd ed (Chicago: University of Chicago Press, 2000), 996.

3. Karl Barth, *Church Dogmatics: The Doctrine of the Word of God, Part I*, vol. 1, eds. G. W. Bromiley and T. F. Torrance (Edinburgh: T&T Clark, 1975), 299. Hereafter *CD I/1*.

4. Sergeï Bulgakov, *The Lamb of God*, trans. Boris Jakim (Grand Rapids, MI: Eerdmans, 2002), 111–40.

5. Wolfhart Pannenberg, *Systematic Theology*, volume 1, trans. Geoffrey W. Bromiley (Grand Rapids, MI: Eerdmans, 1991), 308. Hereafter referred to as *ST1*.

6. Nicene Creed, anglicansonline.org/basics/nicene.html.

7. Barth prefers the phrase "mode of being" so as not to confuse the modern conception of "personhood" with a person of the Godhead. See Barth, *CD I/1*, 348ff. Karl Rahner utilizes the phrase "three distinct ways of subsisting" in Karl Rahner, *The Trinity*, trans. Joseph Donceel (London: Herder and Herder, 1970),103–15. While I recognize the varied historical uses of the terms hypostasis and person (*prosópon*), this book uses the terms hypostasis and person interchangeably. For more information regarding the distinctions between hypostasis and person see John. D. Zizioulas, *Being as Communion: Studies in Personhood and the Church* (London: Darton, Longman & Todd, 1985), 27–65.

8. For more information on fourth century Trinitarian controversies see Lewis Ayres, *Nicaea and its Legacy: An Approach to Fourth-Century Trinitarian Theology* (Oxford: Oxford University Press, 2004).

9. Arius wrote in *Thalia* "The one without beginning established the Son as the beginning of all creatures . . . he [the Son] is not equal to God, nor yet is he of the same substance . . . there exists a Trinity in unequal glories." Translation provided by Rowan Williams, *Arius: Heresy and Tradition* (London: Darton, Longman & Todd, 1987), 101. Young and Teal point out, however, that "Arius was guilty perhaps not so much of demoting the Son as exalting the Father." See Frances Young and Andrew Teal, *From Nicaea to Chalcedon: A Guide to the Literature and Its Background*, 2nd edn (London: SCM Press, 2010). For more information regarding the Arian heresy

see Rowan Williams, *Arius: Heresy and Tradition* (London: Darton, Longman & Todd), 1987.

10. The Nicene Creed specifically used the term "one" essence rather than "same" essence. The Son is one substance/essence with the Father. "One" essence safeguards against Ebionite and Docetic heresies and against polytheism where there is multiplication of God's essence into separate beings. See Barth, *CD I/1*, 439.

11. The axiom is used in the Council of Florence (1438–1445). See Marc. A. Pugliese, "How Important Is the Filioque for Reformed Orthodoxy?" *The Westminster Theological Journal* 66, no. 1 (Spring 2004): 168. See also Barth, *CD I/1*, 299.

12. Barth, *CD I/1*, 299.

13. Barth, *CD I/1*, 299.

14. St Gregory of Nazianzus, *The Oration on Holy Baptism, §XL*, newadvent.org/fathers/310240.htm. See also St Gregory of Nazianzus, *Festal Orations*, trans. Nonna Verna Harrison (New York: St Vladimir's Press, 2008), 137.

15. For more details regarding perichoresis and its historical development see Verna Harrison, "Perichoresis in the Greek Fathers," *St. Vladimir's Theological Quarterly* 35, no.1 (1991): 53–65, EBSCOhost; Slobodan Stamatović, "The Meaning of Perichoresis," *Open Theology* 2, no. 1 (2016): 303–23, doi.org/10.1515/opth-2016-0026; and Danut Manastireanu, "Perichoresis and the Early Church Doctrine," *ARCHÆVS XI–XII* (2007–2008): 61–93, academia.edu/4794642/Perichoresis_and_the_Early_Christian_Doctrine_of_God.

16. Catherine LaCugna refers to Augustine's "point of departure" for his Trinitarianism as "the unity of the divine substance shared by the three divine Persons." See Catherine Mowry LaCugna, *God for Us: The Trinity and Christian Life* (San Francisco: HarperSanFrancisco, 1991), 214. The alleged deficiency of Western Trinitarian theology, attributed to Augustine's influence, is an unbalanced focus on the unity of God at the expense of the personal relations of the divine communion, where the divine essence is postulated prior to the three divine Persons. Such a rhetoric is based on Théodore de Régnon's assertion that Latin theology began with the divine nature (oneness) to contrive divine "threeness"; while Greek theology commenced with the Persons (threeness) to contrive divine "oneness." See Michel Barnes, "De Régnon Reconsidered," *Augustinian Studies* 26, no. 2 (1995): 51–79. Ayres, has, however, questioned whether De Régnon's divide was ever as sharp. Ayres concludes that Gregory of Nyssa and Augustine "offer two compatible articulations of the legacy bequeathed to later generations by pro-Nicene Christians" (p. 383). Ayres therefore argues for a reading of Augustine that confirms a "pro-Nicene Trinitarianism" that demonstrates how "Augustine consistently and specifically rules out the idea that the divine essence is prior to the divine Persons." See Ayres, "The Grammar of Augustine's Trinitarian Theology," in *Nicaea and Its Legacy*, 381, 383.

17. Gregory of Nazianzus and Gregory of Nyssa were first among the Cappadocian Fathers to utilize the concept περιχώρησις theologically. The concept was affirmed by St Maximus the Confessor, while Pseudo-Cyril of Alexandria was the first to use the term in relation to Trinitarian theology in his *De Trinitate*. See Verna Harrison, "Perichoresis in the Greek Fathers," *St. Vladimir's Theological Quarterly* 35

(1991): 53–65; Daniel F. Stramara, "Gregory of Nyssa's Terminology for Trinitarian Perichoresis," *Vigiliae Christianae* 52, no. 3 (1998): 257–63, doi:10.2307/1584502.

18. John Webster, "Non ex aequo: God's Relation to Creatures," In *Within the Love of God: Essays on the Doctrine of God in Honour of Paul S. Fiddes*, eds. Anthony Clarke, and Andrew Moore (Oxford: Oxford University Press, 2014), 12.

19. Webster, "Non ex aequo," 12.

20. Colin Gunton, *The One, the Three and the Many: God, Creation and the Culture of Modernity—The Brampton Lectures 1992* (Cambridge: Cambridge University Press, 1993), 152.

21. Jürgen Moltmann, *The Trinity and the Kingdom of God: The Doctrine of God*, trans. Margaret Kohl (Minneapolis: Fortress Press, 1993), 175. Originally published as *Trinität und Reich Gottes* (Munich: Chr. Kaiser Verlag, 1980).

22. Cornelius Plantinga, Jr., "Social Trinity and Tritheism," in *Trinity, Incarnation and Atonement*, eds. Ronald J. Feenstra and Cornelius Plantinga Jr. (Notre Dame: University of Notre Dame Press, 1989), 28.

23. Moltmann, *The Trinity and the Kingdom*.

24. Zizioulas, *Being as Communion*.

25. Cornelius Plantinga, Jr., "Gregory of Nyssa and the Social Analogy of the Trinity," *The Thomist* 50 (1986): 325–52.

26. Karen Kilby, "Perichoresis and Projection: Problems with Social Doctrines of the Trinity," *New Blackfriars* 81, no. 957 (2000): 442. Kilby continues to express her concerns in *God, Evil and the Limits of Theology* (London: T&T Clark Bloomsbury, 2020).

27. Fred Sanders, "Redefining Progress in Trinitarian Theology: Stephen R. Holmes on the Trinity," *Evangelical Quarterly* 86, no. 1 (2014): 19.

28. Pannenberg, *ST1*, 308.

29. Bulgakov, *Lamb of God*, 111–40.

30. Pannenberg, *Jesus—God and Man*, 2nd edn., trans. Lewis L. Wilkins and Duane A. Priebe (Philadelphia: Westminster, 1977), 181–83. Originally published as *Grundzuge der Christologie* (Giitersloh: Gerd Mohn, 1964). Also see Veli-Matti Kärkkäinen, "The Trinitarian Doctrines of Jürgen Moltmann and Wolfhart Pannenberg in the Context of Contemporary Discussion," in *The Cambridge Companion to Trinity*, ed. Peter Phan (Cambridge: Cambridge University Press, 2011), 240.

31. Pannenberg, *ST1*, 308.

32. Kärkkäinen, "The Trinitarian Doctrines," 231. Ted Peters names this same conceptualization of the interior life of God as "dependent divinity." See Ted Peters, *God as Trinity: Relationality and Temporality in the Divine Life* (Louisville, KY: Westminster Press, 1993), 135.

33. Pannenberg, *ST1*, 312–13.

34. Pannenberg, *ST1*, 312–13. It is worth noting that in this work, the term "mutual" will be preferred over "reciprocal" to emphasize the freedom of the divine relations' freedom rather than potentially inferring an obligatory *quid pro quo*. Asle Eikrem is helpful in regard to this distinction in *God as Sacrificial Love: A Systematic Exploration of a Controversial Notion* (London: Bloomsbury T&T Clark, 2018), 99–100.

35. Aristotle Papanikolaou, "Sophia, Apophasis, and Communion: The Trinity in Contemporary Orthodox Theology," in *The Cambridge Companion to the Trinity*, ed. Peter Phan (Cambridge: Cambridge University Press, 2011), 245.

36. Bulgakov is careful though to note the difference between Creator and the created in regard to time and space. See Bulgakov, *The Lamb of God*, 89–101.

37. Bulgakov, *Lamb of God*, 111–40.

38. Papanikolaou, "Sophia, Apophasis and Communion," 245.

39. Sergeĭ Bulgakov, *The Comforter*, trans. Boris Jakim (Grand Rapids, MI: Eerdmans, 2004), 54–55. Originally published as *Uteshitel'* [The Comforter], pt 2 of *O bogochelovechestve* (Paris: YMCA-Press, 1936).

40. Papanikolaou, "Sophia, Apophasis, and Communion," 245. My italics.

41. Rahner and Barth brought these categories to the fore in the twentieth century. Rahner's axiom is "The 'economic' Trinity is the 'immanent' Trinity and the 'immanent' Trinity is the 'economic' Trinity." Rahner, *The Trinity*, 21–22. The immanent Trinity for Barth constitutes the ontological ground for the economic and this is not reversible (as it is with Rahner). Barth commences noetically with the economic but the immanent has ontic precedence. Barth, *CD I/I*, 479.

42. Katherine Sonderegger, "The God We Worship; The Worship We Owe God," *St Mark's Review*, no. 250 (2019): 6–19.

43. LaCugna, *God for Us*.

44. Paul D. Molnar, *Divine Freedom and the Doctrine of the Immanent Trinity: In Dialogue with Karl Barth and Contemporary Theology* [Rev. ed.] (London: T&T Clark, 2005).

45. LaCugna, *God For Us*, 221.

46. Molnar, *Divine Freedom*, 4.

47. A similarity of logic may be seen in Jürgen Moltmann and Ted Peters. Jürgen Moltmann, *The Crucified God: The Cross of Christ as the Foundation and Criticism of Christian Theology*, trans. R .A. Wilson and John Bowden (London: SCM Press, 1974). Originally published as *Der gekreuzigte Gott*, 2nd ed. (Munich: Chr. Kaiser Verlag, 1973); Peters, *God as Trinity*.

48. Molnar uses a similar term—"pseudo-distinction"—to refer to the disjunction between the economic and immanent Trinity. Molnar, *Divine Freedom*, 137.

49. According to Leighton, Hegel's philosophy as "pre-eminently a philosophy based on experience" gave eloquence to a logic of divine manifestation in the temporality of the world. See J. A. Leighton, "Hegel's Conception of God," *The Philosophical Review* 5, no. 6 (1896), 602. For Hegel, this divine manifestation was conceived in a manner where the "immanent trinitarian sphere requires the economy in order to be real or 'actual.'" A consequence of this divine dependency on creation "is that it effectively abolishes the classical immanent-economic Trinity schema, since it makes the immanent Trinity something like the first moment of a process of divine self-development from the less to the more real." O'Regan points out that Hegel's *The Phenomenology of Spirit* constitutes a fundamental change of direction for construing the immanent/economic Trinity than Augustine's *De Trinitate* or Aquinas' *Summa*. Hegel's Trinitarian concept as a "perfect symbol for a dynamic, self-differentiating divine who necessarily becomes in and through history" has, for many modern

theologians, become a default theological construct to fuse divine "stasis and becoming." See Cyril O'Regan, "The Trinity in Kant, Hegel and Schelling," in *The Oxford Handbook of the Trinity*, eds. Gilles Emery and Matthew Levering (Oxford: Oxford University Press, 2011).

50. For example, see Robert W. Jenson, *Systematic Theology: The Triune God*, vol. 1 (New York: Oxford University Press, 2001); R. Goetz. "The Suffering God: The Rise of a New Orthodoxy," *Christian Century* 103, no.13 (1986): 385–89. EBSCOhost ATLA Serials; Moltmann, *The Crucified God*, 246–49; Ted Peters, *God as Trinity*.

51. See for example, Paul Molnar, *Faith, Freedom and the Spirit: The Economic Trinity in Barth, Torrance and Contemporary Theology* (Downers Grove, IL: InterVarsity Press, 2015), 130.

52. LaCugna, *God For Us*, 8.

53. LaCugna, *God For Us*, 1.

54. LaCugna, *God For Us*, 210. See also Catherine Mowry LaCugna, "The Relational God: Aquinas and Beyond," *Theological Studies* 46, no. 4 (1985): 647.

55. LaCugna, *God For Us*, 227.

56. Molnar, *Divine Freedom*, 4.

57. Molnar, *Divine Freedom*, 4. Philosopher John Macmurray emphasizes how "relations of persons is constitutive of personal existence; that there can be no man until there are at least two men in communion." John Macmurray, *Persons in Relation: Being the Gifford Lectures Delivered in the University of Glasgow in 1954* (London: Faber, 1970), 12. LaCugna's insights regarding the orientation toward the "other" in both human and divine being and her Trinitarian conclusions regarding persons-in-relation are indebted in part to Macmurray. See LaCugna, *God For Us*, 259.

58. Thomas G. Weinandy, *The Father's Spirit of Sonship: Reconceiving the Trinity* (Edinburgh: T&T Clark, 1995), 130.

59. Weinandy, *The Father's Spirit*, 129.

60. LaCugna, *God For Us*, 299. My italics.

61. Contra Barth is who argues that God "does not will to exist for Himself, to exist alone. On the contrary, He is Father, Son and Holy Spirit and therefore alive in His unique being with and for and in another . . . He does not exist in solitude but in fellowship." See Karl Barth, *Church Dogmatics: The Doctrine of God, Part I*, vol. 2, eds. G. W. Bromiley and T. F. Torrance (Edinburgh: T. & T. Clark, 1957). Hereafter *CD II/1*.

62. LaCugna, *God For Us*, 299. My italics.

63. Jacqueline Service, "Trinity, Aseity, and the Commensurability of the Incommensurate One," *St Mark's Review*, no. 250 (2019): 71.

64. Jürgen Moltmann also refers to God's eternal being as love but equates this, like LaCugna, with the act of creation, viewed as a form of divine necessity. Although Moltmann does attempt to nuance his views saying, "there is no external necessity which occasions his creativity, and no inner compulsion which could determine it." Jürgen Moltmann, *God in Creation: A New Theology of Creation and the Spirit of God*, trans. Margaret Kohl (New York: Harper & Row, 1985), 75. However, Molnar argues that Moltmann's reasoning that "in loving the world God is 'entirely himself'"

ultimately renders God contingent on creation for his being. See Molnar, *Divine Freedom*, 211–16.

65. For more on divine persons as subsistent relations see James E. Dolezal, "Trinity, Simplicity and the Status of God's Personal Relations," *International Journal of Systematic Theology* 16, no. 1 (2014): 88–91.

66. Weinandy, *The Father's Spirit*, 130. See also Jacqueline Clark [Service], "'A Disabled Trinity' Help or Hindrance to Disability Theology?" *St. Mark's Review*, no. 232 (2015): 58–59.

67. Barth maintains that one does not achieve a doctrine of God the other way around i.e., considering creation first. While Barth rejects Augustine's triune vestiges in creation as being unable to serve as a second root for the doctrine of the Trinity, he does concede that these vestiges can be illustrative as long as they are preceded by revelation. See Barth, *CD I/1*, 334–44.

68. Barth, *CD I/1*, 342.

69. Hans Urs von Balthasar, *Theo-Drama: Theological Dramatic Theory: The Action*, vol. 4, trans. Graham Harrison (San Francisco, CA: Ignatius, 1994), 322. Hereafter *ThDrIV*. Originally published as *Theodramatik: Bd. III: Die Handlung* (Einsiedeln: Johannes Verlag, 1980).

70. Barth means by "effect" what God "accomplishes, creates and gives in His revelation." See Barth, *CD I/1*, 297.

71. Justin Stratis, "Speculating about Divinity? God's Immanent Life and Actualistic Ontology," *International Journal of Systematic Theology* 12, no. 1 (2010): 23. Original italics.

72. Geoffrey W. Bromiley, *Introduction to the Theology of Karl Barth* (Edinburgh: T&T Clark, 2001), 21. Barth's link between the immanent and economic Trinity is summed up in his phrase "antecedently in himself"—the Son in the economy is the eternal Son; he is Word because he is "antecedently" the Word. Barth, *CD I/1*, 441, 457, 466.

73. LaCugna, *God For Us*, 212.

74. Piet Schoonenberg, "Trinity—the Consummated Covenant: Theses on the Doctrine of the Trinitarian God," *Studies in Religion* 5, no. 2 (1975): 111–16.

75. LaCugna, *God For Us*, 219. Original italics.

76. Volf argues that God's perfect being is not a mere repetition but translation into the economy of the world. See Miroslav Volf, "The Trinity Is Our Social Program: The Doctrine of the Trinity and the Shape of Social Engagement," *Modern Theology* 14, no.3 (1998): 414–15.

77. LaCugna, *God For Us*, 227.

78. Gordon D. Kaufman, *Systematic Theology: A Historicist Perspective* (New York: Scribner, 1968), 102 at footnote 9.

79. LaCugna, *God For Us*, 200.

80. LaCugna, *God For Us*, 221.

81. LaCugna states, "every attempt to describe the immanent Trinity pertains to the face of God turned towards us. *Therefore the economy of salvation is just as ineffable as is the eternal mystery of God (theologia).*" LaCugna, *God For Us*, 230. Italics original. Gilles Emery makes a similar nuanced observation—"The doctrine of the

economic Trinity is no less speculative than that of the immanent Trinity . . . it is rather the last fruit of a reflection founded in the speculative reading of the documents of revelation, when doctrinal speculative principles are applied to the agency of the Persons as taught by Scriptures." Gilles Emery, *Trinity in Aquinas*, 2nd ed. (Ann Arbor: Sapientia Press, 2006), 294.

82. Weinandy, *The Father's Spirit*, 130–31.

83. Kant states "noumena is quite incomprehensible, and beyond the sphere of phenomena . . . the class of noumena have no determinate object corresponding to them, and cannot therefore possess objective validity." Immanuel Kant, *The Critique of Pure Reason* (Auckland: The Floating Press, 1969), 345–46. See also John M. A. Frame, *History of Western Philosophy and Theology*, 1st ed. (Phillipsburg, NJ: P&R Publishing, 2015), 256.

84. Weinandy, *The Father's Spirit*, 131.

85. Molnar, *Divine Freedom*, 134.

86. Molnar, *Divine Freedom*, 134. Barth argues that panentheism was worse than pantheism saying that "The mythology of a merely partial . . . and selected identity of God with the world, which under the name of panentheism has been regarded as a better possibility than undiluted pantheism, is really in a worse case than is that of the latter." Barth, *CD II/1*, 312.

87. LaCugna, *God For Us*, 227.

88. LaCugna, *God For Us*, 227. My emphasis.

89. Stratis, "Speculating about Divinity," 24.

90. LaCugna, *God For Us*, 219.

91. Yves Congar, *I Believe in the Holy Spirit*, trans. David Smith, vol. 3 (New York: Seabury Press, 1983), 15. LaCugna, *God For Us*, 219.

92. This point is decisive for my arguments, and is further extrapolated through Bulgakov, Pannenberg, and Von Balthasar's theology in chapters 4, 5, and 6.

93. Weinandy, *The Father's Spirit*, 130.

94. Scott Harrower, "Bruce Ware's Trinitarian Methodology," in *Trinity without Hierarchy: Reclaiming Nicene Orthodoxy in Evangelical Theology* eds. Michael F. Bird and Scott D. Harrower (Grand Rapids, MI: Kregel Academic, 2019), 311.

95. For example, John 3:16; 6:38; 15:26; Acts 2:33; 1 Cor 11:3; Gal 4:4. Bruce A. Ware, "How Shall We Think about the Trinity?" in *God under Fire*, eds. Douglas S. Huffman and Eric L. Johnson (Grand Rapids, MI: Zondervan, 2002); Bruce A. Ware, *Father, Son and Holy Spirit: Relationships, Roles and Relevance* (Wheaton. IL: Crossway, 2005); Wayne Grudem, *Systematic Theology: An Introduction to Biblical Doctrine* (Grand Rapids, MI: Zondervan, 1994); Wayne Grudem, *Biblical Foundation for Manhood and Womanhood* (Wheaton, IL: Crossway, 2002).

96. Various issues are raised in Kevin Giles, *The Trinity & Subordinationism: The Doctrine of God and the Contemporary Gender Debate* (Downers Grove, IL: InterVarsity Press, 2002); and Kevin Giles, *The Headship of Men and the Abuse of Women: Are They Related in Any Way?* (Eugene, OR: Cascade Books, 2020).

97. Michael F. Bird and Scott D. Harrower, eds., *Trinity without Hierarchy: Reclaiming Nicene Orthodoxy in Evangelical Theology* (Grand Rapids, MI: Kregal Academic, 2019).

98. Millard J. Erickson, *Who Is Tampering with the Trinity? An Assessment of the Subordination Debate (*Grand Rapids, MI: Kregel, 2009).

99. Erickson, *Who Is Tampering with the Trinity?* 250. My italics. See also page 81 of the same work.

100. Letham, regarding ontological implications, says the idea "that God decreed for redemptive purposes that the Son appear in a way different than He eternally is . . . would cast a huge question over the reality of our knowledge of God." Letham and Giles, "Is the Son Eternally Submissive to the Father?" 5. Ware also states "If our knowledge of God is limited to his economic and historical self-disclosure . . . we would be fully in the dark" as to revelation of the divine nature. Ware, "How Shall We Think about the Trinity?" 258–59.

101. Ware and Grudem both arguably align with human constructions. However, Michael Gorman argues that the Apostle Paul understood divine power as expressed in Christ's kenosis of "self-humbling and self-giving" not the power of "influence" or "self-interested control." Michael J. Gorman, *Cruciformity: Paul's Narrative Spirituality of the Cross* (Grand Rapids, MI: W.B. Eerdmans Pub., 2001), 303. See also Michael J. Gorman, *Inhabiting the Cruciform God: Kenosis, Justification, and Theosis in Paul's Narrative Soteriology* (Grand Rapids, MI: William B. Eerdmans Publishing, 2009).

102. Fred Sanders, *The Triune God*, New Studies in Dogmatics (Grand Rapids, MI: Zondervan, 2016), 156.

103. Sanders, *The Triune God*, 156.

104. Sanders reflects usefully on the interplay between the use of reductive exegetical proof-texting and what he calls the "apprehensions of the total witness of Scripture" in the development of Trinitarian hermeneutics in Fred Sanders, *The Triune God*, New Studies in Dogmatics (Grand Rapids, MI: Zondervan, 2016), 155–89.

105. Scott Harrower, *Trinitarian Self and Salvation: An Evangelical Engagement with Rahner's Rule* (Eugene, OR: Pickwick, 2012), 156. Fred Sanders likewise raises similar concerns, saying: "If the relation of economic to immanent is one of strong identity, then it becomes difficult to explain the sequence and variation of economic relationships . . . How can these diverse or changing relationships all be attributed to the one eternal life of God? Evenhanded theological interpretation of all the economic occurrences would soon generate multiple doctrines: a *spirituque* formula at the incarnation, a *filioque* at Pentecost, and a strange near-collapse of the persons into each other in the eschaton, when the Son returns the kingdom to the Father (1 Cor 15)." Fred Sanders, *The Image of the Immanent Trinity: Rahner's Rule and the Theological Interpretation of Scripture,* Issues in Systematic Theology 12 (New York: Peter Lang, 2005), 167–68.

106. Harrower, *Trinitarian Self and Salvation,* 156.
107. Harrower, *Trinitarian Self and Salvation,* 156.
108. Harrower, *Trinitarian Self and Salvation,* 158.
109. Harrower, *Trinitarian Self and Salvation,* 158.
110. Pannenberg, *ST1*, 305.
111. Pannenberg, *ST1*, 320.

112. Christiaan Mostert, *God and the Future: Wolfhart Pannenberg's Eschatological Doctrine of God* (London: Bloomsbury Publishing Plc, 2002), 229. My italics.

113. Pannenberg, *ST1*, 320.

114. Barth, *CD II/1*, 327.

115. Scholars who argue for the concept of kenosis to be limited to the Son alone include Wolfhart Pannenberg, "God's Love and The Kenosis of the Son: A Response to Masao Abe," in *Divine Emptiness and Historical Fullness: A Buddhist-Jewish-Christian Conversation with Masao Abe*, ed. Christopher Ives (Valley Forge, PA: Trinity Press International, 1995), 244–50; and Bruce Lindley McCormack, *The Humility of the Eternal Son: Reformed Kenoticism and the Repair of Chalcedon*, Current Issues in Theology (Cambridge: Cambridge University Press, 2021).

Chapter 2

Beyond Static Perfection

Divine Self-Enrichment and Classical Theism

DIVINE DYNAMISM AND CHRISTIAN CLASSICAL THEISM

> "There is but one only living and true God, who is infinite in being and perfection, a most pure spirit, invisible, without body, parts, or passions; immutable, immense, eternal." (Westminster Confession. II.i)

There was a time when the divine perfections of classical theism were sine qua non for a Christian doctrine of God, where the interrelated concepts of simplicity, aseity, immutability and impassibility served as primary qualifiers of divine being.[1] Recent debate, however, has cast doubt on the relevance and accuracy of ascribing these terms to the Christian God.[2] A contemporary chorus strenuously rejects the classical divine attributes as antithetical to advocating a dynamic divine relationality. At first glance, such a rejection may seem beneficial for the envisioned dynamism of Divine Self-Enrichment, in its alleged support of a logic of divine attributes unhindered by the alleged straight-jacket of classical theism. However, such a rationale is not the architecture for the constructive theology at hand. Rather, this chapter's intent is to establish that the logic of intratrinitarian enrichment not only has theological continuity with classical Christian theism, but is, in fact, secured by it. A primary reflection of this chapter is the Christian reconfiguration of the Greek metaphysic of simplicity (and its correlates of aseity, immutability and impassibility) in light of the Incarnation. Such a reconfiguration, unlike a strict Greek view of simplicity that commits to a notion of a static singularity, is not only consistent with triune dynamism, but is necessary to posit the infinite and abundant animation of the One triune God. A Christianly-configured divine simplicity undergirds both the dynamism of triunity and a distinct divine ontology while avoiding the illation of tritheism or restricting God's relationality with creation. Before turning to the substantive core of these issues let me briefly provide some definitional clarity.[3]

Definitional Clarity

Divine simplicity is a foundational premise undergirding divine aseity, immutability and impassibility.[4] Stemming from "Neoplatonic and Aristotelian frameworks,"[5] simplicity renders the divine free of composition and is invoked to preserve the undividedness of divine ontology necessary for divine perfection. James E. Dolezal defines simplicity in an apophatic sense, "as God's *lack* of parts . . . he is [not] physically, logically, or metaphysically composite."[6] As such, there is "no diversity or change or multiplicity of parts, or accidents, or . . . any other forms" in the divine essence.[7] As Anselm of Canterbury states, "that which has parts can be divided either actually or conceivably, and division in either way is totally foreign to God."[8] The ontological perfection of simplicity expresses "completion, definiteness, limit, intelligibility, and exemption from motion."[9] For Aristotle, simplicity indicates "actualized potential" and is primary for the logic of perfection. Frederick Sontag explains: "Potentiality comes to be ruled out of the Divine nature because of its opposition to actuality; and change, time, motion, and incompleteness are left to represent a lack of perfection."[10] Dolezal, denoting simplicity as the lack of composition by substance or accidents,[11] explains its *theological* importance:

> If God were to be so determined one would have to say that there are aspects of God's being that are true in virtue of something other than his divine substance. That is, God as *divine* would not be sufficient to account for the full range of his actuality—he would depend upon something non-divine (i.e., the accident) for some aspect of his being. The doctrine of God's simplicity aims to rule out just such dependence.[12]

Stemming from the primary metaphysic of simplicity, the other perfections of divine aseity, immutability and impassibility receive their clarification. Augustine highlights the nexus—"nothing simple is changeable,"[13] and again, "there is nothing accidental in God, because there is nothing changeable or that may be lost."[14] Richard Creel similarly outlines the interconnected reasoning for divine immutability—"Anything that is absolutely perfect cannot change by getting better, nor can it change by getting worse . . . Therefore, since God is absolutely perfect, God cannot change."[15] Likewise, the correlated concept of impassibility retains a similar proximity of meaning as a property "insusceptible to causation."[16] Thus, Creel states, "to say that God is impassible is to say that God cannot be affected by anything."[17] Thomas Weinandy expands the definition of impassibility as he relates it to the nature of the contemporary debate regarding divine attributes, stating, "From the dawn of the Patristic period Christian theology has held as axiomatic that God is impassible—that is, He does not undergo emotional changes of state, and so cannot suffer."[18] It is important, however, to emphasize that immutability and impassibility do not correlate in meaning to mere immobility or impassivity.[19] Indeed, Christian theology has traditionally accepted the parameters of simplicity and its associated metaphysical constructs not only as part of the necessary landscape to map the logic of a doctrine of God, but to specifically locate a monotheistic triunity that is profoundly relationally dynamic.

SIMPLICITY AND DIVINE SELF-ENRICHMENT

It is on two accounts that divine simplicity is necessary for construing a theology of Divine Self-Enrichment. First, it provides the deep logic by which to sustain an argument that the triune God relationally constitutes well-being *ad intra* while simultaneously avoiding the charge of tritheism; and second, it provides a *desideratum* of logic to expound a distinct ontology of divine well-being. That is, simplicity secures the concept of a *Divine-self* that is the subject of intra-enriching movements. This stands in contrast to certain modern theological perspectives that regard God's (well-) being as contingent on creation. As I will argue, however, simplicity and the related theistic concepts of the tradition are necessary to repudiate the imputation of accidental potentiality into divine being; a state that necessarily implies divine deficiency and undermines a concept of the pleroma of divine *all*-blessedness. Before focusing on this core contention, two issues require attention. The first addresses the contemporary theological objection that classical theism is incongruent with biblical revelation and represents an uncritical acquiescence to Greek philosophy. The second, responds to arguments that divine simplicity is incoherent with a dynamic of triune well-being.

The Contemporary Divine Perfections Debate

In the contemporary debate over the divine perfections, both sides express disquiet about the implications not only for who God is and how God acts in the economy but also for construing human-divine relations. The debate is broadly drawn as an unbridgeable dialectic of two viewpoints. On the one hand, the modern revisionist view that allegedly champions a dynamically relational God based on a "biblical" hermeneutic (the "new orthodoxy"), and on the other, a "static" and relationally deficient God derived from categories of Greek metaphysics (classical theism). Inherent to this dialectic is the overarching allegation promoted by modern revisionists that early and consecutive eras of the church uncritically, and without qualification, endorsed and embraced a Greek philosophical paradigm to shape theological conviction regarding the divine perfections and, as a consequence, distorted the "biblical" attributes of God. This, alongside theological anxiety concerning the relationship of the Christian God to creation and *vice versa*, precipitates what Kevin Vanhoozer describes as "the demise of the classical paradigm,"[20] and leads Ronald Goetz to herald the "rise of a new orthodoxy"[21] in relation to understanding the divine perfections. This "new orthodoxy" argues for a rejection of simplicity, aseity, immutability, and, in particular, impassibility, as untenable propositions for the Christian God.[22] John Sanders, advocating the perspective of the "openness of God," locates the need for a revision of the classical divine perfections in his assertion that immutability and impassibility restrict theological contemplation of a relational, responsive and loving God.[23] Likewise, Moltmann's negative construal of divine impassibility generates a similar contemporary push for censure, particularly his logic that the dynamic of divine love is incompatible with impassibility—"Were God incapable of suffering in any respect, and therefore in an absolute sense, then He would also be incapable of love."[24]

In response to these allegations, a rigorous refutation has been delivered by scholars who contend for the continued theological relevance of classical theistic categories. These scholars consider that the "new orthodoxy," in fact, exerts a greater detrimental impact to the theological enterprise. Weinandy is forthright in his polemic, stating, "I believe that the entire project on behalf of a passible and so suffering God is utterly misconceived, philosophically and theologically. It wreaks total havoc upon the authentic Christian gospel."[25] David Bentley Hart, highlighting "the haste with which we have tried to free ourselves from the constraints placed upon our discourse by classical Christian thought,"[26] argues that those who reject the divine perfections "have not sufficiently thought through the implications."[27] For Hart, when the divine perfections of Christian tradition are misunderstood and rejected, negative implications abound for theodicy and for understanding the relation and nature of God and humanity.[28] Gavrilyuk also highlights negative implications, arguing that "unqualified passibility" imperils divine transcendence and renders "the assumption of the human nature in the Incarnation" redundant.[29] While Hunsinger emphasizes how a rejection of divine simplicity logically results in the turn to "metaphysical historicism" (where God's being is determined by divine historic action in creation) that "strongly conditions" if not "compromises" divine freedom.[30] These negative implications, particularly for a theology of Divine Self-Enrichment, will be discussed in more depth shortly, but given the significance of the scholarly caution, a degree of circumspection toward an uninterrogated rejection of classical theistic categories appears warranted. Not only so but, in the final assessment, this circumspection bears out that the "new orthodoxy" not only fails to deliver on its promise of a creative revision of alleged past errors but contributes to the demise of theological substructures that secure Christianity's distinct divine narrative. An unexamined and hasty corrective to expunge the classical perfections from Christian discourse, in fact, undermines concepts of divine freedom, transcendence, faithfulness, relationality and love, and holds significant negative ramifications for a theology of triune well-being.

Christianity and Greek Metaphysics

One problematic aspect of the turn to a "new orthodoxy" is that the justifying arguments often fail to accurately engage the reasoning they ostensibly admonish. Rather than sparring with the nuanced views of theologians regarding the *theological function* of the classical perfections, revisionists tend toward establishing a "straw-man" argument of a philosophically assembled God that is statically impervious to the created order. In due course, this straw-man is then dismantled with minimal resistance. Gavrilyuk identifies that the basis of the "convenient polemical starting point for the subsequent elaboration of a passibilist position"[31] tends to be a caricature that the early church delineated flawed attributes to the Christian God based on mere Greek metaphysics. He describes this polemical starting point as the uncritically received "Theory of Theology's Fall into Hellenistic Philosophy."[32] Gunton typifies what Gavrilyuk exposes when he reasons: "one of the tragedies . . . of Christian theological history [is] that the Old Testament was effectively displaced by Greek philosophy as the theological basis of the doctrine of God, certainly so far as the doctrine of the divine attributes is concerned."[33] Commensurate with this alleged displacement of Hebraic divine qualities it is also argued that the early church appropriated Hellenic impersonal qualities to describe the God of Abraham. On this basis, scholars assert that influential theologians, such as Anselm, contorted the revelation of God in the gospels to fit preconceived Greek metaphysics.[34] Such metaphysics are then impugned with ascribing false "classical" perfections to God that result in a divine caricature of the following ilk: this God "takes no interest in human affairs and is entirely immune from suffering. This deity cannot be influenced by anything external. It is useless to pray to it, except for the psychological benefit of moral exercise. Being incapable of feelings and emotions, such a God is also incapable of love and care."[35] On such a view one can empathize with the position Oswald Bayer reaches as he reacts to this supposed metaphysically-distorted divine depiction. He asserts that a theology of the Incarnation cannot but destroy "the axiom of divine impassibility (apathy)" because impassibility (like simplicity) has "its source in Greek metaphysics which held that God, the unmoved mover, is immutable and therefore incapable of suffering."[36] While biblical and metaphysical aspects of the divine nature undoubtedly remained un-synthesized, to indict earlier church theology *carte blanche* with merely ceding to the "God of the Philosophers" is more than somewhat misleading. It amounts to an inaccurate portrayal.

An attentive reading of early church theology explicates that here was no mere acquiesce to Greek metaphysical conceptions. Rather, biblical contemplation and the material reality of the Incarnation transformed the metaphysical cogency of the divine perfections. Although Gavrilyuk concedes that "it has almost become commonplace in contemporary theological works to pass a negative judgment upon the patristic concept of divine impassibility,"[37] his research demonstrates these judgments are made "without any serious analysis of its actual function in the thought of the Fathers."[38] Gavrilyuk delivers a compelling case for emending what he perceives to be the contemporary misinterpretation of divine simplicity's metaphysical sister—divine impassibility. Weinandy, likewise, considers the popular rejection of impassibility as an "utterly misconceived"[39] critique of early church theology and argues:

> The present critique of the Fathers is then entirely misconceived. Contemporary theologians wrongly hold that the attribute of impassibility is ascribing something positive to God, that is, that He is static, lifeless, and inert, and so completely devoid of passion. This the Fathers never countenanced. The Fathers were merely denying of God those passions that would imperil or impair those biblical attributes that were constitutive of His divine being. They wished to preserve the wholly other-ness of God, as found in Scripture, and equally . . . to profess and enrich, in keeping with His complete otherness, an understanding of His passionate love and perfect goodness.[40]

Muller also delivers a similar objection to the contemporary shift that treats the core metaphysic underlying impassibility, that of simplicity, "as purely philosophical," arguing that such a reduction completely misses the point of simplicity's treatment in the tradition.[41] Namely, that simplicity served a fundamental theological purpose to safeguard the distinction between the Creator and the creature, or as Hunsinger explains, "to undergird God's sovereignty."[42] Contra modern caricatures, the early church advocated a dynamic and relational God, both *ad intra* and *ad extra*. However, this advocacy was not at the expense of God's transcendence and "otherness," derived in consonance with a simple divine ontology.

A Dynamic and Triune Simplicity

Even if we accept that divine simplicity is not some mere foreign philosophical interloper, but a primary category reconfigured and utilized by theologians to uphold various theological guardrails, a further contention immediately arises. Specifically, whether the very logic of simplicity is incongruous with upholding a dynamism of triune well-being. The objection might run like this: a theology of Divine Self-Enrichment implies divine composition in its advocacy of distinct movements between the persons of the Trinity, therefore, it undermines the staple concept of an unmoved-singularity ensuant to simplicity. At face value, the objection implies that divine simplicity and the dynamism of triune self-enrichment are mutually exclusive and logically incongruent.[43] Certainly, such a conundrum leads John Cooper to argue that the classical doctrine of simplicity "denies the genuine distinctions among the Persons of the Trinity."[44] While Mullins advocates that "Christians must choose either the doctrine of the Trinity or the doctrine of divine simplicity."[45] The following question therefore arises in connection with the logic of Divine Self-Enrichment—How, in the face of the alleged conflict between simplicity and Trinity can the idea of the distinct persons of the Trinity enriching one another be consistent with the metaphysical root of classical Christian theism (divine simplicity)?

Underlying the anxieties expressed by opponents of simplicity appears to be a strict adherence to a metaphysic that envisages divine simplicity as the static lack of composite parts, rather than a Christian semantic that entails "a recognition of God's rich and integral wholeness."[46] These opponents rightly reject a metaphysically static and non-relational God as incompatible with the Christian God. However, to propose that simplicity is a foreign concept at odds with the biblical revelation of a relational God, is, I believe, a misconception of the biblical nature of God's *abundant* and relationally configured simplicity. God is God's act. As Crisp maintains, "Theological claims that classical theism is 'static' or 'inert,' and should therefore be replaced . . . betray an inadequate understanding of the notion of God as *actus purus*, a staple of the classical theistic tradition."[47] Unfortunately, some interpretations of divine simplicity seem to result from an understanding of divine "ontology which sees the One as prior to the many,"[48] locating a metaphysic that is static, not dynamic, and certainly not triune. Such interpretations of divine simplicity, likewise, appear abstracted from the historical acts of God and a doctrine of revelation.

Mindful of the temptation of considering divine qualities apart from the revelation of divine acting, Barth proposes the term "perfections" instead of "attributes" when describing divine characteristics. He emphasizes that humanity never "ascribes" attributes to God, but rather God *reveals* God's own perfections.[49] Webster, likewise, insists that definitions of divine perfections must take their cue from the "places where God enacts and therefore declares his perfect being."[50] Thus, one cannot propose some "abstract deity apart from God's works."[51] God sets the ambit of what defines divine perfection, and for the Christian God, such definition is never independent from the revelation of triune identity. This means the nature of God's triune perfection is located in the economy of divine revelation. With this in mind, two types of divine simplicity may be identified—a "false simplicity" based purely on Greek metaphysics and a "genuine simplicity" based on biblical revelation of divine acts.[52] For the early church, Scriptural revelation, not mere philosophical reasoning, regulated any suspicion of a theological anomaly between Trinity and simplicity. In particular, the revelation of God through the Incarnation distinguished the Christian God from the pagan gods of antiquity and challenged the categories of a Greek metaphysical framework for perfect being. In light of the Incarnation and the subsequent elaboration of the doctrine of the Trinity, any assumption that Greek metaphysical concepts "underwent no significant critical transformation at the hands of the Christian theologians who appropriated it"[53] is difficult to sustain. As we will explore in the next section, theological reinterpretations of metaphysics led to a broader perception of the Christian God's divine simplicity as a *concentrated abundance of triune wholeness*, not a sterility of singularity. Therefore, a conclusion that "Christians must choose either the doctrine of the Trinity or the doctrine of divine simplicity"[54] only gains traction if the notion of simplicity draws from a static conception closer to a strict Greek metaphysic rather than the location of triune revelation. A reconfigured Christian metaphysic, however, frames the logic to advocate for the abundant dynamic fullness of the Trinity who depends on no accident to determine some further actuality not yet divinely possessed. Such a view optimally articulates a key precept of Divine Self-Enrichment—that *God enriches God* in, and from, the fullness of simple triune perfection. It is to this coherence of triune dynamism and divine simplicity, verified and affirmed by key theological thinkers of the patristic, medieval, and modern eras, we now turn.

Trinity and Simplicity: Patristic Period

During the patristic era, Christian theologians from both the East and West did not merely acquiesce, as is often alleged, to an inherited Greek metaphysical concept of simplicity.[55] Instead, an examination of the function of divine simplicity demonstrates that, in view of the revelation of the Trinity through Christ, they significantly reconfigured the concept. A Christianly-baptized simplicity became essential for maintaining a dynamic and relational triune unity[56] and providing a theological guardrail against tritheism, modalism and subordinationism.[57] The Nicene Creed's affirmation of the *homoousion* of the Son and the Holy Spirit with the Father asserts the triune vibrancy of the Christian interpretation of simplicity. Through a Christian reconfiguration, simplicity no longer denoted "an absence of distinctions, but only and strictly an absence of composition."[58] The early patristic writers understood the divine relations of the distinct persons of the Trinity not as accidents in God, nor composition of substance, but as "identical with the divine essence."[59] This contention is the logical nucleus of perichoresis. Dolezal clarifies: "Insofar as the divine relations are identical with the divine nature we may say that God is relation itself and, as such, God is more intimately and perfectly personal and relational than any creature."[60] In plain terms, God's relational triune life *is* God's simplicity.

As early as Irenaeus, Christian theologians regarded simplicity as the presupposition for understanding God's nature. Irenaeus asserts that God is "a simple, uncompounded Being, without diverse members."[61] Augustine likewise perceives God's unified essence not as "an abstract principle of unity" but defined in concert with the simple triune relations. His integration of the concepts of simplicity and the inseparable operations of the triune persons enabled him to reason that divinity could not be "conceived apart from the Trinity of persons."[62] Indeed, Hunsinger argues that Augustine is not given enough credit for "refashioning the idea of divine simplicity in conformance with the biblical depiction of God."[63] He regards Augustine's view of divine simplicity in *De Trinitate* as "critically reconceived . . . so as to include real multiplicity (and therefore love and life) within itself."[64] Ayres similarly emphasizes that patristic contemplations of the Trinity resulted in the transformation of the concept of divine simplicity to include the idea that triune activity is inseparably unified.[65] He presents the argument that in conjunction with their rejection of *Homoian* theology, "Basil, Gregory, Hilary, and Augustine all use a conception of divine simplicity to explore and bolster the doctrine of inseparable operations" of the Trinity.[66] In other words, simplicity became essential for advocating a triune dynamism without giving rise to a divine being that is composite and tritheistic.

Stephen Holmes, considering the charge that the early church distorted the doctrine of God through acquiescence to a static simplicity derived from Greek metaphysics, proposes that contemporary theologians incorrectly attribute an interpretation to divine simplicity that was not present in early church theology. Using John of Damascus' theology as an example, Holmes argues that John, following earlier Church Fathers, weaves the doctrine of simplicity, Incarnation, and Trinity "so thoroughly that one must assume that he regarded them as necessarily linked doctrines."[67] Holmes argues that John of Damascus' theology in no way adopts an uncritical Greek view of divine simplicity based on an ontologically "eternal unchanging monad."[68] Instead, he argues that John reconfigures simplicity through his doctrine of the Trinity to assert that the perfection of the hypostases "prevent[s] division of the ousia," as only imperfect properties are multifarious, thus "from perfect subsistences [hypostases] no compound can arise."[69] Unlike Cooper's assessment that simplicity denies the distinctions of the Trinity,[70] John of Damascus perceives that triune perichoresis fundamentally redefines divine simplicity.[71] John's advanced contemplation is on full view as he construes that the definition of divine simplicity derives from the revelation of the Trinity, not vice versa. Such a position precipitates John's conclusion that the divine *ousia* is not compound, but "one, simple essence, surpassing and preceding perfection, existing in three perfect subsistences."[72]

A comparable correlation between divine simplicity and the complex fullness of the Trinity is also detected in John's predecessors, Gregory of Nazianzus. Nazianzus, understanding divine simplicity in harmony with the Trinity, maintains "To us there is One God, for the Godhead is One, and all that proceedeth from Him is referred to One, though we believe in Three Persons. . . . nor are They divided in will or parted in power; nor can you find here any of the qualities of divisible things; but the Godhead is, to speak concisely, undivided in separate Persons."[73] Gregory of Nyssa likewise appeals to triune simplicity when he affirms the "operation of the Father, Son and the Holy Spirit is one."[74] Significantly, Nyssa describes the dynamism of divine simplicity in a manner that resonates with Divine Self-Enrichment when he explains that "the divine nature exceeds each [finite] good, and the good is wholly beloved by the good, and thus it follows that when it looks upon itself it desires what it possesses and possesses what it desires, and receives nothing from outside itself . . . the life of that transcendent nature is love."[75] Basil of Caesarea likewise states of the Trinity that, "the divine nature is simple, not composed of various parts . . . [God] does not increase by additions, but is always complete, self-established, and present everywhere . . . He is simple in being."[76] None of these patristic views were apologetics for a rigid Greek metaphysic of simplicity. Rather, they depict the thorough transformation of the concept of simplicity in light of triune revelation. It was only with a Trinitarian-shaped simplicity that the early church could contend for key theological propositions that secured the distinctive dogmatics of a *Christian* theology. These included the inseparable operations of the triune persons codified in the Nicene Creed,[77] the concept of perichoresis that upheld triune dynamism and relationality, and a distinct divine ontology from creation. These propositions are, likewise, key to a theology of Divine Self-Enrichment.

Trinity and Simplicity: Nicolas of Cusa

A brief examination of Nicolas of Cusa's (Cusanus) medieval works, reveals the similar fitting nexus between simplicity and the concentrated abundance of the dynamic Trinity. In *De Ignota Litteratura and Apologia Doctae Ignorantiae*, Cusanus admonishes the "stiff-necked [men]" who propose a simplicity of singularity by which to conceptualize the divine essence. On his estimation, core to their problematic assertion is that they fail to "pay attention to the coincidence of unity and Trinity."[78] Cusanus, swift to pass judgment, concludes that such men possess "no understanding at all regarding theological matters."[79] Putting the matter aright, Cusanus distinguishes the complexity of God's simplicity as the "unsingularly Singular—just as [He is also called] infinite End, limitless Limit, and indistinct Distinction."[80] Employing paradoxical language through his "coincidence of opposites," Cusanus attempts to overcome "the most basic obstacle to our thinking about God: the law of non-contradiction."[81] He argues that a "paradox of opposites," such as allegedly found between simplicity and Trinity, merely exposes the limitations of human reason rather than inconsistencies regarding God's nature. Thus, speaking of the ineffability of the "divine mode,"[82] Cusanus states that: "nothing similar to it can occur to our mind—as Paul said most elegantly in Acts 17. For who can conceive of a mode which is indistinctly distinct?—as Athanasius says, 'neither confounding the Persons nor dividing the substance.'"[83] Furthermore, he opines that "it is not inconsistent with the simplicity of oneness that every number is enfolded in oneness,"[84] thus "[the doctrine of] the Super-blessed Trinity is compatible with this [doctrine of the divine simplicity]. For the infinite simplicity allows that God is one in such way that He is three, and is three in such way that He is one."[85] Simplicity, for Cusanus, is commensurate with the fullness inherent in the "Maximum" (a term he used for the triune God)—an "infinite simplicity," not a static simplicity derived from an uncritical adherence to Greek metaphysics.[86]

Divine Simplicity: Contemporary Discussions

Karl Barth explicates a similar understanding of divine simplicity. Triune simplicity is not an unchanging single barrenness, but an undivided, unchanging, triune life of abundance. Simplicity is, for Barth, a consideration of the "infinitely rich being of God"; a God "whose simplicity is abundance itself and whose abundance is simplicity itself."[87] This God, is far from the God of the "Philosophers"—a desolateness of impersonal mono-being.[88] Pickard, contemplating Barth's doctrine of simplicity, says:

Clearly for Barth, to speak of the divine simplicity is not to posit an abstract, impersonal absolute; rather the true and genuine simplicity of God—God's indivisible, indissoluble and inflexible being—is the implicate of the being of the God who loves in freedom. God's simplicity is demonstrated and confirmed in God's covenant of loving faithfulness with the creature. God's essence, revealed in God's act, is trustworthy; this is God's simpleness . . . The simplicity of God is, in this way, *transposed from bare essence to dynamic act*; from the realm of metaphysics to implicate of revelation.[89]

Advocating a similar configuration, Hart delineates the fullness of divine simplicity as commensurate with the unity and distinction of the Trinity, where "[E]ach person is fully gathered and reflected in the mode of the other; as other, as community and unity at once."[90] Interestingly, Hart's definition of divine simplicity simultaneously adduces an active mutuality between the divine Persons that indicates movements of triune enrichment. Hart argues that "the divine simplicity is the result of the self-giving transparency and openness of infinite Persons."[91] He goes on, asking and answering the question: "How is it that such a God is one? It is because each divine person, in the circle of God's knowledge and love of his own goodness . . . is a 'face,' a 'capture,' of the divine essence that is—as must be, given the simplicity and infinity of God—always wholly God, in the full depth of his 'personality.'"[92] Hart provides a contemporary reiteration of the Orthodox position that understands the subsistent relations of the Father, Son and Holy Spirit as the essence of the One God—the concentrated simplicity of the abundant and dynamic Trinity. In a similar vein, Weinandy not only emphasizes the dynamism and abundance of triune simplicity but also corroborates the continuity of the contours of a theology of Divine Self-Enrichment with divine simplicity as he reasons:

> As subsistent relations fully in act, the Persons of the Trinity are utterly and completely dynamic and active in their integral and comprehensive *self-giving to one another*, and could not possibly become any more dynamic or active in their self-giving since they are constituted, and *so subsist, as who they are only in their complete and utter self-giving to one another*.[93]

DIVINE SELF-ENRICHMENT AND SIMPLICITY

This brief selection of theological voices, spanning various Christian eras, provides insight into the complementary nature of Trinity and simplicity. Simplicity is no mere foreign interloper to be dismissed as incongruous with Christianity but rather derives its Christian interpretation from the revelation of the dynamism of the Trinity. One aspect of the challenge in the modern debate concerning the divine perfections is not simplicity *per se* but a static interpretation that remains unconfigured by the revelation of the triune God in Christ. Mullins' suggestion, therefore, that "simplicity is not a possible perfection"[94] of the Christian God only holds true if the underlying ontology of simplicity is conceived as static singularity. However, if divine simplicity is defined through the kaleidoscope of the Trinity, the concept is invested with a richness that reflects a dynamic perfecting of perfection. Accordingly, simplicity provides the logic for complexity to operate in concentrated form. Divine simplicity is therefore not incongruent with a proposal of abundance, life, movement, and enrichment within the Trinity. Rather, divine simplicity is defined as the Trinity's life of unending richness and delightful plenitude of subsistent relations. The dynamism and relationality at the center of a theology of Divine Self-Enrichment requires the logic of a Christianly reconceived simplicity on two fronts—to advocate triune interrelatedness that is not tritheistic and to uphold a divine ontology distinct from creation. The final part of this chapter now reiterates the necessity of the traditional perfections for the logic of Divine Self-Enrichment by addressing some unintended theological problems that ensue when theology rejects the classical Christian perfections.

REJECTING THE DIVINE PERFECTIONS

The preceding section acknowledges that the rejection of the classical divine attributes stems rightly from a desire to advocate a dynamic, relational and loving Creator involved in human affairs. Unfortunately, a significant element of the rejecting logic improperly envisions a static ontology accompanying the classical divine perfections. This results in the faulty view that classical theism and divine dynamism are mutually exclusive. Weinandy, noting this flawed understanding, argues that only since the rise of Hegel and Process Philosophy have theologians "perceived the extent of the deformity" of the traditional notions of divine perfections and offered an all too easy "curative procedure."[95] This procedure he summarizes as follows: "One only needs to hold that God is neither immutable nor impassible, but is both mutable and passible, and so He suffers. Presto, the gospel is once more, philosophically and theologically, its vibrant self."[96] However, beneath this "easy cure" lies a number of theological and philosophical difficulties that undermine (perhaps unintentionally, but nevertheless) the logic of God's own all-blessedness. The irony is that the quest for a dynamic Trinitarianism is mistakenly believed to require the setting aside of traditional Christian theism. Such a conclusion, however, removes the very conditions required to substantiate the perfection of divine well-being. It also results in a confused metaphysical understanding of the God of the "new orthodoxy" and fundamentally undermines a coherent theodicy.

A Confused Divine Metaphysic

Scholars who collapse the immanent Trinity with the economic Trinity are usually committed to emphasizing the interdependency between God and creation. Yet, one serious consequence that flows from this approach is that it disrupts the traditional theological interpretations of divine triune simplicity and its associated correlates—divine aseity, immutability, and impassibility. Those who reject the traditional Christian reappropriation of triune simplicity and render God's relational dynamism contingent on the world, however, arguably sacrifice the very metaphysical logic necessary for advocating a profound relationality between God and creation. Expressed differently, in rejecting divine simplicity on the reasoning that it hinders divine relationality with the world, theologians remove the necessary condition for God to actually be the divine "other" that the world may relate to. These scholars opt for a Hegelian "panentheistic historicism"[97]—where God must necessarily exist *with* creation. In an unexpected twist, theologians who make these moves arguably render God metaphysically "simple" *with* creation by removing any real distinguishing markers between God and the creation, resulting in both God and the cosmos becoming absolutely necessary. While advocates may argue that panentheism can be upheld instead of pantheism, the metaphysical effect of both constructions is to remove the "otherness" and aseity of God. Thus, Gunton contends: "panentheism cannot finally be distinguished from pantheism, because it does not allow the other space to be itself."[98] On closer examination of the reasoning behind the rejection of a reconfigured Christian theism, what becomes evident is the presence of a confused metaphysic and an inconsistency of logic.

This confusion is unveiled more specifically through a consideration of simplicity. According to classical theism, simplicity contains *no* un-actualized potential; simplicity is actualized potential. Thus, if one maintains that divine ontology necessarily exists with creation, and *vice versa*, the divine and the cosmos is imputed with actualized potential (what can be necessarily is—therefore—an absolute necessity or modal collapse). This logic results in a situation where the mutual contingency of God and creation offers no demarcation between beings (and therefore no composition). This logic thus unwittingly affirms a notion of God and the cosmos more akin to a singularity of actualized potential or a version of simplicity derived from an unconfigured Greek metaphysic. Mullins follows the logical conclusion of such a view, and concludes that divine simplicity (a strict simplicity deprived of a theological abundance of Trinitarian reality) "pushes us to modal collapse where God must necessarily exist with creation in order to be who He is."[99] This conclusion follows because if God and the world are conflated and exist necessarily together then God is actualized potential with the cosmos (simple). In other words, the world and God are contrived as a singularity of simple being of absolute necessity.

Such a collapse imperils, among other things, the very concept of divine freedom—for how can God be free if all things are absolutely necessary? Certainly, Mullins rejects divine simplicity on the basis that it restricts God's freedom (although in another forum I would want to theologically press his definition of freedom a little more) as it results "modal collapse" and is therefore inconsistent with a doctrine of the Trinity that seeks to maintain divine distinction.[100] Mullins' interpretation (and rejection) of simplicity appears, however, more akin to a static singular Greek metaphysical conception rather than the simplicity reconceived by the early church—a simplicity crafted in light of the biblical witness to God's triune dynamic self. This type of singularly-conceived, as opposed to Christianly-appropriated, understanding of divinity is ironically and unwittingly the underlying logic common to the arguments of those who reject "simplicity" and advocate that God is conditioned by creation (the "new orthodoxy"). Yet, by contending that God is ontologically conditioned by creation to be God, and that creation has eternally existed (in some form) in God, one arguably (and inadvertently) embraces a notion of divine simplicity more comparable to Greek metaphysics rather than the biblical narrative.[101] So while theologians reject a simplicity they believe is the classical Christian view, they may in fact be unintentionally embracing a logic of "simplicity" more aligned with Greek philosophy, as they uphold an endpoint that condenses into modal collapse; "where God must necessarily exist with creation in order to be who He is."[102]

To complicate things further, those who advocate for a panentheistic theology, that necessarily results in the actualized potential of modal collapse, also curiously want to presuppose a divine ontology that allows them to attribute change to God (i.e., un-actualized potential). For example, Jürgen Moltmann, rejecting "the traditional distinction between the immanent and economic Trinity,"[103] maintains that "the world is inherent in the nature of God himself from eternity"[104] (actualized potential/absolute necessity). However, he also argues that the Cross has a retroactive effect on God, and the "pain of the cross *determines* the inner life of the triune God"[105] (un-actualized potential/contingent possibility). Similarly, Ted Peters suggests that "the whole of temporal history is factored into the inner life of God"[106] (actualized potential/modal collapse) yet he also holds to a divine ontology that is not actualized by affirming that "God is in the process of becoming Godself through relationship with the temporal creation"[107] (un-actualized potential). These examples demonstrate how an unexamined metaphysical logic inadvertently renders theological statements as confused or inconsistent. How is the divine to be ontologically understood—as "actualized potential" (where the divine is defined in relation to the actuality of creation) or as "un-actualized potential" (where the divine has potentiality, thus, God continues to change in relation to the world)? When the traditional function of divine triune simplicity (to guard the distinction between the Creator and creature and to uphold God's abundant Oneness in Threeness) is inadequately considered, logical inconsistency transfers throughout the connected sinews of broader theology.

One such problem located downstream of the divine nature is in relation to what we might say of humanity made in this divine image. Let us consider some of the (il)logic. Bruce Epperly advocates that God "is shaped by all things" and "the world contributes to and shapes God's experience."[108] These statements imply that God does not ontologically have free self-determination, God has no replete aseity of being. Epperly, though, simultaneously espouses that humans are "self-determining creatures" and that "God has a vision that God seeks to embody in the context of *creaturely freedom* and *self-determination*."[109] This begs the question—How can creatures (made in the divine image) be characterized by change carried out by free will when ontologically the divine has no free will, but is rather defined by a necessary relation with the world?[110] If the ontic source of being has no free self-determination, then it follows that humanity, the *imago Dei*, would have none either. The definition provided by Mullins and Byrd is useful here. They explain:

> The source of the universe's contingency is grounded in the free and contingent will of God. If God's will to create the universe is absolutely necessary, and thus not contingent, then the grounds for the contingency of the universe will disappear . . . if God necessarily creates the universe, then everything that happens in the history of the universe is also necessary.[111]

It appears that a theology that rejects the traditional divine perfections and casts God as dependent on the creation (through the necessity of what is) unwittingly comprises God's and the creature's freedom. God, ironically, is rendered the metaphysical ground for denying human freedom and self-determination. Not only so, but as we will see, the "ramifications for this [modal collapse] for the problem of evil, grace, God's goodness . . . are disastrous."[112] Considering these ramifications, a more compelling contention for maintaining divine freedom is to assert that God's being is not a necessitated *reaction to* creation but rather a *manifestation in* creation. This divine reality then provides the basis to argue that through a creaturely repetition of the divine origin of freedom, the creature is likewise endowed with freedom.

Undermining of Theodicy

A further implication of abandoning the traditional definitions of divine perfections is that God's identity, fashioned in reaction to the world, is deprived of ontological stability to be the secure source of human hope and well-being. Such a God is arguably also incapable of being described as love. David Bentley Hart explicates this point in relation to theologies that ascribe passibility to God. He says that such an ascription does not make God "our companion in pain, but simply the truth of our pain and our only *pathetic* hope of rescue; his intimacy with us has not been affirmed at all: only a truly transcendent and 'passionless' God can be the fullness of love dwelling within our very being."[113] Hart concludes such because a divine passibility that assigns God's identity as dependent on the world logically results in worldly violence, suffering and sin becoming necessary for the expression of God's identity. Hart clarifies—"If God's identity is constituted in his triumph over evil, then evil belongs eternally to his identity, and his goodness is not goodness as such *but a reaction*, an activity that *requires the goad of evil* to come into full being."[114] While it appears counterintuitive, designating God with unqualified passibility, in fact, removes the ontologically required perfections for God *not* to be implicated as the cause of creation's suffering. On such a metaphysical construction, the divine is no longer perfect to contend with suffering and pain but is merely the source of it.

Construing God as an ontological fellow-sufferer not only delineates God as the metaphysical source of suffering but eviscerates the Cross of Christ of its "good news." Embracing an unqualified passibility is to unwittingly advocate God as the affirming entity of misery. The negative implications of such a divine metaphysic for a theological foundation of human well-being are obviously disastrous. Not only is the concept of divine all-blessedness or enrichment eradicated, but locating a human rationale and impetus for well-being sourced in divine ontology becomes elusive. That God's all-blessedness sources and shapes human well-being is severely undermined if divine being has suffering, not the pleroma of enrichment, at its core. Furthermore, if God's love is spurred by suffering how might we understand a human imitation of such a divine being? Would this mean, like the Divine originator, suffering is necessary for humans to desire and do the good? Rather than the doctrine of God offering a robust rationale for human well-being, an opposite deduction arises; where humanity, made in the image of such a God, requires impoverishment as the stimulus for goodness. On this logic, human ill-being, discomfort or distress become necessary evils to compel or initiate enriching activity. Such perverse conclusions clearly undermine Christian theology's ability to provide resources capable of alleviating human suffering or to advocate for human *well*-being.

CONCLUSION

The grave consequences of uncritically rejecting traditional theological boundaries underscore that a Christian theism, defined by the revelation of the abundant simplicity of the all-blessed Trinity, provides the optimal ground for a theology of Divine Self-Enrichment. A modern capitulation to a Hegelian metaphysic simply cannot serve as the basis for advocating a divine ontology of well-being or for offering a divine source for human resonance and imitation on three main accounts. First, it removes the "otherness" for both Creator and creation. Second, it restricts divine and human freedom. Third, it significantly undermines the central concept of a divine-*self* that may enrich itself from antecedent richness. In contradistinction, upholding classical theistic concepts allows Divine Self-Enrichment to avoid inconsistencies of logic and downstream theological consequences associated with the proposed "new orthodoxy." Divine Self-Enrichment is therefore premised on the notion that God's simplicity is triune, dynamic, complex and concentrated. Upholding triune simplicity averts a confused metaphysics and denies a divine dependency on the world, all the while upholding an intimate extensity of divine relationality with the world. Ultimately, this God is the distinct, trustworthy and perfectly good origin of the fullness of love, capable of furnishing the entirety of creation's well-being.

NOTES

1. Paul Gavrilyuk identifies the coalesced nature of these terms and argues that "divine impassibility should be located among the predicates of immutability, invisibility, incorporeality, indivisibility, incorruptibility, incomprehensibility, and the like. The interpretive difficulties that arise in the case of divine impassibility have family resemblances to those that arise in the case of other apophatic qualifiers." Paul Gavrilyuk, *The Suffering of the Impassible God* (Oxford: Oxford University Press, 2004), 61.

2. Ronald Goetz has called the rejection of the traditional perfections the "new orthodoxy" and states, in relation to impassibility, that the "ancient theopaschite heresy that God suffers has, in fact, become the new orthodoxy." R. Goetz, "The Suffering God: The Rise of a New Orthodoxy," *Christian Century* 103, no. 13 (1986): 385, EBSCOhost ATLA Serials. See also R. T. Mullins' opposition to divine simplicity in "Simply Impossible: A Case against Divine Simplicity," *Journal of Reformed Theology* 7, no. 2 (2013): 181–203. For those defending the theological importance of classical theism, see Stephen R. Holmes, "'Something Much Too Plain to Say': Towards a Defence of the Doctrine of Divine Simplicity," *Neue Zeitschrift für systematische Theologie und Religionsphilosophie* 43, no. 1 (2001): 137–54. James. E. Dolezal, *God without Parts: Divine Simplicity and the Metaphysics of God's Absoluteness*

(Eugene, OR: Wipf and Stock Publishers, 2011); Christopher Franks, "The Simplicity of the Living God: Aquinas, Barth and Some Philosophers," *Modern Theology* 21, no. 2 (2005): 275–300; David Bentley Hart, *Beauty of the Infinite: The Aesthetics of Christian Truth* (Grand Rapids, MI: Eerdmans, 2003).

3. While I say "clarity," it is acknowledged that these philosophical categories are dense and complex and have been debated extensively by great thinkers from Aristotle, Philo, Augustine to Aquinas. My intention here is to give a brief categorization. For further detailed discussion regarding these terms, see R. E. Creel, *Divine Impassibility* (Cambridge: Cambridge University Press, 1986); J. W. Richards, *The Untamed God: A Philosophical Exploration of Divine Perfection, Simplicity and Immutability* (Downers Grove, IL: Intervarsity Press, 2003); Thomas H. McCall, "Trinity Doctrine, Plain and Simple," in *Advancing Trinitarian Theology: Explorations in Constructive Dogmatics*, eds. Oliver D. Crisp and Fred Sanders (Grand Rapids, MI: Zondervan, 2014), 53–54; and Barry D. Smith, *The Oneness and Simplicity of God* (Eugene, OR: Wipf and Stock Publishers, 2014), 71.

4. See Wolfhart Pannenberg, *Basic Questions in Theology*, trans. George H. Kehm, vol. 2 (London: SCM, 1971), 165–73. Originally published as *Grundfragen systematischer Theologie*, Bd i. (Gottingen: Vandenhoeck &t Ruprecht, 1967); T. Morris, *Our Idea of God: An Introduction to Philosophical Theology* (Notre Dame: University of Notre Dame Press, 1991), 113–18. George Hunsinger highlights how the concept of divine simplicity is, for theologian Robert Jenson, the "real culprit behind the ideas, so unacceptable to the Hegelian Jenson, of divine immutability, impassibility, and timelessness." George Hunsinger, "Robert Jenson's Systematic Theology: A Review Essay," *Scottish Journal of Theology* 55, no. 2 (2002): 189.

5. Stephen Pickard, *The In-Between God: Theology, Community and Discipleship* (Hindmarsh: ATF Press, 2011), 196.

6. Dolezal, *God Without Parts*, 31.

7. Peter Lombard, *Sentences 1*, Dist. VIII.3, www.franciscan-archive.org/lombardus/I-Sent.html.

8. Anselm, "Incarnation of the Word," in *The Complete Philosophical and Theological Treatises of Anselm of Canterbury*, trans. Jasper Hopkins and Herbert Richardson, vol. 7 (Minneapolis: Arthur J. Banning Press, 2000).

9. Frederick Sontag, *Divine Perfections: Possible Ideas of God* (New York: Harper & Brothers: 1962), 23.

10. Sontag, *Divine Perfections*, 26.

11. James E. Dolezal, "Trinity, Simplicity and the Status of God," *International Journal of Systematic Theology* 16, no. 1 (Jan 2014), 81.

12. Dolezal, "Trinity, Simplicity," 81. Original italics.

13. Augustine, "On The Trinity," in *A Select Library of Nicene and Post-Nicene Fathers of the Christian Church, 1886–1889*, 28 vols. in 2 series, eds. Philip Schaff and H. Wace (Reprinted Grand Rapids, MI: Eerdmans, 1956), VI.8. (Herein *NPNF*).

14. Augustine, "On The Trinity," *NPNF*: V:IV.5.

15. Richard E. Creel, "Immutability and Impassibility," in *A Companion to Philosophy of Religion*, eds. Philip L. Quinn and Charles Taliaferro (Oxford: Blackwell Publishing, 1997), 322.

16. Creel, "Immutability and Impassibility," 314.
17. Creel, "Immutability and Impassibility," 323.
18. Thomas. G. Weinandy, "Does God Suffer?" *First Things: A Monthly Journal of Religion & Public Life* 11. no. 117 (2001): 35.
19. Kevin J. Vanhoozer, *Nothing Greater, Nothing Better: Theological Essays on the Love of God* (Grand Rapids, MI: Eerdmans, 2001), 6.
20. Vanhoozer, *Nothing Greater, Nothing Better*, 7.
21. Goetz, "The Rise of a New Orthodoxy," 385.
22. Gavrilyuk argues that "with a few significant exceptions modern theologians advocate the claim that God suffers. Scholarly opinion shows a remarkable consensus on this issue." Gavrilyuk, *The Suffering of the Impassible God*, 1.
23. In particular, Sanders states, "Though the tradition, with good intentions, employed immutability and impassibility to protect God's freedom, they were taken too far and left no room for speaking of divine openness where God, in vulnerability, binds himself to others in love." John Sanders, "Historical Considerations," in *The Openness of God: A Biblical Challenge to the Traditional Understanding of God*, ed. Clark H. Pinnock (Downers Grove, IL: Intervarsity Press, 1994), 100.
24. Jürgen Moltmann, *The Trinity and the Kingdom of God: The Doctrine of God*, trans. Margaret Kohl (Minneapolis: Fortress Press, 1993), 23. Originally published as *Trinität und Reich Gottes* (Munich: Chr. Kaiser Verlag, 1980).
25. Weinandy, "Does God Suffer?" 36.
26. Hart, *Beauty of the Infinite*, 166.
27. Hart, *Beauty of the Infinite*, 166.
28. Hart, *Beauty of the Infinite*, 164–65.
29. Gavrilyuk, *The Suffering of the Impassible God*, 20.
30. Hunsinger, "Robert Jenson's Systematic Theology," 198.
31. Gavrilyuk, *The Suffering of the Impassible God*, 2.
32. Gavrilyuk, *The Suffering of the Impassible God*, 5. Gavrilyuk outlines the widely accepted interpretation of the passibilist argument and defines it as the "Theory of Theology's Fall into Hellenistic Philosophy." According to Gavrilyuk, the main elements of the argument are: "1) divine impassibility is an attribute of God in Greek and Hellenistic philosophy; 2) divine impassibility was adopted by the early Fathers uncritically from the philosophers; 3) divine impassibility does not leave room for any sound account of divine emotions and divine involvement in history, as attested in the Bible; 4) divine impassibility is incompatible with the revelation of the suffering God in Jesus Christ; 5) the latter fact was recognized by a minority group of theologians who affirmed that God is passible, going against the majority opinion." For further details of this argument see Gavrilyuk, *The Suffering of the Impassible God*, 21–45.
33. Colin Gunton, *Act and Being: Towards a Theology of The Divine Attributes* (Grand Rapids, MI: Eerdmans, 2002), 3. The basis for this argument can be traced to Adolf von Harnack (1851–1930). Adolf von Harnack, *What is Christianity?* (Philadelphia: Fortress, 1986), 211–12.
34. Gunton, *Act and Being*, 23.
35. Gavrilyuk, *The Suffering of the Impassible God*, 2.

36. Oswald Bayer, *Theology the Lutheran Way*, trans. and eds. Jeffrey Silcock and Mark Mattes (Grand Rapids, MI: Eerdmans, 2007), 9.

37. Gavrilyuk, *The Suffering of the Impassible God*, 9.

38. Gavrilyuk, *The Suffering of the Impassible God*, 2.

39. Weinandy, "Does God Suffer?" 36.

40. Weinandy, "Does God Suffer?" 38. Weinandy refers to Justin Martyr, Irenaeus, Clement of Alexandria, Origen, Tertullian, and Novatian as the "Fathers" here.

41. Richard A. Muller, *Post-Reformation Reformed Dogmatics: The Rise and Development of Reformed Orthodoxy, ca. 1520–1725*, vol. 4 (Grand Rapids, MI: Baker Academic, 2003), 199.

42. Hunsinger, "Robert Jenson's Systematic Theology," 198.

43. Robert Jenson espouses this dialectical position when he says God "is not eternal in that he adamantly remains as he began, but in that he always creatively opens to what he will be . . . not in that he perfectly persists, but in that he perfectly anticipates." Robert W. Jenson, *Systematic Theology: The Triune God*, vol. 1 (New York: Oxford University Press, 2001), 217. Hunsinger says of Jenson's conclusion: "Why these distinctions should necessarily be alternatives is never adequately explained. Their contrariety is far from obvious." Hunsinger, "Robert Jenson's Systematic Theology," 183.

44. John W. Cooper, *Panentheism, the Other God of the Philosophers: From Plato to the Present* (Grand Rapids, MI: Baker Academic, 2006), 326.

45. Mullins, "Simply Impossible," 199. For further discussion regarding simplicity and Trinity see Richards, *The Untamed God*, 229.

46. Pickard, *The In-Between God*, 197.

47. Oliver D. Crisp, Review of *The Untamed God*—by J. W. Richards, *Scottish Journal of Theology* 58, no. 4 (2005): 493, doi:10.1017/S0036930605251578.

48. Holmes, "Something Much Too Plain to Say," 152.

49. Karl Barth, *Church Dogmatics: The Doctrine of God. Part 1*, vol. 2, eds. G. W. Bromiley and T. F. Torrance (Edinburgh: T. & T. Clark, 1957), 322. Hereafter *CD II/1*. Barth states: "there is no possibility of knowing the perfect God without knowing his perfections." Barth, *CD II/1*, 322.

50. John Webster, "God's Perfect Life," in *God's Life in Trinity*, ed. Miroslav Volf and Michael Welker (Minneapolis: Fortress Press, 2006), 144.

51. Webster, "God's Perfect Life," 145.

52. Pickard, *The In-Between God*, 198.

53. Hunsinger, "Robert Jenson's Systematic Theology," 189.

54. Mullins, "Simply Impossible," 199.

55. Ayres, commenting on the nexus between the inseparable operations of the Trinity and simplicity, notes that it was a principle found in both Latin and Greek theology. Lewis Ayres, "The Fundamental Grammar of Augustine's Trinitarian Theology," in *Augustine and His Critics*, ed. Robert Dodaro and George Lawless (London: Routledge, 2000), 51–76.

56. Karl Barth recognizes the clarification of divine simplicity through the early church's affirmation of the *homoousion* of Father, Son and Holy Spirit. Barth, *CD II/1*, 446.

57. For further argument about the use of the concept of simplicity by the Church Fathers to guard monotheistic Trinitarianism see Keith Goad, "Simplicity and Trinity in Harmony," *Eusebeia* 8, no.1 (2007): 97–118. Gilles Emery likewise discusses the nexus between simplicity and Trinity. He argues that "divine simplicity is a Trinitarian doctrine. It is essential for grasping the identity of substance of the three Persons." Gilles Emery, *The Trinity: An Introduction to Catholic Doctrine on the Triune God*, trans. Matthew Levering (Washington, DC: Catholic University Press, 2011), 91.

58. Muller, "Post-Reformation," 57.

59. Dolezal, "Trinity, Simplicity," 88.

60. Dolezal, "Trinity, Simplicity," 94.

61. Irenaeus, "Against Heresies Part 11, Chpt XIII, 3" in *The Ante-Nicene Fathers: Translations of the Writings of the Fathers Down to A.D. 325. 10 vols. 1885–1887*, eds. A. Cleveland Coxe, Alexander Roberts and James Donaldson (Reprinted, Grand Rapids, MI: Eerdmans, 1987), 374.

62. Rowan Williams, "*Sapientia* and the Trinity: Reflections on the De Trinitate," *Augustiniana* 40, no. 1 (1990): 325. Ayres argues that Augustine's "adherence to the doctrine [of inseparable operation] not only indicates his deep indebtedness to his immediate Latin predecessors, but also indicated some fundamental lines of continuity with pro-Nicene Greek theologians." Lewis Ayres, "Remember That You Are Catholic (serm. 52.2): Augustine on the Unity of the Triune God," *Journal of Early Christian Studies* 8, no. 1 (2000), 78.

63. Hunsinger, "Robert Jenson's Systematic Theology," 189.

64. Hunsinger, "Robert Jenson's Systematic Theology," 189. However, questions remain as to Augustine's un-synthesized dependence on Neoplatonism. For further discussion see Ayres, "Remember That You Are Catholic," 78.

65. Ayres, "The Fundamental Grammar," 56.

66. Ayres, "Remember That You Are Catholic," 80.

67. Holmes, "Something Much Too Plain to Say," 148.

68. Holmes, "Something Much Too Plain to Say," 146.

69. John of Damascus, *Exposition of Faith*, "Concerning the Holy Trinity," Book 1. VIII. *NPNF* 2/9: 6–11.

70. Cooper, *Panentheism*, 326.

71. Holmes, "Something Much Too Plain to Say," 149.

72. John of Damascus, "Concerning the Holy Trinity," *NPNF* 2/9: 6–11.

73. Gregory of Nazianzus, *The Fifth Theological Oration Or. 31.14. NPNF* 2/7: 322.

74. Gregory of Nyssa, *On the Holy Trinity*, *NPNF* 2/5: 328.

75. Gregory of Nyssa, *De Anima et Resurrection*, 46:93–96 translated in Hart, *The Beauty of the Infinite*, 173. See also Gregory of Nyssa "On the Soul and the Resurrection," *NPNF* 2/5: 450.

76. Basil, *On the Holy Spirit*, trans. David Anderson (New York: St Vladimir's Seminary Press, 1980), 8.21; 9.22.

77. For more information see R. P. C. Hanson, *The Search for the Christian Doctrine of God*, 694–99, 734–37.

78. Nicholas of Cusa, *Nicholas of Cusa's Debate with John Wenck: A Translation and an Appraisal of De Ignota Litteratura and Apologia Doctae Ignorantiae*, ed. Jasper Hopkins (Minneapolis: The Arthur J Banning Press, 1981), n. 23.

79. Cusa, *De Ignota Litteratura and Apologia Doctae Ignorantiae*, n. 23.

80. Cusa, *De Ignota Litteratura and Apologia Doctae Ignorantiae*, n.10. See also *Nicholas of Cusa: Selected Spiritual Writings*, ed. H. Lawrence Bond (Mahwah, NJ: Paulist Press, 1997), 122.

81. Louis Dupre and Nancy Hudson, *Nicholas of Cusa*, in *A Companion to Philosophy in the Middle Ages*, eds. Jorge J.E. Gracia and Timothy B. Noone (Malden: Blackwell, 2002), 468.

82. Cusanus speaks of "learned ignorance" of the infinite God (which he refers to as "the Maximum"). Learned ignorance is not mere ignorance but rather it acknowledges that the Maximum cannot be entirely comprehended by the finite. While we may learn about the Maximum, "our learnedness consists of knowing that we do not know." Dupre and Hudson, *Nicholas of Cusa*, 467.

83. Cusa, *De Ignota Litteratura and Apologia Doctae Ignorantiae*, n. 24.

84. Cusa, *De Ignota Litteratura and Apologia Doctae Ignorantiae*, n. 27.

85. Cusa, *De Ignota Litteratura and Apologia Doctae Ignorantiae*, n. 23. See also Nicholas of Cusa, "How an Understanding of Trinity in Unity Transcends All Things," in *Nicholas of Cusa: Selected Spiritual Writings*, 98–99.

86. Cusa, *De Ignota Litteratura and Apologia Doctae Ignorantiae*, n. 22–23. On the "maximum" see Nicholas of Cusa "On Learned Ignorance" in *Nicholas of Cusa: Selected Spiritual Writings*, 122.

87. Barth, *CD II/1*, 406.

88. See Barth *CD II/1*, 448. Barth considers monotheism "the religious glorification of the number 'one.'" He says that "we must say that God is the absolutely One . . . we cannot say that the absolutely one is God." In this manner he identifies the gulf between Christianity and Islamic proclamation of the "One God."

89. Pickard, *The In-Between God*, 201. My italics.

90. Hart, *The Beauty of the Infinite*, 174.

91. Hart, *The Beauty of the Infinite*, 173

92. Hart, *The Beauty of the Infinite*, 174.

93. Thomas Weinandy, *Does God Suffer?* (T&T Clark: Edinburgh: 2000), 48. My italics.

94. Mullins, "Simply Impossible," 194.

95. Weinandy, "Does God Suffer?" 36.

96. Weinandy, "Does God Suffer?" 36.

97. Hunsinger, "Robert Jenson's Systematic Theology," 189.

98. Colin Gunton, *The Triune Creator: A Historical and Systematic Study* (Grand Rapids, MI: Eerdmans, 1998), 142. Barth certainly equated panentheism and pantheism and objected to panentheism as much, if not more, than pantheism. He argues that "the name of panentheism has been regarded as a better possibility than undiluted pantheism, is really in a worse case than is that of the latter." See Barth, *CD II/1*, 312.

99. Mullins, "Simply Impossible," 197. Kraay explains modal collapse, in relation to the world, as "nothing could possibly be otherwise than it is." Klaas J. Kraay "Theism and Modal Collapse," *American Philosophical Quarterly* 48 (2011): 364.

100. Ryan Mullins, "In Search of a Timeless God" (PhD diss, University of St. Andrews, 2013), 199. Mullins defines modal collapse in the following terms: "A view suffers from a modal collapse when everything becomes necessary and all contingency is eradicated. One way of putting this is that there is only one possible world. The way the world is the only way things could be." Mullins, "In Search of a Timeless God," 154. I argue that Mullins' assertion—that divine simplicity results in modal collapse and must therefore be rejected as inconsistent with the doctrine of the Trinity—only gains traction if simplicity is conceived in greater continuity with a statically-singular metaphysic akin to Greek conceptions, rather than through the theological depth of the simple abundance of triune being. One does not arrive at this position if simplicity is construed through the active dynamism of triune being. For various other arguments against Mullins' argument see Joseph C. Schmid, "The Fruitful Death of Modal Collapse Arguments," *International Journal for Philosophy of Religion* 91, no. 1 (2, 2022): 3–22.

101. For a discussion of the various categories of simplicity—hard and soft simplicity see Richards, *The Untamed God*.

102. Mullins, "Simply Impossible," 197.

103. Moltmann, *Trinity and Kingdom*, 160.

104. Moltmann, *Trinity and Kingdom*, 106

105. Moltmann, *Trinity and Kingdom*, 160.

106. Ted Peters, *God as Trinity: Relationality and Temporality in the Divine Life* (Louisville, KY: Westminster Press, 1993), 181.

107. Peters, *God as Trinity*, 92.

108. Bruce G. Epperly, *Process Theology: Guide for the Perplexed* (London: T & T Clark International, 2011), 49–50.

109. Epperly, *Process Theology*, 66. My italics.

110. Such arguments are also seen more generally in process theology (with some nuancing of opinion). Whitehead broadly advocates that "God creates the World as that the World created God." Alfred North Whitehead, *Process and Reality: An Essay in Cosmology*, Gifford Lectures 1927–1928, eds. David Ray Griffin and Donald W. Sherburne (New York: Free Press, 1978), 348. Epperly says that God is "shaped by the dynamic interdependence of the temporal world." Epperly, *Process Theology*, 50. Alongside these propositions, Cobb and Griffin argue that the "universe is characterised by change carried out by free-will," whereby the "universe also refers to God." John Cobb and David Griffin, *Process Theology: An Introductory Exposition* (Philadelphia: Westminster Press, 1976), 14–16.

111. Ryan Mullins and Shannon Byrd, "Divine Simplicity and Modal Collapse: A Persistent Problem," *European Journal for Philosophy of Religion* 14, no. 3 (2022): 27.

112. Mullins, "Simply Impossible," 197.

113. David Bentley Hart, *The Hidden and the Manifest: Essays in Theology and Metaphysics* (Grand Rapids, MI: Eerdmans, 2017), 54.

114. Hart, *The Beauty of the Infinite*, 165. My italics.

Chapter 3

Beyond Deficiency

Enrichment from Divine Fullness

As the previous chapter has argued, the divine perfections of the Christian tradition serve as the optimal theological and metaphysical framework by which to sustain a Trinitarian dynamism integral to the concept of Divine Self-Enrichment. The onus within this chapter is now to address possible objections to the concept of "God *enriching* Godself" on the basis that Divine Self-Enrichment implies divine deficiency. If God *enriches* Godself, one might conclude that this implies that God requires some further accidental property for being. Such a requirement would impute the notion of a divine inadequacy, or paucity of perfection. However, despite such a semantic first impression, it is imperative to emphasize that a theology of Divine Self-Enrichment does not denote deficiency within God. The concept rather affirms an infinite movement of fullness that is God's self-sufficient life (aseity). As I have previously asserted, God is not a being that is replete in some singularly static manner. Rather, the triune God of Christianity is the personal, infinite and immeasurable abundance of dynamic life.

Undergirding a logic of divine abundance is not only the perfection of simplicity but the parallel metaphysic of aseity. Divine aseity is essential to adduce that Divine Self-Enrichment is actualized in the concentrated abundance of divine life. If God's well-being is the ontological predicate for human well-being, then it must first be a self-sufficient capacity of God's eternal nature. If divine being is not a *well*-being of fullness and abundance, how would a commensurate well-being be offered as a potentiality to humanity? How would the words of Christ Jesus—"I came that they may have life and have it abundantly" (Jn 10:10)—be a creaturely possibility if God did not have God's own fullness of life? Speaking of God's active *enrichment* is not, however, the invocation of a divine intra-activity that enriches the poor, fills the empty or enhances that which is deficient. These activities are what God graces in the creature, not divinity. Instead, Divine Self-Enrichment conveys

God's full and ever-expansive living life. It is not God becoming God from deficiency but the being of God as fullness. Divine Self-Enrichment of God's eternal full life is not a deficiency made whole but the actualization of the abundance of divine self-sufficiency. The enrichment of God, from God's simple, self-sufficient and concentrated fullness might best be likened to a "divine Becoming" articulated by Thomas F. Torrance, who argues: "This does not mean that God ever becomes other than he eternally is . . . but rather that he continues unceasingly to be what he always is and ever will be in the living movement of his eternal Being."[1]

THE ASEITY OF GOD: DIVINE SELF-ENRICHMENT FROM DIVINE SELF-SUFFICIENCY

Proposing that God's life is the fullness of an enriched and enriching life of aseity, that is, God's all-blessedness is self-sufficient, may raise two objections in light of the "new orthodoxy's" rejection of classical theism. First, it may be insinuated that divine aseity imputes the divine with intra-vertedness and self-enclosed narcissism, core attributes of a non-relational God of self-love. Such a "perfection," it may well be argued, is surely the antipathy of the self-giving (kenotic) God of the Incarnation. The second demurral may propose that aseity conceptually prevents God from receiving enrichment from that which is created, raising a number of questions regarding the nature of the Christian believer's relationship with God. With these objections in mind, what is contended here is that triune aseity is not only necessary for divine ontology to be regarded as the complete, stable source and telos for human well-being, but that it is theologically necessary for divine love and faithful relationality toward the creation.

John Webster's definition usefully abbreviates the concept of divine aseity[2] or self-sufficiency—"no perfection of God would be lost, no triune bliss compromised, were the world not to exist."[3] In the same vein, Jay Richards describes divine aseity as "the conviction that God is the one reality that exists *a se* (from and of himself) and is dependent on nothing outside of himself for his essence and existence."[4] Traditionally, divine aseity functioned theologically to maintain the distinction between the Creator and creature. Its biblical foundation is highlighted by the fact that "only God says 'I Am' (Ex 3:14); everything else that exists says 'I am *because* . . . ' God alone exists *a se*, everything else that exists does so in reliance upon him."[5] Nevertheless, some contemporary theologians are swift to reject aseity as incongruent with the "biblical" God by equating it with divine solitariness, narcissism, self-indulgence and non-relationality. Catherine LaCugna, for instance, bases her rejection of aseity on the view that God's perfection is "the perfection of love, of communion, of personhood" and these perfections are the "antithesis of self-sufficiency."[6] For LaCugna, God is "alive in communion with the creature";[7] therefore, God's love, communion, and personhood are derived through relationship *with* the creature. Consequently, the proposition that God is self-sufficient in triune love, communion and personhood is necessarily rejected. Disability theologian, Nancy Eiesland, asserting the same underlying assumption as LaCugna, also regards aseity as incompatible with a God who is in relationship with the creature. Eiesland couples "belief in the transcendence of God constituted as radical otherness"[8] (in other words, aseity) with a "god whose attention we cannot get."[9] LaCugna and Eiesland both regard relationality and aseity as mutually exclusive. Their common conclusion necessarily results from their chain of logic—they converge the immanent and economic Trinity, conflate the noetic and ontological, and designate God's relationship *with the creature* as determinative for God's being.

Various theologians, committed to a distinction between the immanent and economic Trinity, argue, however, that God's aseity does not infer some distant, non-relational God. Rather, aseity conveys God's self-sufficient freedom, elemental for God to truly relate to the world in a freedom defined by divinity rather than absolute necessity.[10] While the traditional Christian understanding of divine aseity signals a God obtaining composition *from the world*, the doctrine itself does not inhibit God's dynamic involvement *with the world*. A conflation of these two propositions is a misnomer. George Hunsinger highlights the error born of equating divine aseity with non-relationality, that is, of equating "commitment with strong dependence, as if a metaphysically independent God could not freely commit himself to the world, or as if God's free commitment to the world necessarily made him dependent upon it."[11] Karl Barth also recognizes that it is not contradictory to affirm both the replete satisfaction of God's own intratrinitarian being and a God who loves the world. Barth states,

> While He [God] could be everything only for Himself (and His life would not on that account be pointless, motionless and unmotivated, nor would it be any less majestic or any less the life of love), He wills—and this is for us the ever-wonderful twofold dynamic of his love—to have it not only for Himself, but also for us.[12]

The complete actuality of love within the intratrinitarian movement of God propels the demonstration of eternal "love" in and toward the creation. This love grounds the bestowal of the "fullness of life" (Jn 10:10) to humanity, as "only a truly transcendent . . . God can be the fullness of love dwelling within our very being."[13] And yet, the challenge remains—Does the proposition that God is the fullness of aseity in the eternal loving and enriching relations of Father, Son and Holy Spirit, run the risk of casting God's love as narcissistic self-love, thereby evacuating the harmony of such a concept with the biblical revelation of God's nature? I argue no; endorsing a fullness of divine aseity does not affirm divine narcissism. To illustrate this point, let me engage briefly with Jürgen Moltmann's theology for the very reason that it continues to exert considerable influence in connecting divine aseity with divine narcissism.

DIVINE ASEITY AND NARCISSISM? CONSIDERING JÜRGEN MOLTMANN'S INFLUENCE

Moltmann's theology, particularly his theology of the Cross (where suffering is ascribed into the divine being), is strongly influenced by his rejection of divine aseity. Aseity, for Moltmann, is incompatible with God's self-giving love evidenced in the economy: "God cannot find bliss in eternal self-love if selflessness is part of love's very nature."[14] For Moltmann, the creation is a necessary determinant of God's love because "Creation is a fruit of God's longing for 'his Other.'"[15] Moltmann argues for a complete repudiation of divine aseity, that is for him, a primary metaphysical culprit implicated in shaping the parameters for a narcissistic God. He contends that aseity is incongruent with a God who is selflessly for the "other."[16] In Moltmann's perspective, God's engagement with creation's "otherness" safeguards against accusations that God is narcissistic, consumed with "self-love." As such, the nature of God's self-giving love toward the "other" is an emphasized trajectory in Moltmann's work. The following quotation succinctly encapsulates Moltmann's view on this point:

> [God's] very existence is love. He constitutes himself as love. That is what happens on the cross . . . Jesus' forsakenness on the cross, the surrender of the Son by the Father and the love which does everything—gives everything—suffers everything—for lost men and women. God is love. That means God is self-giving. It means *he exists for us*.[17]

While there is much to affirm in Moltmann here, a problem weaves throughout his reasoning on the basis of his interpretation of the nature of God's self-giving love that conflates the economic and immanent Trinity. This leads him to the conclusion that it is the "pain of the cross" that determines "the inner life of the triune God from eternity to eternity."[18] In other words, something outside of Godself, an accidental property not essential to God's being, determines the nature of God's self-emptying love.[19] Significantly, the cry of Jesus' forsakenness—"My God, my God, why have you forsaken me?" (Mt

27:46) (also at the heart of Moltmann's theology of the Cross)[20]—is not only demonstrative of God's solidarity with humanity but conditions the self-emptying nature of divine love with "active suffering."[21] On Moltmann's account, such a divine nature demands that one reject an impassible and self-sufficient God. In *The Crucified God*, he reasons: "a God who cannot suffer is poorer than any man. For a God who is incapable of suffering is a being who cannot be involved . . . But the one who cannot suffer cannot love either. So, he is a loveless being."[22] The theme is also transparent in *The Trinity and the Kingdom of God*, where Moltmann's logic again results in divine ontology being imputed with pain and suffering—"[I]f God were incapable of suffering in every respect, then he would also be incapable of love. He would at most be capable of loving himself, but not loving another as himself."[23] For Moltmann, the two key factors that prevent God from being construed as a God of narcissistic and uninvolved self-love are: (1) God's love for creation; and (2) the eternal divine pain of the Cross that suffers in solidarity with the creation.

The ultimate goal of the self-emptying divine activity that Moltmann endorses is the healing restoration of humanity; a telos that most theologians would likewise affirm. Yet, given the metaphysical parameters Moltmann employs, where the cry of dereliction determines God's being, how this might result is far from clear. A significant challenge is posed by the manner in which Moltmann regards the cry of forsakenness as imputing hypostatic alienation within God's being. The self-giving of Christ on the Cross, necessary for humanity's restoration is, for Moltmann, simultaneously an abandonment of the filial relation Jesus has with the divine Father. Moltmann paints the picture for us—"If we take the relinquishment of the Father's name in Jesus' death seriously, then this is even the breakdown of the relationship that constitutes the very life of the Trinity . . . the Son does not merely lose his sonship . . . The Father loses his fatherhood as well."[24] Thomas McCall refers to this understanding as the "broken-Trinity view" and argues that it is "biblically unwarranted and theologically impossible."[25] Samuel Youngs is likewise hesitant toward Moltmann's radical conclusion, saying that its severing of the relational life of the Trinity "raises a tremendous question mark over Moltmann's system."[26] Despite Moltmann's insights, one wonders whether the ontological significance imputed to the "abandoned" cry of Christ is unbalanced. Although we can surmise that humans suffer and die, which the God-man Jesus did, it is quite another thing to hold that the cry of "forsakenness," arising from Psalm 22, is an abandonment of the subsistent relations of the Son and Father. The reference to Psalm 22 on Jesus' lips commences with this cry but abandonment is not the culminating focus of the Psalm, as verse 24 crescendos with the comfort that "he [God] has not hidden his face from him."[27] Mostert rightly questions whether the cry of abandonment "can bear the weight of an entire doctrine of God."[28] Certainly, one could sketch a far more fecund nature of divine ontology from other recorded words of Christ on the Cross. Take, for instance, "today you will be with me in Paradise" (Lk 23:43). In the Lukan declaration, we find no rent-Trinity, nor the shape of a divine ontology defined by suffering and abandonment.

While Moltmann's theological perspective encourages a renewed focus on the significance of the Cross in Christian thought, his assertion that God's self-giving love is determined by and dependent on the creation remains problematic. Moltmann arrives at such a conclusion, in part, because he correlates divine aseity with narcissism. Moltmann's statement that—"God cannot find bliss in eternal self-love if selflessness is part of love's very nature"[29]—reveals an interpretation that "eternal self-love" is incongruent with divine "selflessness." It is, though far from evident, that a self-sufficiency of divine self-love is mutually exclusive from divine self-giving. Yet, rejecting the fullness of God's aseity, he proposes that the historicity of the Cross is determinative for construing divine kenosis. He says:

> Christ's death on the cross acts from below upwards, from without inwards, out of time back into the divine eternity "He is the Lamb slain, and the Lamb slain from the foundation of the world. For this reason, the crucified Jesus is the 'image of the invisible God.'" The meaning of the cross of the Son on Golgotha reaches right into the heart of the immanent Trinity. From the very beginning, no immanent Trinity and no divine glory is conceivable without "the Lamb who was slain" . . . God is from eternity to eternity "the crucified God."[30]

Here, it appears that the divine kenosis encountered in salvation history necessarily *determines* who God is, rather than being the astonishing *demonstration of* the eternal nature of the kenotic Trinity.

Contra Moltmann, and upholding divine aseity, it is possible to maintain that the Cross reaches into the "heart of the immanent Trinity," not because the Cross changes God[31] nor because God becomes determined by its pain. Rather, because the Cross and the "Lamb slain" reflect God's eternal kenotically-enriching *life*. God is "the crucified God" in history, and salvation is accomplished through self-giving, because it is a faithful manifestation and revelation of who God is eternally—the kenotic and ecstatic God of self-sufficient triune enriching relations. God reveals Godself to the creation in fidelity to who God is. The Cross manifests resounding self-giving because the nature of God *is* eternally kenotic. Simply put, the Father, Son and Holy Spirit live the enriching life of divinity in the aseity of tri-hypostatic self-giving. Moreover, the kenotic act of God through Incarnation and atonement has salvific efficacy, it is life-giving and enriching because it manifests and shares the self-giving of triune *life* in and with the created order. God's "other-centered" love within the triune nature is manifest in Christ as love to the "other" of creation. On these terms, God's aseity is no harbinger of "bad news," but is the fullness of God that ensures the "good news" of God's work in the world. In contrast, serious questions remain for a Moltmannian view. How might imputing pain and suffering into the being of divinity elicit "good news" for humanity? Does not such a construction render God as the metaphysical ground of all suffering?[32] Furthermore, why is the *pain* of the Cross determinative for the construal of divine ontology? Could not the embrace of suffering on the Cross reflect the fullness of God's love rather than eternal pain? Christiaan Mostert comments on such considerations: "While love often entails suffering, it is not a constitutive element of love . . . We are willing to suffer with or on account of someone we love, which is a good, 'but it is precisely the love that is good and not the suffering itself.'"[33]

Divine aseity, rather than a recipe for narcissism, is a requisite metaphysic for understanding God's life as eternally constituted by self-giving love—where kenotic love, "other" centered love, *is* the enriching and self-sufficient life of the Father, Son and Spirit. Self-giving is the definitive manner by which God receives divine enrichment *in se*, and the constitutive feature of divine love revealed in the economy. Kenosis and enrichment are, in God's aseity, eternally symbiotic. Without aseity, God is arguably imputed with a deficiency requiring completion from the creation. Ironically, rather than guarding against a charge of divine narcissism, this type of relationality could be construed as the ultimate narcissism, where God uses creation for God's own well-being and completion. Divine aseity, however, removes this possible conclusion. God's self-sufficiency is altogether different from narcissism because the nature of divine life is the replete actualization of tri-hypostatic selflessness, the turning of Father, Son and Spirit in endless othering love. As Barth argues, "Why should God not also be able, as eternal love, to be sufficient unto Himself? In His life as Father, Son and Holy Spirit He would in truth be no lonesome, *no egotistical God* even without man, yes even without the whole created universe."[34] God's life is not constituted by egoistic-enrichment but by the eternal kenosis of the triune persons. Divine life and love are therefore commensurate with triune self-giving. Moltmann's charge that God is narcissistic without the "other" of creation might hold true for a purely mono-God. However, the Christian God's abundant Tri-unity of enriching relations means that the ontological being of God is eternally other-centered, a point highlighted again by Barth:

> As He is the Father who begets the Son He brings forth the Spirit of love, for as He begets the Son, God already negates in Himself, from eternity, in His absolute simplicity, all loneliness, self-containment, or self-isolation. Also and precisely in Himself, from eternity, in His absolute simplicity, God is oriented

to the Other, does not will to be without the Other, will have himself only as He has Himself with the Other and indeed in the Other.[35]

The logic of Divine Self-Enrichment is fashioned on quite a different premise of divine self-giving (kenosis) than found in Moltmann. It underscores the primary importance of affirming aseity to advocate the fullness and perfection of divine love manifest in intra-hypostatic self-giving. This divine self-sufficient fullness of enriching self-giving (not always equated with suffering), in turn, provides the logical basis for understanding the Cross of Christ as a *demonstration* consistent with God's interior eternal life. Not only is the Cross a demonstration of the nature of God's life of kenotic-enrichment, but we can extrapolate that the acts of creation, the Covenants, the Incarnation, the Resurrection, the Parousia and consummation of the Kingdom likewise resonate and reveal the beauty of triune kenotic-enrichment.[36] The economic acts of God in history are constituted by, from and for God's abundant fullness of aseity.

DIVINE SELF-ENRICHMENT AND CREATION'S PARTICIPATION

This chapter has proposed that God's life is the fullness of an enriched and enriching life that is self-sufficient and not dependent on the non-divine for divine being. Furthermore, God's fullness of aseity constituted by intratrinitarian other-centered and self-giving love (ecstatic and kenotic love between the divine hypostases) refutes the charge that aseity constitutes divine narcissism. These concepts frame the nature of God's own enriched life and are necessary if divine ontology is to provide the theological rationale for human enrichment. One final issue, however, remains to be considered here: How does the concept of the fullness of divine aseity enable God to receive enrichment from that which is created?

Elaine Padilla, in *Divine Enjoyment: A Theology of Passion and Exuberance*,[37] using the trope of "divine erotic love," constructs a "model of divine enjoyment that allows for *reciprocal* forms of enjoyment between God and all living beings."[38] Her methodology employs "poetic imagination [and] . . . mystically embedded philosophy" mixed with a sensitivity toward Latin American feminist thought to address the important question of whether there is receptivity within God from creation.[39] Her thesis question— "whether a divine enjoyment can also stem from a *give-and-take* with the created order" is pertinent to the present discussion.[40]

In contrast to my argument, however, Padilla prosecutes her thesis through rejecting divine aseity and impassibility based on what I have described earlier as the stereotypical "straw-man" argument, or Gavrilyuk's "Theory of Theology's Fall into Hellenistic Philosophy."[41] While I appreciate her desire to quicken in humanity a "passion for enjoying the *whole* of life,"[42] and the advocacy of well-being of others based on a God of "enjoyment" in whose presence is "fullness of joy [and] . . . pleasures forevermore—Psalm 16:11,"[43] the route that Padilla traverses does not adequately circumnavigate the theological issues involved. Her work arguably falls into the category, which Hart describes, as too hastily rejecting the Christian conceptions of divine perfections without engaging with the consequences of the logic.[44] The manner by which Padilla understands and rejects the divine perfections of aseity and impassibility, to assert that God receives enjoyment from creation, reflects the caricature discussed in chapter 2 rather than a Christian reconfiguration.[45] Thus, we see her rejection founded on the erroneous interpretation that the divine perfections are "categories . . . that have become too insular and static."[46] Divine aseity and impassibility are interpreted by Padilla in such a way to render God as "enclosed within the divine self."[47] Yet, as we have already canvassed, Christian interpretations of the perfections do not normatively embrace insular and static divine categories.[48] A more nuanced contemplation could have opened another avenue for Padilla's overall contentions. As it stands, Padilla's interpretation of the God shaped by classical theism appears more mono than triune, in a "lonely affair with the self"[49] and is therefore, not surprisingly, rejected in maintenance of her thesis that God receives enjoyment *from* creation. Contrary to Padilla's constructions, I want to posit that a Christian interpretation of divine aseity does not prevent an understanding that God receives enrichment from that which is created; it merely precludes that God is determined or made replete by it.

Webster's definition of God's self-sufficiency provides a theologically invaluable understanding of the fullness of God's life where "the triune God could be without the world; no perfection of God would be lost, no triune bliss compromised, were the world not to exist; no enhancement of God is achieved by the world's existence."[50] This last statement, "no enhancement of God by the creature," contains, however, a theological problem in light of the fact that God's salvation of humanity culminates in the outpouring of the Holy Spirit to believers by which they praise God. Webster's formula of "no enhancement of God by the creature" does not adequately capture the reconciled relations between God and believers that is supremely manifested in worship. Webster's definition reflects a determination to preserve God's aseity by disallowing any concept that God's being contains a deficiency which requires enhancement by the creation. This polemic is understandable given some contemporary theologies that mythologize God through pantheistic and panentheistic tendencies foreign to Christianity. However, envisaging the "enhancement" of God by the renewed creature does not necessarily impute deficiency within God that requires satisfaction. Could we not rather hold a nuanced view that advocates that redeemed humanity enhances that which is fully enhanced, magnifies that which is magnificent, and enriches that which is eternally rich by its participation in the divine life? Hart, explicates Gregory of Nyssa's contemplation that affirms both *reception* of creaturely participation into the divine life as well as the ontological distinction of God and not-God:

> Gregory's grasp of the radical ontological disparity between God and creation is balanced by his understanding of the union of God with creation in the economy of salvation; and thus he means what he says when he calls the practice of virtue participation in God and the presence of God to the soul: he means, in a word, deification . . . despite the ontological distance between God and creation: . . . [Gregory shows] that it is not an uncrossable abyss but a genuine distance, reconciled and yet preserved in the incarnate Logos, crossed from the divine side so that it may be crossed forever from the side of the creature, and by showing that God who is infinite, for this reason, cannot be made absent by any distance.[51]

We can draw out two points from this insight. First, the creature participates in the life of God, but God does not become God because of creaturely participation. God remains God. And second, the creature, by voluntary participation in deification, by becoming like God through the act of God, magnifies the essence of divine all-blessedness.

God's own glory, recognized, participated in and conformed to by the creature, is confirmed as worthy and essential to the creature's own well-being. Such a concept is likewise highlighted by the words of the Apostle Paul, "And all of us, with unveiled faces, seeing the glory of the Lord as though reflected in a mirror, are being transformed into the same image from one degree of glory to another; for this comes from the Lord, the Spirit" (2 Cor 3:18). Humanity is enveloped into the eternal pattern that is the delight of triune self-giving love. The creature's self-giving praise and worship enriches, blesses and glorifies God through an act of God, the Holy Spirit, who enables humanity to gift to God, from the gift of God. Such a giving is in harmony with the mode of God's kenotic love; the creature participates in self-giving worship which is simultaneously life-giving. An apt designation of this patterning of the human-divine union, ontologically conditioned by the very life of God, is that creation's "praise perfects perfection."[52] The concept of the fullness of divine aseity allows creation both to receive enrichment from a replete source of well-being, and to gift enrichment to the antecedently enriched God. Understanding that creation enriches the unlimitedly enriched God through fellowship in the fullness of God's own self-sufficiency means that we do not need to enter the muddy waters of some contemporary theologies that panentheistically merge God with creation, nor disparage the early Church's advocacy of the traditional divine perfections, nor disregard the creature's worshipful self-surrender that is lovingly received by the Creator.

When we apprehend that the nature of God's kenotic-enrichment is utterly self-actualized in the fullness of aseity, and that God engages with the world consistent with who God is eternally, a further perception unfurls. We perceive that God is "actively enacting his own well-being in the world,"[53] as well as "bringing the world to its fullness *by sharing his own fullness with it.*"[54] The self-giving of God demonstrated in the acts of creation is not only a sharing of God's eternal enriching life toward creation, but is the simultaneous gift of well-being or enrichment within God. In other words, God continues to live the liveliness of God's being as he shares his life with the creation. The Apostle Paul touches on such a concept when he says, "all things have been created by Him *and for Him*" (Col 1:16). Likewise, the Son's self-emptying on the Cross not only ensures the well-being and enrichment of humanity but continues God's own eternal self-sufficient enrichment as the Son's act redeems humanity back to God—"by your blood you ransomed *for God* saints from every tribe and language and people and nation; you have made them to be a kingdom and priests serving our God" (Rev 5:9–10). None of these perceptions, however, entertain a notion that God receives "enjoyment" or "enrichment" from the cosmos as formative for God's being. Rather, what we see in the divine activity in the world is the ongoing life of God, where God is ever faithful to God's nature. God continues to receive enrichment in the eternal fullness of the triune dynamics, yet now shares the enveloping fullness of well-being with the created order.

CONCLUSION

As we have seen the replete self-sufficiency of God is yet another elemental perfection necessary to construe a cogent theology of Divine Self-Enrichment. Contra to the allegations of some contemporary theology, aseity does not undermine God's intense relationality with the world by positing a narcissistic, isolated God. Instead, upholding divine self-sufficiency secures both the active relationality of God with creation and a stable and replete divine ontology. Aseity safeguards the logic that God is the fullness of well-being actualized in the concentrated abundance of divine life. Through the lens of aseity, the enrichment of the life and love that the Trinity enjoys may be understood as the perfecting of perfection. Divine Self-Enrichment on these terms is far from the human experience of enrichment; that of enrichment from deficiency. Divine Self-Enrichment is not advocacy of a deficiency within God that requires repletion from an external, nor an internal, accidental property. To suggest so is to impute limitation into the nature of God, leaving a serious doubt as to how a God who has no self-sufficiency of well-being might be the source of well-being for the creature. The central contention of this chapter is rather that God's enriching life derives from God's fullness and self-sufficiency, and in this way explicates a further element of my axiomatic definition of Divine Self-Enrichment—God enriching God in the *perfection and fullness of God*.

NOTES

1. T. F. Torrance, *The Christian Doctrine of God: One Being Three Persons* (Edinburgh: T&T Clark, 1996), 242.

2. It is important to note here that my definition of divine aseity is connected to my interpretation of divine simplicity; that is, divine aseity is a hallmark of the "unbreakable communion (koinonia)" of the divine persons so that "none of them can be conceived apart from the rest." For the quotes above see John D. Zizioulas, "The Doctrine of the Holy Trinity: The Significance of the Cappadocian Contribution," in *Trinitarian Theology Today: Essays on Divine Act and Being*, ed. Christoph Schwöbel (Edinburgh: T&T Clark, 1995), 48. I do not, however, agree with Zizioulas' theology that ascribes aseity to the "Father" alone. For criticism of Zizioulas' ascription of aseity to the Father see Tom McCall, "Holy Love and Divine Aseity in the Theology of John Zizioulas," *Scottish Journal of Theology*, 61, no. 2 (2008): 191–205, doi:10.1017/S0036930608003955.

3. John Webster, "Trinity and Creation," *International Journal of Systematic Theology* 12, no. 1 (2010): 12.

4. J. W. Richards, *The Untamed God: A Philosophical Exploration of Divine Perfection, Simplicity and Immutability* (Downers Grove, IL: Intervarsity Press, 2003), 33.

5. McCall, "Holy Love and Divine Aseity," 196.

6. Catherine Mowry LaCugna, *God for Us: The Trinity and Christian Life* (San Francisco: HarperSanFrancisco, 1991), 304. These objections arise because modern notions of "self" are so highly problematic when applied to God. One can see the reaction against contemporary individualism influenced by Kant's autonomous self.

7. LaCugna, *God For Us*, 304.

8. Nancy Eiesland, *The Disabled God: Toward a Liberatory Theology of Disability* (Nashville, TN: Abingdon Press, 1994), 104.

9. Eiesland, *The Disabled God*, 105.

10. See for example, Paul Molnar, *Faith, Freedom and the Spirit: The Economic Trinity in Barth, Torrance and Contemporary Theology* (Downers Grove, IL: InterVarsity Press, 2015), 275–76; and George Hunsinger, "Election and Trinity: Twenty-Five Theses on the Theology of Karl Barth," *Modern Theology* 24, no. 2 (2008): 179–98.

11. Hunsinger, "Election and Trinity," 177.

12. Karl Barth, *Church Dogmatics: The Doctrine of God. Part 1*, vol. 2, eds. G. W. Bromiley and T. F. Torrance (Edinburgh: T. & T. Clark, 1957), 280–81. Hereafter *CD II/1*.

13. Hart, *The Beauty of the Infinite*, 165–66.

14. Jürgen Moltmann, *The Trinity and the Kingdom of God: The Doctrine of God*, trans. Margaret Kohl (Minneapolis: Fortress Press, 1993), 106. Originally published as *Trinität und Reich Gottes* (Munich: Chr. Kaiser Verlag, 1980).

15. Moltmann, *Trinity and Kingdom*, 106.

16. See Daniel Castelo, "Moltmann's Dismissal of Divine Impassibility: Warranted?" *Scottish Journal of Theology* 61, no. 4 (2008): 396–407.

17. Moltmann, *Trinity and Kingdom*, 82–83. My italics.

18. Moltmann, *Trinity and Kingdom*, 160.

19. Jürgen Moltmann, *The Crucified God: The Cross of Christ as the Foundation and Criticism of Christian Theology*, trans. R. A. Wilson and John Bowden (London: SCM Press, 1974), 246–49. Originally published as *Der gekreuzigte Gott*, 2nd ed. (Munich: Chr. Kaiser Verlag, 1973).

20. Moltmann's theology of the Cross is also a reflection on theodicy. Farrow places Moltmann's theology in the context of his questions in post-war Germany and the horrors of the Holocaust. Thus, for Moltmann, "theology means also theodicy: 'The question about God and the question about suffering are joint, a common question. And they can only find a common answer'... He insists that the universal significance of the cross can be understood only within the framework of the theodicy question." In Douglas B. Farrow, "Review Essay: In the End is the Beginning: A Review of Jürgen Moltmann's Systematic Contributions," *Modern Theology* 14, no. 3 (1998): 435.

21. Moltmann, *The Crucified God*, 245–47. See also Jürgen Moltmann, *A Broad Place: An Autobiography* (Minneapolis: Fortress Press, 2008), 191.

22. Moltmann, *The Crucified God*, 222.

23. Moltmann, *Trinity and Kingdom*, 23.

24. Moltmann, *Trinity and Kingdom*, 80.

25. Thomas H. McCall, *Forsaken: The Trinity and the Cross, and Why it Matters* (Downers Grove, IL: IVP Academic, 2012), 46. Mostert maintains that Moltmann is more nuanced when he argues in *The Crucified God* that the Cross "contains community between Jesus and his Father in separation, and separation in community." Christiaan Mostert, "Moltmann's Crucified God." *Journal of Reformed Theology* 7, no. 2 (2013), 176, where he quotes Moltmann, *The Crucified God*, 244. However, one cannot help but note the pneumatological depletion in the content of Moltmann's *Trinity and The Kingdom of God* and *The Crucified God* and ponder whether this contributes to the theological deficiency that evolves into the rent-Trinity problem.

26. Samuel J. Youngs, "Wounds of the Emptied God: The Role of Kenosis at the Cross in the Christologies of Jürgen Moltmann and Sergius Bulgakov," *American Theological Inquiry* 4, no. 2 (2011): 56.

27. N. T. Wright, *Jesus and the Victory of God: Christian Origins and the Question of God*, volume 2 (London: SPCK, 1996), 600–601.

28. Mostert "Moltmann's Crucified God," 166.

29. Moltmann, *Trinity and Kingdom*, 106.

30. Moltmann, *Trinity and Kingdom*, 159–61. Here, Moltmann is quoting Karl Barth, *Church Dogmatics: The Doctrine of God. Part 2*, vol. 2, eds. G. W. Bromiley and T. F. Torrance (Edinburgh: T. & T. Clark, 1957), 123. Hereafter *CD II/2*.

31. See also Kathryn Tanner's condemnation of this type of view—"God is not changing God's relation to us in Christ but changing our relation to God." Kathryn Tanner, *Jesus, Humanity and the Trinity: A Brief Systematic Theology* (Edinburgh: T&T Clark, 2001), 15.

32. Hart, *The Beauty of the Infinite*, 160.

33. Mostert, "Moltmann's Crucified God," 177.

34. Barth likewise affirms the absolute relatedness of God in his aseity to the creation, arguing that "He wants in His freedom actually not to be without man but *with* him and in the same freedom not against him but *for* him." Karl Barth, *The Humanity of God*, trans. Thomas Wieser and John Newton Thomas (Richmond: John Knox Press, 1968), 50. Original italics.

35. Karl Barth, *Church Dogmatics: The Doctrine of the Word of God. Part 1*, vol. 1, eds. G. W. Bromiley and T. F. Torrance (Edinburgh: T&T Clark, 1975), 483.

36. While using Divine Self-Enrichment as a hermeneutic by which to read the acts of God in the world is beyond the scope of this book, such a project awaits future contemplation. Certainly, the concept of triune kenotic-enrichment could form the basis for a more thorough systematic inquiry.

37. Elaine Padilla, *Divine Enjoyment: A Theology of Passion and Exuberance* (New York: Fordham University Press, 2015).

38. Padilla, *Divine Enjoyment*, 2.

39. Padilla, *Divine Enjoyment*, 6.

40. Padilla, *Divine Enjoyment*, 13.

41. Paul Gavrilyuk, *The Suffering of the Impassible God* (Oxford: Oxford University Press, 2004), 5.

42. Padilla, *Divine Enjoyment*, 2.

43. Padilla, *Divine Enjoyment*, 1.

44. Hart, *The Beauty of the Infinite,* 166. For example, following Moltmann, Padilla in *Divine Enjoyment* asserts that "divine suffering is divine fullness and an aspect of divine perfect love" (p. 25). She then argues, on the basis of ontological divine solidarity with human suffering, that this concept challenges the "idea of a totalitarian God and the totalitarian regimes that justify torture, mass murders, and disappearance" (p. 28). However, a consequence of her logic is that if suffering is attributed to God's love then one could logically (and perversely) justify the infliction of suffering on the basis that it allows humanity to know God. On this basis, attributing suffering into God's being makes God the source and cause of suffering rather than its liberator. Furthermore, Padilla rejects divine aseity and places the cosmos "within the inner existence of God" (p. 5) but then she refers to the "vulnerability of God that results from the inner life within God" (p. 7). The logic of her argument begs the question as to how one can speak of the "inner life" of God if God is comingled with the cosmos? Which is God and which is the cosmos? Further, Padilla argues, "For God to truly enjoy Godself with creation, God would need to welcome true otherness . . . into the

divine self" (p. 84). However, this logically implies a difference, a distance between God and the "other." Her argument is confusing—how can there be "true otherness" from God if God's being is intermingled with the cosmos? Contra Padilla, my argument is that only through a radical distinction between God and creation can there be a welcoming of "true otherness."

45. Padilla, *Divine Enjoyment*, 4.

46. Padilla, *Divine Enjoyment*, 4.

47. Padilla, *Divine Enjoyment*, 6.

48. Padilla equates a static Greek metaphysical interpretation of God, that God "is a self-subsisting unmoved-mover, is impassive and unalterable" (p. 18), with Gregory of Nyssa's theology that asserts God as unchangeable and free of passion. However, Nyssa's understanding of God does not have the Aristotelian unmoved-mover in mind but rather the dynamics of the Trinity. See Gregory of Nyssa, "On the Soul and the Resurrection," in *A Select Library of the Nicene and Post-Nicene Fathers of the Christian Church, 1886–1889*, 28 vols. in 2 series, eds. Philip Schaff and H. Wace (Reprinted Grand Rapids, MI: Eerdmans, 1956), 2/5: 450.

49. Padilla, *Divine Enjoyment*, 9. Padilla equates aseity with divine narcissism that requires the "cosmos" as its antidote.

50. Webster, "Trinity and Creation," 12.

51. Hart, *The Beauty of the Infinite*, 198–99.

52. Daniel W. Hardy, *Jubilate: Theology in Praise*, ed. David Ford (London: Darton, Longman & Todd, 1984), 6.

53. Hardy, *God's Ways with the World*, 26.

54. Hardy, *God's Ways with the World*, 29. My italics. Ford and Hardy also assert that "perfection would not be perfect if it had to require praise for its completion," in David Ford and Daniel W. Hardy, *Living in Praise: Worshipping and Knowing God*, rev. ed. (London: Darton, Longman & Todd, 2005), 9.

PART II

The Ecumenical Thread of Divine Self-Enrichment

Part I of this work has outlined core metaphysical and theological parameters by which to establish a theology of Divine Self-Enrichment. The examination of this part II now reflects on how the patterning integral to the nature of divine enrichment arises in contemporary Trinitarian theology across denominational lines. Here, I explore the work of three ecumenically diverse and influential theologians of the twentieth Century: Sergeĭ Bulgakov (Orthodox), Hans Urs von Balthasar (Catholic) and Wolfhart Pannenberg (Lutheran). These theologians provide a point of departure due to their influence on the contemporary landscape of Trinitarian theology, their insightfulness in allowing the Trinity to regulate their wider theological commitments, and the fact that the logic of Divine Self-Enrichment resonates with each of their projects. My examination over the next three chapters focuses specifically on the content espoused by each theologian that accords with the theological elements of Divine Self-Enrichment. Significantly, each of these theologians affirm, not only the concept of divine well-being, but the dynamism of Trinitarian mutuality that gives rise to this enriched state. Moreover, of marked importance to this work, contained in the logic of each of their unique theological projects, Bulgakov, Pannenberg and Balthasar identify characteristic traits that fill out the theological choreography of the perichoretic "divine-dance" of all-blessedness. That is, amid the diverse ecumenical perspectives of Trinitarian theologies, discernible patterns of "dance-steps" emerge, shedding light on the inherent dynamics of triune life.

Chapter 4

Divine Self-Enrichment in Sergeĭ Bulgakov

At the heart of his complex and controversial exposition of the Trinity, Russian Orthodox theologian and philosopher Fr. Sergeĭ Bulgakov (1871–1944) situates an inherent divine kenosis. At the core of this Trinitarian kenosis is the deep influence of the Russian sophiology tradition.[1] Through this tradition, Bulgakov reinterprets Chalcedonian Christology by incorporating the concept of Sophia (divine wisdom). Through Sophia, he affirms the two natures of Christ (God and human) as a way of apprehending God's relation to, and communion with, that which is not-God—the creation. Alongside his Christological cosmology and throughout his sophiologically-inspired trilogy—*The Lamb of God*, *The Comforter*, and *The Bride of the Lamb*—Bulgakov also articulates a dynamism within the triune relations that resonates with Divine Self-Enrichment.[2] In these two entwined facets of Bulgakov's Christological and Trinitarian theology, valuable insights arise. These insights serve to not only verify the theological conditions for Divine Self-Enrichment but also to illustrate how the economic acts of God inform interpretations of the dynamics within intratrinitarian life. Of particular significance is Bulgakov's interpretation of divine action in the world as the manifestation of a profound ontic *triune*-kenosis. For Bulgakov, divine tri-hypostatic kenosis constitutes the Glory of God. In this, his theology recognizes a dynamic similar to the formulation of "kenotic-enrichment" developed in this work. That is, where kenotic giving and receiving among Father, Son and Holy Spirit constitutes the life or all-blessedness of God (what Bulgakov chronicles as the "Glory of God"). To understand the theological elements that compose Bulgakov's kenotic Trinitarianism, it is necessary to first place it within the broader context of his sophiology.

DIVINE SOPHIA: BULGAKOV'S TRINITARIANISM

According to Bulgakov, Divine Sophia is the "self-revelation of the Holy Trinity,"[3] construed as an "exhaustive self-revelation" and is, therefore, "the fullness of divinity."[4] Divine Sophia is, for Bulgakov, *ousia*—the divine essence revealed.[5] Aristotle Papanikolaou provides a useful distillation of Bulgakov's correlation of Sophia and Trinity:

> The Trinity is thus the self-revelation of God to Godself, the self-revelation of the Father mediated through Godself, the revealing hypostases of the Son and the Holy Spirit . . . Sophia is the *ousia* of God hypostatised in trihypostatic self-revelation of God, but as such it is no longer simply *ousia*.[6]

For Bulgakov, the Father is the principal source of the Trinity and as such is the self-revealing hypostasis.[7] The self-revelation of the Father is the Son and the Holy Spirit.[8] Revealing himself in the Son, the Father eternally originates the content of the Son, with the Father's self-revelation in the Son being affirmed and completed by the hypostasis of the Holy Spirit. Divine Sophia, as triune self-revelation, is therefore an "event of love" between the Father, the Son and the Holy Spirit.[9] Again, as Papanikolaou clarifies: "In the self-revelation of the Father in the Son, the Father breathes forth the Spirit, who proceeds from the Father as the hypostatic love of the Father for the Son; the Holy Spirit returns to the Father 'through the Son' as the loving answer to the self-revelation of the Father in the Son."[10]

Drawing his connection between divine and created beings, Bulgakov differentiates between "Divine Sophia" and "Creaturely Sophia." Such a differential is important to avoid two potential pitfalls—either imputing a deficiency in divine being through a Hegelian-type logic or depreciating the profound relationality between the divine and human. Divine Sophia is the fullness of the immanent Trinity in its self-revelation. Creaturely Sophia, on the other hand, explicates God's self-revelation in the created world, a revelation that is simultaneously a continuation of God's eternal self-actualization.[11] Creaturely Sophia is not identical in essence to Divine Sophia; rather, it is a replication of God's life in creation.[12] One of the key distinguishing markers Bulgakov identifies between the two Sophias is that "creaturely Sophia is present and identical to the Divine Sophia in potentiality, not in actuality."[13] Unlike divinity, creatures are conditioned in life by the world, where becoming and unactualized potential are emblematic of human life. As Bulgakov asserts, "conditionedness is the mark of *creatureliness*."[14] It is through his use of Sophia, both divine and creaturely, that Bulgakov forges a theological congruence of *distinction and affinity* between God and the world without introducing an external limitation on God nor obscuring the conditions of creatureliness. Sophia serves as the "ontological bridge to effect this union . . . between God and the creature"[15] as Sophia is both "the place of encounter among the three hypostases of the Trinity and between God and man."[16] Bulgakov's theological vision of Sophia endorses both the transcendence of God from all that is not-God, while maintaining the relational immanence of God in the world.

DIVINE SELF-ENRICHMENT IN BULGAKOV'S TRINITARIAN THEOLOGY

Bulgakov's sophiologically-inspired Trinitarian theology offers three core components that resonate with the logic of a theology of Divine Self-Enrichment. These are: (1) the requisite of Divine self-positing by which he comprehends intratrinitarian mutuality; (2) the self-sufficiency of Divine Sophia; and (3) the ontological priority of the immanent Trinity. Before turning to a more detailed review of Bulgakov's overall kenotic Trinitarianism, let us briefly consider these coordinates for their pertinence to Divine Self-Enrichment.

Divine Self-Positing of Gift and Receipt

Bulgakov's logic of the hypostatic "event" of Divine Sophia is closely tied to his understanding of God as a "self-positing absolute subject"[17] (discussed earlier in chapter 1). Here, Bulgakov posits that the Father, Son and Holy Spirit are their "own person centres," and their dynamic self-revelatory relations constitute the "we" of the Trinity.[18] Importantly, this divine self-revelation is identified by Bulgakov as a *kenotic* manifestation of gift and receipt between the hypostases. The event of intratrinitarian self-revelation is a "movement of mutual self-giving, sacrifice, effacement, and reception."[19] This movement allows for the understanding that God's being is "realised dynamically, as the eternal act of Trinitarian self-positing in another."[20] For Bulgakov, God is not a static, petrified edifice of perfection. By integrating both Sophia and "divine self-positing" as necessary a priori theological conditions, Bulgakov is able to identify the movement of Trinitarian kenosis as integral to divine life while maintaining both the unity and distinction of God's tri-hypostatic being. This logic enables a movement of divine-hypostatic gift and receipt without succumbing to tritheism or modalism. Bulgakov's logic provides further theological justification for construing the concept of Divine Self-Enrichment in a contiguous manner that upholds a kenotically centered symbiosis of divine unity and hypostatic distinction.

The Self-Sufficiency of Divine Sophia

While cognisant of the Hegelian pull, Bulgakov is careful not to cede to a path of logic that results in a divine deficiency requiring fulfillment by creation. Rather, Bulgakov's concept of Divine Sophia is premised on the perfection and fullness of God in Godself. He says: "the living I has its *own life*. It is the source of this life and *its fullness* . . . it lives ceaselessly realizing itself for itself."[21] Bulgakov argues that the life of God is the fullness of Trinitarian self-positing as love. The persons of the Trinity are manifested, realized and known by "each going out of itself into the others, in the ardour of self-renouncing personal love."[22] Divine Sophia is, therefore, self-constituting; divine self-revelation of the Father in the Logos and the Spirit constitute the "fullness of divinity."[23] In this manner, God is "fully manifested and actualised . . . as the eternal act of Trinitarian self-positing in another."[24] Such an approach to Divine Sophia supports two aspects of the logic of Divine Self-Enrichment. First, it is possible to maintain that God's well-being is a ceaseless dynamic actualized through the simple and self-sufficient triune intra-relations. And second, God's self-constituting all-blessedness—the fullness of Divine Sophia (divine well-being or the Glory of God)—is not imputed with deficiency through ontological dependency on creation.

While espousing the fullness of self-constituting divinity, Bulgakov never, though, seeks to undermine the "unbreakable mutual relatedness of God and the world."[25] Through an interpretive analogy of a positive—rather than apophatic—Chalcedonianism, Bulgakov clarifies the archetypical nexus between God and the world seen in the hypostatic union, saying, "The transcendent God has united himself with the world, has become God and the world, and this *And* is the union of the two natures in one divine hypostasis, divine and human, without division and without confusion, in a single life."[26] Here, Bulgakov asserts not only the fullness of divine aseity in Divine Sophia, but God's uncompromising union with the world, arguing that "there is no God without the world and no world outside of God."[27] While Bulgakov could be interpreted here as affirming a contemporary Hegelian turn, there is a vital difference. He does not view the created world as constitutive for God's being.[28] Upholding notions of divine simplicity and aseity,[29] Bulgakov considers that the fullness of divine being is not contingent on the world to realize itself, because in God "there is no nocturnal twilight of half-being . . . for that would signify that the Divine life is limited. It would contradict the all-blessedness, unchangeability, and fullness of the Divine life."[30] Bulgakov is clearly cognisant of the metaphysical and theological difficulties for affirming divine all-blessedness if God's being is construed as being contingent on not-God. And yet, Bulgakov's articulation of the fullness of Divine Sophia does not exclude or reduce the relationality between God and not-God. For

Bulgakov, the traditional concepts of aseity and simplicity are congruent with, and necessary for, the profound relationality between the all-blessed God and creation. Katy Leamy affirms this, stating: "Sophia . . . enables him to hold together Greek metaphysical principles and German idealism to reinterpret traditional Christian formulations . . . in a way that is both consistent with traditional orthodoxy as well as relevant in the modern philosophical context."[31] Simply put, Bulgakov maintains the ontological pleroma of divinity and Orthodox distinction between divine and creaturely natures while also confirming a dynamic union between them. Bulgakov's insights again confirm that the framework of traditional Christian theism provides an optimal theological basis for Divine Self-Enrichment.

Bulgakov on the Immanent Trinity in the Economy

Bulgakov's Trinitarian framework affirms a further presupposition for the logic of Divine Self-Enrichment—the continuity between the life of divine self-revelation (immanent Trinity) and the life of God demonstrated in the world (economic Trinity). For Bulgakov, God's eternal being is the constituent foundation for God's economic acts in the world. Bulgakov proposes that God's revelation in the world is such that it "presupposes the self-revelation of the Absolute in itself, which in turn is included in the revelation of the Absolute to the world."[32] God, therefore, reveals himself in the world because God is eternally self-revealing. On this premise Bulgakov establishes the grounds for God's communion with humanity, as God is "free to commune with what is not God because God's life is one of self-positing as self-revelation."[33] That is to say, God reveals Godself to humanity because that is the nature of divine being. Bulgakov similarly argues that God is the eternal Creator, not because the world exists, but because of "the intra-Trinitarian *kenosis* of mutual self-giving and reception."[34] Intratrinitarian kenosis is an a priori presupposition for God "to give God's life, Sophia, kenotically to created existence."[35] This does not admit of a dualism between the immanent and economic acts of God but is rather the expression of "a Trinitarian metaphysics with Sophia as a 'common' nature between God and creation that maintains both the absolute contingency of creation and the simplicity of the triune act that is the life of God."[36] Thus, for Bulgakov the immanent Trinity has ontological precedence to, but also continuity with, the economic Trinity. Bulgakov's understanding of the nature of the relationship between the Creator and the created supports the contention that a correlation exists between the patterning of divine well-being and created well-being. Divine action in relation to the created realm of well-being and human enrichment, in fact, arises from the nature of God's immanent ontological existence.

TRINITARIAN KENOSIS AND ENRICHMENT

One of the most significant aspects of Bulgakov's Trinitarian theology, relevant to a constructive dogmatic of Divine Self-Enrichment, is his identification of kenosis as a determinative characteristic by which God lives "Divine Sophia." Bulgakov's sophiology is replete with the notion that kenosis is expressed through the traditional relations of origin. Inherent to Bulgakov's delineation of the hypostatic movement commensurate with the relations of unbegotten, begotten and proceeding is a discernible pattern of hypostatic self-giving and self-actualization. For Bulgakov, the Father acquires himself by going outside himself and (kenotically) begets the Son and spirates the Spirit.[37] Bulgakov thus determines the begetting power as "the ecstasy of a going out of oneself, of a kind of self-emptying, which at the same time is self-actualisation."[38] Here, in Bulgakov's construal we can identify a link between giving-of-self and "self-actualization" (enrichment) for the Father. Yet, Bulgakov locates a similar kenotic intratrinitarian manifestation for the Son and Spirit. The Son, in his begotteness, offers his "personal selfhood in sacrifice to the Father, and being the Word, He [becomes] mute for Himself, as it were, making Himself the *Father's* Word."[39] And, the Spirit, as "the very movement of love" between the Father and Son, is expressed by Bulgakov as having,

> its *own* hypostatic life, its own kenosis, which consists precisely in hypostatic *self-abolition*, as it were: By its procession from the Father upon the Son, the Third hypostasis loses itself, as it were, becomes only a *copula*, the living bridge of love between the Father and the Son, the hypostatic *Between*. But in this kenosis the Third hypostasis finds itself as the Life of the other hypostases, as the Love of the Others and as the Comfort of the Others, which then becomes for it too its own Comfort, its self-comfort.[40]

From Bulgakov's theology we glimpse his insight that confirms a symbiotic interrelation between kenosis and the perfection of divine enriching life. This interrelation allows us to reconfigure the defining content of kenosis. No longer should kenosis be associated with divine depletion and mere vacuous emptying (key issues often attending interpretations of the *Carmen Christi* in Philippians 2)[41] but should be unified with its divine purpose—enrichment. The nature of divine kenosis should more aptly be understood as "enriching-kenosis" or "kenotic-enrichment"; where enrichment and kenosis symbiotically constitute the hypostatic essence of God's being. Bulgakov voices the core of how we can begin to understand the basic elements of kenotic-enrichment when he says: "sacrifice not only does not contradict the Divine all-blessedness but, on the contrary, *is its foundation*, for this all-blessedness would be empty and unreal if it were not based on authentic sacrifice . . . mutual sacrifice . . . cannot be separated or excluded from this bliss, for it is its hidden foundation."[42]

Bulgakov characterizes the relations of origin as a pattern of "mutually sacrificial love"[43] among the hypostases. In recognizing that each divine hypostasis "has its own kenosis of love,"[44] he also identifies a unified communicable nature that resonates with kenotic-enrichment. He identifies a mutuality between the Son and Father marked by "*self-depleting* ideality and *self-accomplishing* reality,"[45] with the Spirit's nature likewise revealed as "hypostatic depletion and self-acquisition, kenosis and glorification."[46] This nascent patterning of an enriching-kenosis inherent to the divine life is perhaps most poignantly identified in Bulgakov's scriptural contemplation of the Holy Spirit (Jn 16:13, 14, 17–19),[47] where he detects "a special self-abolition of its personality . . . becoming perfectly transparent for the other hypostases, but in this it *acquires the perfection of Divine life: Glory.*"[48] Condensed in Bulgakov's insight lies the central contention of this book, that the glorified life of divine bliss is actualized through Trinitarian kenosis. This is no mere one-sided self-emptying. Kenosis achieves its telos of the divine life of love.[49] Through the relations of origin, Bulgakov identifies the tri-hypostatized unity of divine being that is the revelation of *ousia*. The revelation of *ousia* discloses a compelling nexus between acts of kenosis with the event of divine being. Put plainly, divine well-being is constituted in tri-hypostatic kenosis.

Symbiosis of Kenosis and Enrichment in the Holy Spirit

According to Bulgakov, the "self-renouncing love"[50] between the Father and Son is conjoined through the Holy Spirit, where divine life is unified as the "joy of sacrificial love."[51] The Holy Spirit as an intra-divine intermediary, symbiotically actualizes kenosis and enrichment or, in Bulgakov's words, the Spirit "answers the depletion of the Logos with glorification."[52] Through the Holy Spirit the symbiosis of divine kenosis and enrichment is catalyzed. This, for Bulgakov, is the content of glorification. On this basis one could argue that absent the Holy Spirit no possibility for a symbiosis of kenosis and enrichment can arise. Rather, divine kenosis would be particularized by destructive depletion and diminution, and divine enrichment epitomized by narcissism.[53] This accords with what I refer to as "truncated-kenosis" and "egoistic-enrichment." Although such conclusions are provisional regarding divine being, they do provide a useful heuristic for understanding the possible dynamics relevant to the demise and renewal of human well-being. Using Bulgakov's view of the repetition of "Divine Sophia" in "Creaturely Sophia," we could conclude that, as in the divine life, where in the movement of the Holy Spirit kenosis and enrichment symbiotically coinhere, so also in created life. Yet, in the absence of the Spirit's dynamism, truncated-kenosis and egoistic-enrichment become the markers of human existence. These are arguably core traits of missing the divine mark (*harmatia*)—the archetypal dynamics of sin.

Active or Passive Kenotic-Enrichment?

In the course of our discussion so far, we briefly noted how Bulgakov recognizes a kenosis inherent to the expression of each hypostasis. This view is consistent with his affirmation of hypostatic differentiation resonant with the Chalcedonian dogma of "without separation *and without confusion*."[54] However, according to Bulgakov, the Son and Spirit's kenosis differs from that of the Father. Bulgakov posits that the kenotic differentiation between the divine persons is manifested in an "active and passive" manner.[55] Although he does argue for the "equal dignity and equal divinity" of Father, Son and Holy Spirit, due to his affirmation of the monarchy of the Father as the cause "of eternal interrelation,"[56] he maintains that "they [the Trinity] manifest equality with inequality."[57] This results in the Father being characterized through "active begetting,"[58] the Son as "passive and obedient 'begottenness,'"[59] and the Spirit as humble and invisible procession.[60]

Bulgakov's characterization here—where the Son and the Holy Spirit are construed passively to the Father's activity—could be charged with imputing a type of hierarchical subordinationism into the Trinity.[61] Certainly, it does appear that the actualization of hypostatic content is actively constituted from the Father alone, not from an eternal unity of tri-hypostatic causative action. While Bulgakov does challenge the deficiency of "any doctrine that transforms the Holy Trinity into a system of originations and dyads"[62] and views the Father and Son united in the Holy Spirit,[63] he stops short of expressing the radical mutuality of relations later expressed by Pannenberg, whereby the Son and Spirit actively determine the Father's deity (see chapter 5). Bulgakov understands the Son and Spirit as a "dyadic union" that is a self-revelation of the Father (against the "falsely expressed . . . doctrine of two originations")[64] with the two hypostases "correlated with the Father as their Principle."[65] The Son and the Spirit depend not only on the Father for their being but each other as "co-revealing" hypostases.[66] Bulgakov does not, however, construe the content of the Father as being likewise dependent on the active or operative agency of the Son and Spirit. While Son and Spirit reveal the Father, the second and third hypostases do not assertively constitute what is revealed. Bulgakov argues that "the Son, as the Son, has Himself and His own not as himself and His own but as the Father's."[67] Here, Bulgakov appears to view the Son as *passively receiving* self-realization as the *logos* from the Father.

On this view, Bulgakov could be interpreted as amputating from the Son a capacity intrinsic to the fullness of deity; that of *active giving*. In Bulgakov's account, the Son seems to relate to the Father solely through passivity or depleting. There appears no *active* initiation of gift to the Father consistent with the Son's own fullness of divinity, nor a corresponding reception by the Father. The Son's possession of personhood rather appears silenced in the actualization of the Father, where the Son becomes "mute" for himself, as He becomes the "Word" of the Father.[68] At this point, we need to consider whether Bulgakov's interpretation limits the full divinity of the Son (and Spirit), where they are free to receive from the Father's divinity but not to actively construe it. On this account do we conclude that the second and third hypostases are divinity that are passively determined and limited in their determination? Moreover, would this conclusion not introduce a differentiation of divine will and attributes, thereby jeopardizing divine unity?

At this point, Bulgakov's views require some clarification to align with the nature of hypostatic gift and receipt envisaged by the constructive theology of Divine Self-Enrichment. Bulgakov's conceptions, although replete with insightful content, skirt close to imputing an uneasy inequality between the active determinations of the divine hypostases. However, it is possible to reinterpret Bulgakov's insights by considering of the nature of the Son and Spirit's kenotic depletion more closely. Instead of affirming Bulgakov's kenosis of the Second and Third hypostases as merely passive or the negative removal of agency, a more fruitful construction opens when we view this kenosis as an *active*-acceptance, a voluntary, not forced kenosis. On this construction, the assumption of a mere docile "passivity" is reconceived as the active exercise of agency consistent with the communicable nature of divine kenotic love. In part, this alternative view could alleviate the unfortunate standardization of a narrow interpretation of kenosis as negative agency or mere depletion, seen particularly in contemporary feminist critiques.[69] Instead of the passive-kenosis of the Son and the Spirit being understood as mere reductive and crude diminishment of divinity, a reenvisaged concept places the movement as congruent with an active-kenosis consistent with the type that Bulgakov accords to the Father's generative energy of begetting. In the unity of divinity, the passive or receptive activity of the Son and the Spirit may be understood as *acts* of agency, active gifting that enriches the movement of divine love. Gilles Emery confirms such a concept, saying:

> When we consider the generation of the Son and the procession of the Holy Spirit, it is necessary to avoid any idea of passivity ... It is by one operation that the Father begets and that the Son is born from all eternity, but this operation is in the Father and in the Son under distinct relations ... Therefore, the Father's act of begetting the Son implies no passivity in the Son.[70]

Indeed, Emery considers the Holy Spirit's so-called passivity as actualized-reception,[71] asserting that "the Holy Spirit exists in a proper mode that is relative to the Father and to the Son, from whom he receives himself. This does not imply any 'passivity' in the Holy Spirit, any more than generation implies 'passivity' in the Son who is begotten. To proceed is an act."[72]

Emery's observations are, of course, undergirded by the notion of divine simplicity and necessarily counteracts any temporal concept of passivity as diminishment of divine agency or a passive potency requiring actuality. Because divine simplicity is actualized potential, where divinity is not defined with "passive potency," the so-called "passivity" of the Son and the Spirit can be more powerfully understood as a self-determined actualized act, not involuntary submission.[73] Viewed through the lens of simplicity and the subsistent relations of actualized receptive agency, hypostatic divine kenosis does not have to be construed as a restriction of shared divine identity or Bulgakov's somewhat unsatisfactory assertion of hypostatic passivity that results in an "equality with inequality."[74] Rather, Bulgakov's "passivity" of the Son and the Spirit could be reinterpreted more akin to what Sarah Coakley refers to as "power-in-vulnerability,"[75] where humble receptivity (as well as humble *activity*) is the hidden kenotic manifestation of the *power* of life. Nuancing Bulgakov's theological insights allows us to reconceive voluntary reception and activism within the Trinity as commensurate expressions of divine fullness, hypostatic self-actualization and the enrichment of the unified life of divinity. The movement of both gift *and* receipt in the unity of divine love demonstrates the possibility of a tri-hypostatic mutuality of kenosis and enrichment, that neither divides the will nor the attributes of divinity, nor "ends in cancelling out any distinction" of the personal agency of the hypostases.[76]

Enriching-Kenosis: Divine and Creaturely Modes

Bulgakov's kenotic Trinitarianism is a valuable tool for distinguishing between divine and creaturely enrichment. On Bulgakov's terms, the "All-Blessedness" of divine simplicity, characterized as the kenotic revelation of God's Glory or Sophia, is the fullness of divinity (Col 2:9).[77] God's glory is an "intradivine principle" not derived from creatures through acts of glorification.[78] Extrapolating his thought, divine enrichment may be characterized in terms of an *immediate* symbiosis of kenosis and well-being. For example, if we consider that the Father's self-revelation (correlated, on Bulgakov's terms, with glory or all-blessedness) is realized through kenosis we inherently acknowledge a concept of an immediate interrelation occurring between the Father's kenosis and his self-actualization. In other words, the Father's self-giving toward the other hypostases is eternally symbiotic with divine self-actualization. This occurs immediately within the simplicity and aseity of divine being; there is no delayed enrichment nor mere diminution of the Father in the Father's self-giving in the Son and Spirit, nor vice versa. As Bulgakov contends: "God glorifies himself . . . This is God's joy about himself. It is God admiring himself, being comforted by Himself, seeing Himself in Beauty . . . This is the all-blessedness of God, the joy of Divine life as self-knowledge and self-revelation."[79] This self-glory is not, however, relatable to narcissistic self-love inherent to created beings because it has trihypostatic kenosis as its nucleus. Bulgakov clarifies the difference to created contingent beings, saying: "In a unihypostatic created being, such self-glorification would be inevitably egocentric . . . But in a trihypostatic God, in virtue of his trihypostatic character, all self-love or egocentric self-affirmation is excluded."[80] Creaturely enrichment is, however, premised quite differently from divine ontology. Enrichment for the creature is subject to *delayed* well-being; where kenosis and enrichment have an intervallic or interrupted symbiosis. For creatures, kenosis and enrichment are not unified in simplicity but are rather incrementally realized, characterized by unactualized-potential.

Bulgakov's consideration of the nature of divine self-giving in the Incarnation provides a further useful framework to understand the ontological difference between divine and creaturely kenotic-enrichment. Positing the question—What does God empty himself of in the acts of self-revelation in creation and Incarnation?[81]—Bulgakov contemplates not only the self-giving side of divine life, but importantly for my purposes, the enriched side of divine life. Considering the kenosis of the Son in Philippians 2:6–8, Bulgakov opines that the "descent from heaven" (and the subsequent glorification) reveals the depths of divinity itself.[82] The voluntary impoverishment of the Son through the Incarnation consists, not of a change in the unchangeable God, but a demonstration of the eternal kenotic nature of God. The Son empties himself of the "norm of divine life" which Bulgakov identifies, in part, as an emptying of the glory or all-blessedness of God.[83] Bulgakov maintains that "God voluntarily renounced his Divine glory. He removed it, bared Himself, emptied and impoverished Himself . . . He put Himself in a *creaturely* relation to God."[84] In assuming a human nature, the Son became subject to the processes of incremental development inherent to the temporal order.[85] This was not due to God the Son being emptied of divinity, signifying a change in divine nature, but rather as a contiguous *expression of* the divine nature. Thus, Bulgakov states that the self-limitation inherent to the Incarnation, depicted in Philippians 2, "does not contradict God's absoluteness, aseity, and all-blessedness, for this self-limitation is not a consequence of limitedness and is not imposed from outside. Rather, it is a proper, voluntary self-definition of the Absolute."[86] On Bulgakov's account, we can deduce that the "descent from heaven" might be characterized as a descent from the divine life of Glory. Unlike human existence and well-being, which are marked by potentiality and becoming, the divine life of Glory is actualized and replete. Referencing the high-priestly prayer of John 17:5 ("Father, glorify me in your own presence with the glory that I had in your presence before the world existed"), Bulgakov concludes that the Son in his kenosis "retains of the potential of glory, which must be actualised anew."[87] The Son, through Incarnation, enters the creaturely reality of delayed enrichment (temporal glory) until his risen glorification—"Glory and Divinity in Sophia pre-eternally shine in heaven for the Holy Trinity; but the Second hypostasis, in descending from heaven, abandons this shining . . . He retains only the nature of Divinity, not its glory."[88]

Bulgakov's insights, when applied through the lens of Divine Self-Enrichment, are a useful way to begin to interpret the Son's Incarnation as a voluntary depletion from the *immediate* symbiosis between kenosis and divine glory "to the domain of the unfullness of creaturely being."[89] The Son, through Incarnation, embraces an incremental enrichment,[90] or a delayed and contingent well-being that is common to humanity. For Bulgakov, Christ's ascension is, therefore, the completion of his kenosis; where the Son passes from humiliation to return to his eternal life of glory (enriched and enriching life of actualized Trinitarian bliss).[91] However, while Bulgakov posits the full glorification of the Son re-commencing at the ascension, through the broader notion of Divine Self-Enrichment it may be more appropriate to consider whether there is a further enriching-enrichment of divine glorification occurring at the consummation of the eschatological kingdom when God becomes "all in all" (1 Cor 15:28). Perhaps, through the concept of glorification (understood as eternal divine enrichment or well-being) we can extend Bulgakov's initial insight and posit a further glorification yet to come, not only for the creation (which is enrichment from deficiency) but also for the Creator (as the continuing eternal enrichment of full glory).

Kenosis and Suffering

As we have seen, there is significant overlap between Bulgakov's concept of triune-kenosis as the foundation for the all-blessed life of God and the logic of Divine Self-Enrichment. However, on Bulgakov's account kenosis is framed as a sacrifice commensurate with *suffering*. He says: "it is impossible to *not* speak of sacrificial suffering precisely in the Absolute God, as an aspect of intra-Trinitarian divine life."[92] This position arguably anticipated the attempts of theologians in the twentieth century, like Moltmann, to attribute suffering to the divine nature.[93] Despite my agreement with Bulgakov, that self-sacrifice and love are interconnected (*"there is no love without sacrifice"*[94]), questions remain as to whether sacrificial love always entails suffering. If triune life is a replete all-blessedness, it is not immediately clear how divine sacrifice automatically equates to divine suffering. Certainly, in Christ's crucifixion the self-giving love of God engaged with suffering. However, it would be a mistake to reduce this event to divine passibility or bleak tragedy.[95] Rather, the Cross of Christ corresponds with the nature of God, whose self-giving actualizes life. Athanasius emphasizes this truth, saying—"Thus it happened that both things occurred in a paradoxical manner: the death of all was completed in the lordly body, and also *death and corruption were destroyed by the Word* in it . . . the Word, since he was *not able to die for—he was immortal*—took himself a body able to die."[96] It is through divine self-giving that *life* is actualized, where suffering is transfigured, and "death is swallowed up in victory" (1 Cor 15:54).

Divine Self-Enrichment, in consonance with the Athanasian intuition, advances that kenosis is possible without attributing ontological and eternal suffering or pain to divine being. As discussed earlier (chapter 2), the contemporary move toward divine passibility remains problematic for theodicy and for soteriology. However, exorcising eternal suffering from God's being does not posit a disengaged God or evade the horrific crucified-suffering of Jesus Christ. Instead, it corroborates the necessity of assuming a human nature in the Incarnation. In order to suffer and die, the divine must enter the unique human state. Again, Athanasius aptly states the situation: "since he was *not able to die for*—he was immortal—[he] *took himself a body able to die.*"[97] Referring to Cyril of Alexandria's position (in contrast to a Nestorian view), Gavrilyuk states that "impassibility did not make God withdraw to the heavenly realm and supervise the death of Christ . . . but guaranteed that it was God himself who participated in the experiences of the human nature."[98] Indeed, ascribing impassibility to God ensures that "it is actually God, in all his wholly transcendent otherness as God, who suffers, and not 'God' in some mitigated or semi-divine state."[99] In Christ, the self-giving of God is indeed made manifest in the created and fallen world of suffering, yet is not subsumed or defined by it. In the hypostatic union of Jesus of Nazareth, we observe the "suffering of the *incarnate* God."[100] In Christ, fleshly suffering and death is transfigured with life because it is the impassible one who suffers.[101] In essence, when the impassibility of divine kenosis is expressed in the Incarnation and the Cross, God's giving-of-self engages extensively with the creation's pain and suffering. Yet, this manifestation of divine kenosis is no mere truncated-kenosis. It is an *enriching*-kenosis, where the divine giving-of-self results in the life and enrichment of the contingent creation. It also results in the continued enrichment of eternally-enriching God, wherein by the blood of the Son, saints from "every tribe and language and people and nation" are ransomed and made "a kingdom and priests serving our God"

(Rev 5:9–10). In other words, God enriches the eternally replete "divine-dance" by enveloping the dancing of redeemed humanity.

CONCLUSION

Bulgakov's Trinitarian logic is replete with theological propositions that are consistent with, and provide additional content to, the definition of Divine Self-Enrichment: *God* (divine self-positing) *enriching God* (hypostatic self-actualization through kenosis) *from the fullness and perfection of God* (self-constituting divine self-revelation: Divine Sophia). In light of Bulgakov's sophiology and kenotic Trinitarianism, the logic of Divine Self-Enrichment can be nuanced, affirmed and clarified in the following manner:

1. Divine being is dynamically constituted through the eternal triune relations.
2. Divine being is perfect and full, self-constituting, not requiring a deficiency within God to be realized by the creation. God's own well-being is the Glory of God. This is actualized and full, consistent with divine simplicity, and achieved through relational kenosis.
3. Self-positing of the hypostases is not individualistic self-realization (tri-theistic), but rather, the actualization of the Tri-unity of the One God. In other words, enrichment is communal.
4. Self-revelation is an eternal activity within the Trinity and is the "fullness of divinity." Divine self-revelation is demonstrated through kenotic events of tri-hypostatic self-giving and receiving. The eternal act of kenotic self-giving is self-enriching; it is not diminution but the fullness of God's life. There is no self-given Glory (or enrichment) by a hypostasis to themselves in the Trinity.[102]
5. The result of divine kenotic life is joy, bliss, glory, and all-blessedness (enriched life).
6. Divine well-being is rendered through an immediate symbiotic relationship of actualized kenosis and enrichment (actualized potential). Creaturely well-being is, however, defined by a delayed or incremental symbiosis of kenosis and enrichment (unactualizedn-actualized potential).
7. Divine kenosis, while delineated by self-sacrifice and the giving-of-self, is not equated with eternal and ontological suffering in God's being. Suffering in the economy is part of the kenosis of the Son's Incarnation that embraces temporal contingency.

NOTES

1. Sergeï Bulgakov was influenced in his sophiological approach by Soloviev, whom Bulgakov referred to as "the first Russian sophiologist." Sergeï Bulgakov, *The Lamb of God*, trans. Boris Jakim (Grand Rapids, MI: Eerdmans, 2002), 9. For further information regarding Russian Sophiology see J. D. Kornblatt, *Divine Sophia: The Wisdom Writings of Vladimir Solovyov* (Cornell University Press: New York, 2009); Paul Valliere, *Modern Russian Theology: Bukharev, Soloviev, Bulgakov: Orthodox Theology in a New Key* (Grand Rapids, MI: Eerdmans, 2000); Sergeï Bulgakov, *Sophia: The Wisdom of God: An Outline of Sophiology* (Lindisfarne Press: New York, 1993); Mikhail Sergeev, *Sophiology in Russian Orthodoxy: Solov'ev, Bulgakov, Losskii, and Berdiaev* (Lewiston: Edwin Mellen Press, 2006); Michael Martin, ed., *The Heavenly Country: An Anthology of Primary Sources, Poetry, and Critical Essays on Sophiology* (Kettering, OH: Angelico Press, 2016).

2. In 1928 Bulgakov considered the concept of the self-giving kenotic love between the persons of the Trinity in his *Chapters on Trinitarianism* (*Glavy o Troichnosti*) (Moscow: OGI, 2001). This nascent idea was then fruitfully extended through his kenotic Christology in the first volume of his major trilogy, *The Lamb of God* (1933), trans. Boris Jakim (Grand Rapids, MI: Eerdmans, 2002), and then expanded in a further two volumes, *The Comforter* (1936) trans. Boris Jakim (Grand Rapids, MI: Eerdmans, 2004), originally published as *Uteshitel'* [The Comforter]. Pt 2. of *O bogochelovechestve* (Paris: YMCA-Press, 1936) and *The Bride of the Lamb* (1939) trans. Boris Jakim (Grand Rapids, MI: Eerdmans, 2002) originally published as *Nevesta agntsa* [The Bride of the Lamb]. Pt 3 of *O bogochelovechestve* (Paris: YMCA-Press, 1945). For further analysis see also Paul Gavrilyuk, "The Kenotic Theology of Sergius Bulgakov," *Scottish Journal of Theology* 58, no. 3 (2005): 252.

3. Bulgakov, *The Bride of the Lamb*, 23, 26.

4. Bulgakov, *The Bride of the Lamb*, 39.

5. Sergeï Bulgakov, *Sophia*, 54.

6. Aristotle Papanikolaou, "Sophia, Apophasis, and Communion: The Trinity in Contemporary Orthodox Theology," in *The Cambridge Companion to the Trinity*, ed. Peter Phan (Cambridge: Cambridge University Press, 2011), 329. Papanikolaou highlights the similarity of thought in Karl Barth where the Father is the revealing hypostasis, the Son is the revealed and the Spirit the revelation.

7. Bulgakov, *The Comforter*, 177.

8. Bulgakov's construction of Divine *Sophia* has, however, been viewed under the suspicion of introducing a "fourth" into the Trinity, or espousing "a unitarian Godhead of which the Persons are merely modes." Valliere, *Modern Russian Theology*, 329. In 1935 Bulgakov was censured for making Sophia a "fourth hypostasis" in God. Later the charges of heresy were discharged. See Aiden Nichols, "Wisdom from Above? The Sophiology of Father Sergius Bulgakov," *New Blackfriars* 85, no. 1000 (2004): 605. Bulgakov himself refuted the charge saying: "The nature of God (which is in fact Sophia) is a living and therefore loving substance, ground, and 'principle.' But, it might be said, does this not lead to the conception of a 'fourth hypostasis'? The reply is 'certainly not,' for this principle in itself is non-hypostatic,

though capable of being hypostatized in a given Hypostasis, and thereby constituting its life. But, it might still be urged, would this not result in 'another God,' a sort of totally 'other' divine principle within God? Again we reply, no; for no one has ever attempted to maintain such an idea in connection with the divine *Ousia* in its relation to the hypostases, while the very conception of *Ousia* itself is but that of Sophia, less fully developed." Bulgakov, *Sophia*, 35–36.

9. Aristotle Papanikolaou, *Being with God: Trinity, Apophaticism and Divine-Human Communion* (Notre Dame: Notre Dame University, 2006), 152.

10. Papanikolaou, "Sophia, Apophasis and Communion," 244.

11. Bulgakov, *Lamb of God*, 121–22. Bulgakov affirms both a boundary between the Creator and created as well as the intimate relation between the two. Bulgakov, *Lamb of God*, 121.

12. Bulgakov, *Lamb of God*, 159; Bulgakov, *Bride of the Lamb*, 50–60. Bulgakov perceives Divine Sophia as the source of creaturely Sophia where the world expresses Divine self-revelation. Critics, however, view Bulgakov's sophiology as reducing human engagement with God to a natural cosmic process that removes personal transformation through a pneumatic Christology. Bulgakov does not, however, view Sophia as standing between God and the world as some sort of "World Soul." See Rowan Williams, *Sergeĭ Bulgakov: Towards a Russian Political Theology* (Edinburgh: T&T Clark, 1999), 178.

13. Myroslaw Tataryn, "History Matters: Bulgakov's Sophianic Key," *St Vladimir's Theological Quarterly* 49, no. 1–2 (2005): 210.

14. Bulgakov, *Lamb of God*, 91 and 96. Original italics.

15. Bulgakov, *Lamb of God*, 220.

16. Antoine Arjakovsky, "The Sophiology of Father Sergius Bulgakov and Contemporary Western Theology," *St Vladimir's Theological Quarterly* 49, nos. 1–2 (2005): 221.

17. Papanikolaou, "Sophia, Apophasis and Communion," 245.

18. Papanikolaou, "Sophia, Apophasis and Communion," 245.

19. Papanikolaou, "Sophia, Apophasis and Communion," 244.

20. Bulgakov, *Lamb of God*, 94.

21. Bulgakov, *Lamb of God*, 89. My italics.

22. Bulgakov, *Lamb of God*, 95.

23. Bulgakov, *The Bride of the Lamb*, 39.

24. Bulgakov, *Lamb of God*, 94.

25. Valliere, *Modern Russian Theology*, 343.

26. See Valliere, *Modern Russian Theology*, 343. Original italics.

27. Valliere, *Modern Russian Theology*, 305. There is a sense in Bulgakov's thought, however, that God "needs" the world, not as God's self-completion, but rather as the "*necessity of love*, which cannot not love." This is a combination of freedom and necessity because "love is *free* by its nature." Bulgakov, *Lamb of God*, 121.

28. Bulgakov, *Lamb of God*, 220.

29. Bulgakov, *Lamb of God*, 101, 120.

30. Bulgakov, *Lamb of God*, 96.

31. Katy Leamy, *The Holy Trinity: Hans Urs von Balthasar and His Sources* (Eugene, OR: Pickwick Publishing, 2015), 14.

32. Bulgakov, *The Comforter*, 361.

33. Papanikolaou, "Sophia, Apophasis and Communion," 245.

34. Papanikolaou, "Sophia, Apophasis and Communion," 244.

35. Papanikolaou, "Sophia, Apophasis and Communion," 244.

36. Leamy, *The Holy Trinity*, 17–18.

37. Rowan Williams notes Bulgakov's use of the term "self-devastation" in relation to the Father's begetting and highlights how for Bulgakov "The Father begetting the Son 'lays himself waste,' 'empties all that he might hold, so we can never understand the Father independently of that utter bestowal and emptying into the life of the Word or the Son." Rowan Williams, *A Margin of Silence: The Holy Spirit in Russian Orthodox Theology* (Quebec: Éditions du Lys Vert, 2008), 22.

38. Bulgakov, *Lamb of God*, 98.

39. Bulgakov, *Lamb of God*, 99.

40. Bulgakov, *The Comforter*, 180. See also Williams, *A Margin of Silence*, 21–27.

41. David Brown, *Divine Humanity: Kenosis Explored and Defended* (London: SCM, 2011).

42. Bulgakov, *Lamb of God*, 99. My italics.

43. Bulgakov, *The Comforter*, 179.

44. Bulgakov, *The Comforter*, 182.

45. Bulgakov, *The Comforter*, 180. My italics. In reference to the congruence of self-depletion and self-accomplishment in the Spirit, Bulgakov states, "the Third hypostasis has, in its own hypostatic life, its *own* kenosis, which consists precisely in hypostatic *self-abolition*, as it were: By its procession from the Father upon the Son, the Third hypostasis loses itself, as it were, becomes only a *copula*, the living bridge of love between the Father and the Son, the hypostatic *Between*. But in this kenosis the Third hypostasis finds itself as the Life of the other hypostases, as the Love of the Others and as the Comfort of the Others, which then becomes for it too its own Comfort, its self-comfort." Bulgakov, *The Comforter*, 181. Original italics.

46. Bulgakov, *The Comforter*, 180.

47. For more specific reference to these bible verses see Bulgakov, *The Comforter*, 184.

48. Bulgakov, *The Comforter*, 181–82. My italics.

49. As Bulgakov concludes: "Love is *Humility*." Bulgakov, *The Comforter*, 182. Original italics.

50. Bulgakov, *Lamb of God*, 100.

51. Bulgakov, *Lamb of God*, 99.

52. Bulgakov, *Lamb of God*, 111. This comfort is ultimately from the Father to the Son through the Holy Spirit.

53. Perhaps this is the problem with Moltmann's kenotic interpretation of the cry of dereliction and the ensuing issue of the rent-Trinity; there is a need for a fuller pneumatological dimension. Williams also notes how the "potential tragedy of mutual annihilation" of a mutual self-giving of the Father and Son Spirit is "overcome in the

joy of the Spirit" where self-giving is not merely a giving *out* but an *exchange* that engenders life. Williams, *A Margin of Silence*, 24.

54. Bulgakov, *The Comforter*, 178. Original italics.
55. Bulgakov, Lamb of God, 98.
56. Bulgakov, *Lamb of God*, 98.
57. Bulgakov, *Lamb of God*, 110. See also Bulgakov, *The Comforter*, 149 for his views of a "voluntary hierarchism" within the triune relations.
58. Bulgakov, *Lamb of God*, 98.
59. Bulgakov, *Lamb of God*, 98.
60. Bulgakov, *The Comforter*, 179–82.
61. Bulgakov also refers to the Holy Spirit in "passive" terms. Bulgakov, *Lamb of God*, 100.
62. Bulgakov, *The Comforter*, 141.
63. Bulgakov, *The Comforter*, 137–38.
64. Bulgakov, *The Comforter*, 150.
65. Bulgakov, *The Comforter*, 150.
66. Bulgakov, *The Comforter*, 150.
67. Bulgakov, *Lamb of God*, 98–99.
68. Bulgakov, *Lamb of God*, 99.
69. See for example, Daphne Hampson, "On Power and Gender," *Modern Theology* 4, no. 3 (1988): 234–50. And, for a Christian feminist apologetic for kenosis, see Sarah Coakley, *Powers and Submissions: Spirituality, Philosophy and Gender* (Oxford: Blackwell Publishing, 2002), 3–39. See also Aristotle Papanikolaou, "Person, Kenosis, and Abuse: Hans Urs von Balthasar and Feminist Theologies in Conversation," *Modern Theology* 19, no. 1 (2003): 41–65.
70. Gilles Emery, *The Trinity: An Introduction to Catholic Doctrine on the Triune God*, trans. Matthew Levering (Washington, DC: Catholic University Press, 2011), 150.
71. Dolezal claims that we need to remove the "idea of passivity from our notion of receptive relation in God, and . . . instead to hold that the Persons are purely actual 'receivers,' inscrutable as such a notion might be." James E. Dolezal, "Trinity, Simplicity and the Status of God." *International Journal of Systematic Theology* 16, no. 1 (Jan 2014): 92.
72. Emery, *The Trinity*, 149–50.
73. Dolezal, "Trinity, Simplicity," 91.
74. Bulgakov, *Lamb of God*, 110. While not equating the two, such a contortion of terms is reminiscent of Wayne Grudem's evangelical project that looks for a Trinitarian archetype to justify the submission of women to men in Church and marriage. Grudem uses the concept "equal in being but subordinate in role" of Jesus' relationship to the Father as he does of the nature of women's relation to men. See Wayne A. Grudem, *Systematic Theology: An Introduction to Biblical Doctrine* (Grand Rapids, MI: Zondervan, 1994), 251.
75. Coakley, *Powers and Submissions*, 3–39. This concept is interestingly confirmed in the research of secular author Brené Brown, *Daring Greatly: How the*

Courage to Be Vulnerable Transforms the Way We Live, Love, Parent, and Lead (New York: Gotham Books, 2012).

76. Williams, *A Margin of Silence*, 23.

77. Bulgakov, *Lamb of God*, 107ff. For more on Bulgakov's writings articulating the concept of the Glory of God see Sergiĭ Bulgakov, *The Burning Bush: On the Orthodox Veneration of the Mother of God*, ed. T. Allan Smith (Grand Rapids, MI: Eerdmans, 2009). Originally published as *Kupina neopalimaia: opyt dogmaticheskogo istolkovaniia nekotorykh chert v pravoslavnom pochitanii Bogomateri* (Paris: YMCA-Press, 1927).

78. Bulgakov, *Lamb of God*, 109.

79. Bulgakov, *Lamb of God*, 109. Original italics.

80. Bulgakov, *Lamb of God*, 109.

81. Bulgakov, *Lamb of God*, 220.

82. Bulgakov, *Lamb of God*, 219.

83. Bulgakov, *Lamb of God*, 216.

84. Bulgakov, *Lamb of God*, 217. Original italics.

85. Bulgakov, *Lamb of God*, 221.

86. Bulgakov, *Lamb of God*, 223.

87. Bulgakov, *Lamb of God*, 224.

88. Bulgakov, *Lamb of God*, 224.

89. Bulgakov, *Lamb of God*, 223.

90. Bulgakov does not speak in terms of a delayed enrichment, but he interprets the Incarnation as an "uninterrupted self-emptying." Bulgakov, *The Comforter*, 265. His "uninterrupted self-emptying" may, however, be likened to a truncated-kenosis that occurs when detached from the fullness of glory.

91. Bulgakov, *Lamb of God*, 404.

92. Bulgakov, *The Comforter*, 66. Original italics. Thus, Bulgakov perceives that "in the cross of the earthly path is realized the cross of the heavenly kenosis." Bulgakov, *The Lamb of God*, 217. See also Bulgakov, *The Comforter*, 180–81, 384. While these statements appear similar to Moltmann who argues in that "the cross of the Son stands from eternity in the centre of the Trinity," Bulgakov's conception does not conflate the economic and immanent Trinity. Rather, he understands the Cross as the demonstration of an eternal reality within God's being, unlike Moltmann who conceives that the Cross determines God's being. See Jürgen Moltmann, *The Trinity and the Kingdom of God: The Doctrine of God*, trans. Margaret Kohl (Minneapolis: Fortress Press, 1993), xvi, originally published as *Trinität und Reich Gottes* (Munich: Chr. Kaiser Verlag, 1980).

93. Gavrilyuk, "The Kenotic Theology of Sergius Bulgakov," 256.

94. Bulgakov, *The Comforter*, 65. Original italics.

95. Bulgakov uses the phrase the "tragic side of love"—which he views as the sacrificial suffering between the Father and Son. Bulgakov, *The Comforter*, 66.

96. Athanasius, *On the Incarnation*, trans. John Behr (Yonkers, NY: St Vladimir's Seminary Press, 2011), §20, 95. My italics.

97. Athanasius, *On the Incarnation*, §20, 95. My italics.

98. Paul Gavrilyuk, *The Suffering of the Impassible God* (Oxford: Oxford University Press, 2004), 19. See also St Cyril, "Scholia on the Incarnation," in John A. McGuckin, *St. Cyril of Alexandria: The Christological Controversy: Its History, Theology & Texts* (Leiden: E.J. Brill, 1994), 332–33.

99. Thomas, G. Weinandy, "Cyril and the Mystery of the Incarnation," in *The Theology of St. Cyril of Alexandria: A Critical Appreciation*, eds. Thomas G. Weinandy and Daniel A. Keating (London: T&T Clark, 2003), 51.

100. Gavrilyuk, *The Suffering of the Impassible God*, 19. My italics.

101. St Cyril, "Scholia on the Incarnation," 332–33.

102. Bulgakov, *Lamb of God*, 95.

Chapter 5

Divine Self-Enrichment in Wolfhart Pannenberg

Protestant theologian Wolfhart Pannenberg's *Systematic Theology*[1] traverses and connects truth, history and eschatology throughout his doctrine of the Trinity; a doctrine formed through "the historical revelation of Jesus Christ [as] the anticipation of the end of history . . . the final disclosure of all truth."[2] For Pannenberg, truth, known only at the end of history, is proleptically revealed in Jesus the Christ as the anticipatory revelation of the "God of the future" *in history*. Within this context, Pannenberg's triune ontology forms as he reads the scriptural testimony of the Christ event as the revelatory locus of the eternal nature of divine relationality and the future kingdom of God. Significantly, Pannenberg affirms and clarifies that the dynamic content of perichoresis—the nature of the activity between the Persons of the Godhead—is constitutive of God's being. In dialogue with his theology, this chapter explores how Pannenberg's Trinitarian propositions support and provide additional critical content to the broader concept of Divine Self-Enrichment. Identifying the significance of Pannenberg's theology for the axiom of Divine Self-Enrichment is limited to three key areas. First, his concept of the self-distinctions between the triune Persons (*God* enriching *God*); second, the unity and constitution of deity through the gifting and receiving of lordship or God's kingdom (God *enriching* God); and finally, his "retroactive" eschatology that expresses a dynamic fullness and perfection of God's being (in the *fullness* and *perfection* of God).

TRINITARIAN SELF-DISTINCTION

For Pannenberg, the relationality of the divine Persons is essential to the "question of the essence and attributes of God for the doctrine of the Trinity."[3] In consonance with the "mutually determining relational view" derived from

Basil and Athanasius,[4] he argues that the relations of the Trinity mutually determine God's being, where "each person is determined by its relation to the others."[5] He emphasizes that the Trinitarian relations in themselves imbue the essence of God, and opposes Trinitarian theology that derives the plurality of Persons from a single divine subject or essence.[6] Concerning his desire to harmonize the differentiations among the Trinity with "the monotheistic character of the biblical belief in God," Pannenberg utilizes his theory of reciprocal "self-distinction"; whereby hypostatic self-distinction is defined in the sense "that the one who distinguishes himself from another defines himself as also dependent on that other."[7] He concludes that "if the Trinitarian relations among Father, Son and Spirit have the form of mutual self-distinction, they must be understood not merely as different modes of being in the one divine subject but as living realisations of separate centres of action."[8] Thus, deity is understood as dependent on the agency of each of the hypostases for its realization.[9] Crucially for Pannenberg, hypostatic mutual self-distinction is integral to triune actualization; divine difference expresses divine unity and being—thus, the "Father is the Father only vis-à-vis the Son; the Son is Son only vis-à-vis the Father; the Spirit is Spirit only as the bond of community of Father and Son."[10]

Although Pannenberg appropriates the concept of perichoresis, he significantly modifies the traditional doctrine that defined its content, that of the relations of origin. Pannenberg rejects the relations of origin (generation and spiration) as the *sole* determining factor by which to apprehend the distinctions between the divine Persons, stating: "Relations among the three Persons that are defined as mutual self-distinction cannot be reduced to relations of origin in the traditional sense."[11] Rather, he proposes that the relational structure of a one-way movement from the Father to the Son and the Spirit fails to reflect the scriptural witness of the "active relations of the Son and the Spirit *to the Father*."[12] Pannenberg recognizes that each divine person is a "catalyst of many relations" within the Godhead[13] and therefore seeks to understand the "full complexity of the relations among the Father, Son and Spirit."[14] Using Scripture's account of the divine relations he surmises that "begetting and breathing on the one side, sending and gift on the other [can] . . . hardly be justified exegetically."[15] Pannenberg explicates his reasoning as follows:

> When Scripture bears witness to the *active relations of the Son and the Spirit to the Father*, it is not good enough to treat these as not constitutive for their identity and in this respect to look only at the relations of begetting and proceeding (or breathing), viewing solely the relations of origin, which lead from the Father to the Son and Spirit, as applicable to the constitution of the Persons. None of the other relations is merely incidental to the Son and Spirit in their

relation to the Father. All have a place in the distinctiveness and fellowship of the Trinitarian Persons.[16]

Based on the scriptural account of divine self-revelation in Jesus, Pannenberg insists, therefore, that the doctrine of the Trinity must "begin with the way in which Father, Son and Spirit come on the scene and relate to one another in the event of revelation."[17]

TRINITARIAN GIVING AND RECEIVING: DIVINE LORDSHIP AND KINGDOM RULE

"The Reciprocal Self-Distinction of Father, Son and Spirit,"[18] central to Pannenberg's understanding of the essence and attributes of God, receives its ultimate expression in the Kingdom or Rule of God. Divinity is confirmed and demonstrated through a Kingdom motif connected to Jesus. The sending and service of Jesus, referenced in the high-priestly prayer of John 17:4,[19] is "for the glory of the Father and his Lordship," "to establish the lordship of God,"[20] and to give place to the "Father's claim to deity."[21] Yet, for Pannenberg, Jesus' service cannot be reduced to a one-way affirmation of paternal lordship (from Son to the Father). In undertaking his mission, and in affirming the distinction between himself and the Father, Jesus is concurrently determined as the Son of the Father, the Son of God and, thus, "receives his deity from the Father."[22] The lengthy quote below is critical to Pannenberg's view that the relational activity between the Father and the Son in the Spirit establishes the "rule" or kingdom of God, a central marker of divine being. Important to note is the *mutual* dependence of giving and receiving between the divine Persons:

> The *handing over* of the power and rule of the Father to the Son is then to be seen also as a defining of the intratrinitarian relations between the two, as is also their *handing back* by the Son to the Father . . . In the handing over of lordship from the Father to the Son, and its handing back from the Son to the Father, we see a *mutuality in their relationship* that we do not see in the begetting. By handing over lordship to the Son the Father makes his kingship *dependent on* whether the *Son glorifies him* and fulfils his lordship by fulfilling his mission. The self-distinction of the Father from the Son is not just that *he begets* the Son but that he *hands over all things* to him, so that his kingdom and his own deity are now *dependent upon* the Son. The rule or kingdom of God is not so external to his deity that he might be God without his kingdom. The world as the object of his lordship might not be necessary to his deity, since its existence owes its origin to his creative freedom, but the existence of a world is not compatible with his deity apart from his lordship over it. Hence lordship goes hand in hand

with the deity of God. It has its place already in the intratrinitarian life of God, in the reciprocity of the relation between the Son, who *freely subjects* himself to the lordship of the Father, and the Father, who *hands over his lordship* to the Son.[23]

For Pannenberg, these intratrinitarian relations revealed through Scripture are "not just historical or economic but relations which characterise the eternal divine essence."[24] The Lordship of God, constitutive of deity, is an a priori intratrinitarian principle.[25] The dynamism of mutual hypostatic interpenetration that enacts the kingdom rule and Lordship of God over creation is revealed as contiguous with eternal deity. Although Pannenberg rejects the traditional relations of origin as the *sole* precept for divine unity, he does not, however, rescind the monarchy of the Father. On the contrary, "the Son and Spirit serve the monarchy of the Father. Yet the Father does not have his kingdom or monarchy without the Son and Spirit, but only through them."[26] Thus, for Pannenberg the monarchy of the Father remains the "seal of their [Godhead's] unity."[27] It is important to note that the monarchy of the Father is not the "presupposition" of divine unity, but rather the "result of the common operation of the three Persons."[28] Central to Pannenberg's Trinitarian theology is that the *mutual* movement between the Father, Son and Holy Spirit constitutes divine being. Putting aside his characterization of the monarchy of the Father for the moment, this central contention of triune mutuality is, likewise, inherent to the concept of Divine Self-Enrichment.

Although Pannenberg recognizes that the mutuality of the divine relations is constitutive and purposeful for deity he stops short of delineating characteristics inherent to triune activity. A hint as to why this is so is revealed in his contention that "NT statements do not clarify the interrelation of the three but they clearly emphasise the fact that they are interrelated."[29] Nevertheless, despite Pannenberg's hesitation, he does identify dynamic movements of triune relating in the following manner: the Spirit "raises" Jesus (Rom 1:4), "glorifies the Son" (Jn 16:14), bears witness to Jesus (Jn 15:26), searches the depth of God (1 Cor 2:10–11) and teaches humanity to recognize and confess the Son (1 Cor 12:3).[30] The Son "glorifies the Father" (Jn 17:4), praises the Father (Lk 10:21), proclaims the goodness of God (Mk 10:18) and serves the will of the Father (10:36ff).[31] The Father gives all things to the Son (Jn 17:4), gives all judgment to the Son so that he might be honored (Jn 5:23), the Father exalts the Son (Phil 2:9, Heb 2:8), hands over his kingdom (1 Cor 1:24) and raises the Son from death (Acts 2:24).[32] Pannenberg recognizes that through this relating activity one may conclude that "from all eternity the Father loves the Son, the Son loves the Father, and the Spirit loves the Father in the Son and the Son in the Father . . . and each thereby fulfils itself."[33]

While Pannenberg recognizes the myriad of interrelated movements of the triune persons, he ultimately restricts his interpretation of the scriptural "facts" of triune interrelation to the establishment of the rule of God and the concept of triune love. He provides no further interpretation or categorization of the dynamic movements inherent to these relations. Simply put, he modifies the constitution of the "divine-dance" to accord with divine mutuality reflected in Scripture but does not clarify the "dance-steps." However, while the New Testament might not directly clarify the characteristics of the divine relations, it is possible to *interpret* these from the Scriptural accounts, as indeed Pannenberg does when he interprets the mutuality of the triune relations to establish the telos of divine reign and love. It is to this possibility that Divine Self-Enrichment is concerned; to discern inherent characteristics of triune interrelatedness, not merely its fact.

THE ESCHATOLOGICAL TRINITY

Pannenberg's Trinitarian theology is indelibly contoured by Jesus' message of both the eschatological kingdom of God's rule and the eschatological reality of Jesus' resurrection.[34] For Pannenberg, God's rule is commensurate with the being of the triune God, where this God is the "power of the future."[35] Through this lens, he envisions the eschatological rule of the Trinity as having an "ontological priority over present time and past time."[36] Arriving at this conclusion, through philosophical contemplations of being and appearance,[37] Pannenberg advocates that appearance includes both "'the act of coming-into-appearance'" and "the 'something' that appears," which is not exhausted in the act of appearing.[38] With a similar logic, Pannenberg extrapolates from Jesus' teachings that the "kingdom of God is expressed in the present but not exhausted by its presence."[39] Rather, the historical presence of the kingdom of God, says Pannenberg, is "derived from [its futurity] and is itself only the anticipatory glimmer of its coming."[40] Pannenberg therefore asserts a unity between the economic and immanent Trinity, not as a conflation of the immanent and the economic, "a tendency he finds in Moltmann,"[41] but where the economic and immanent Trinity are unified eschatologically. At the eschaton the economic Trinity will be complete in the immanent Trinity, where it will be seen that "the eschatological consummation is only the locus of the decision that the Trinitarian God is always the true God from eternity to eternity. The dependence of [God's] existence on the eschatological consummation of the kingdom changes nothing in this regard."[42] Pannenberg's logic here connects the "eternal triune being of God and the history of the world."[43] It is at this point, however, that Pannenberg attracts the charge of Hegelianism (on the basis that Pannenberg's Trinity appears to only acquire fulfillment in the creation's eschaton).[44] Peters, however, rejects such a charge, arguing that Pannenberg does not advocate a concept of God as "the result of a developmental process. Rather, the eschatological event determines what will have been eternally true."[45] While Pannenberg uses insights from Hegel in order to address what he considers a deficiency of some traditional views, that of a separation of God's action in the world from the eternal life of God, contra Hegel, he maintains that "God and history are to be linked but not fused."[46] As our discussion continues to unfold we will see that Pannenberg envisages that the intratrinitarian establishment of God's rule in the world is derived from a dynamic fullness of divine aseity, not a deficiency reliant on a world process. Pannenberg, therefore, expounds, in a manner similar to the logic of Divine Self-Enrichment, the congruent nexus between divine self-sufficiency and divine relatedness with the world.

PANNENBERG AND DIVINE SELF-ENRICHMENT

So far we have canvassed how, for Pannenberg, the intra-divine relations are constitutive for the unity and purpose of divine being.[47] Likewise, we have observed Pannenberg's desire to expand the terminology used to clarify the relational nature of the Trinity through tri-hypostatic "concepts such as *giving over* and *receiving back*, *obedience* and *glorification*, and *filling* and *glorifying*." This expanded understanding is likewise used by Pannenberg to argue for a reconfiguration of the traditional one-way relations of origin.[48] Furthermore, Pannenberg affirms that the intra-divine relations not only constitute the fullness of divine being but ontologically condition divine relationality with the world. In these ways, Pannenberg's system elucidates and endorses key aspects undergirding the logic of Divine Self-Enrichment. However, there remain elements of Pannenberg's views that compel further discussion. These are: (1) the nature of the reciprocity of the divine relations, including the role of hierarchy and kenosis; (2) the mode by which the fullness of deity is achieved; and (3) the goal and anticipation of the eschatological kingdom. The remainder of this chapter will begin to productively employ the logic of Divine Self-Enrichment to engage, challenge and augment some of these issues. Consequently, Divine Self-Enrichment develops not only as a constructive theology but as a critical hermeneutical tool.

Pannenberg and Hierarchical Divine Relations

Pannenberg's revision of the relations of origin and his advocacy of reciprocal triune self-distinction as constitutive for divinity significantly contribute to the development of new avenues for contemporary Trinitarian theology.

These conceptions also confirm an intratrinitarian logic inherent to Divine Self-Enrichment. However, Pannenberg's emphasis on establishing the monarchy of the Father through the submissively construed activity of the Son, arguably undermines the interpretation of the triune relations as authentically mutual, reciprocal and equal.[49] Although Pannenberg formally eschews subordination of "the deity of the Son and Spirit to that of the Father,"[50] his conception of God's deity hinges on the relative subordination of the activity of the Son in the Spirit to the Father.[51] Thus, Pannenberg holds that the establishment of "the Lordship of God [is] the chief content and primary goal of the mission of Jesus," by which he shows "himself to be the Son who serves the will of the Father."[52] The emphasis on Jesus' obedience to the Father dominates Pannenberg's interpretation of the divine relations. In fact, Pannenberg interprets Jesus' "not knowing the time of the end," not having authority to "assign places of honour at his side in the heavenly kingdom," and subjecting his own will to that of the Father in Gethsemane, as evidence of "*subordination* to the Father."[53] Consequently, by construing the Trinitarian relations in such a manner he arguably binds divinity to a hierarchically-structured framework, impeding further insight into the nature of the relations. Linn Tonstad identifies this problem and argues:

> every relation between Jesus and the Father that Pannenberg mentions . . . is variation on a single theme that of hierarchical subordination that translates as obedience . . . True reciprocity and mutuality do not appear in this picture. Not only do the relations repeat precisely the pattern of the relations of origin, which given Pannenberg's criticism thereof is already problematic, but the relations are also hierarchical and structured by lines of authority and order. It seems, then, that Pannenberg's understanding of mutuality is merely a formal being-in-relation-to rather than a genuine mutuality that could include relations that need no hierarchical structure.[54]

Tonstad thus questions whether the Son's "free submission" is the most appropriate designation by which to cast the relationship between the Son and Father, asserting that such a view is a "narrative that ultimately enshrines difference as hierarchical."[55] Miroslav Volf also suggests, with Pannenberg in mind, that

> hierarchy is not necessary to guard either the divine unity or the distinctions between divine Persons . . . in a community of perfect love between Persons who share all divine attributes a notion of hierarchy is unintelligible. Hierarchical constructions of the Trinitarian relations appear from this perspective as projections of the fascination with earthly hierarchies onto the heavenly community.[56]

Although Pannenberg acknowledges reciprocity in the triune relations, including paternal dependence on the Son for his rule, his articulation of the Father's mode of relating conveys hypostatic distinction derived from paternal hierarchy. While Pannenberg identifies that the *Father glorifies* the Son (Jn 8:50), and all things are given, including judgment and ultimately the kingdom, *to the Son by the Father* (Lk 10:22), these paternal acts are never interpreted by Pannenberg as acts of deference or some form of "submission" of the Father to the Son.[57] Yet, Pannenberg consistently imputes such an interpretation to the Son's similar activity of glorifying and handing over the kingdom to the Father. Pannenberg states that the Son is to proclaim "the lordship of the Father, to glorify him, to subject all things to him" but in this activity the Son is said to not only distinguish "himself from God" but "sets himself as a creature *below God*."[58] The nature of this hypostatic relating is not accorded to the economy alone, but is considered by Pannenberg as having significance for understanding the eternal triune relations. Pannenberg states:

> if the intratrinitarian relations between the Father and the Son are to be inferred from the mutual relations between the historical person of Jesus and the Father, the fulfilment of the sending is an expression of his relation to the Father and the Father's relation to him. The handing over of the power and rule of the Father to the Son is then to be seen also as *a defining of the intratrinitarian relations* between the two, as is also their handing back by the Son to the Father.[59]

It appears for Pannenberg that the replication of giving and receiving from Son to Father and Father to Son is pertinent for redefining the traditional one-way relations of origin, but not for according an equality of attribute that sources these divine actions. There seems to be an unacknowledged resistance to conferring the Father with the same attribute (I argue a kenotic attribute) that gives rise to both the filial *and paternal* acts of giving and receiving. For Pannenberg, that the Son gives glory and honor and hands over the kingdom to the Father is categorized as an attribute of deference or submission. However, the Father's similarly contoured giving of glory, honor and handing over the kingdom to the Son receives quite a different categorization. Although Pannenberg advocates a multi-directional triune relationality for the constitution of divinity he stops short of according a truly communicable unity in the divine nature. As such, Pannenberg cannot avoid rendering a hierarchical asymmetry into the divine nature.

This raises the question of the possibility of a more nuanced characterization by which to interpret the nature of hypostatic relating. To which I maintain that Divine Self-Enrichment (with its pattern of tri-hypostatic mutual kenotic-enrichment) is such a construction. Such a concept provides the theological framework to advocate a truly unified and non-hierarchical understanding of the Son and Spirit's deference to each other and to the Father, as well as providing the appropriate logic to understand the Father's kenotically deferential acts toward the Son and Spirit. A reductive concept of subordination or submission (a truncated-kenosis) is simply not capable of encapsulating the mutual movements of triune relationality found in Scripture. The glory, kingdom and rule gifted to the Son from the Father is, through a theology of Divine Self-Enrichment, more beneficially interpreted as demonstrations of the communicable divine nature of kenotic-enrichment; where the Father submits in faithful trust to the faithfulness of the Son's own kenotically-enriching nature. This construction avoids imputing a hierarchical distortion of the unity of God's nature from a misreading of the economy.

One final consideration requires discussion here—that is, the role that the Son's submissively-interpreted distinction from the Father has in forming Pannenberg's ontological basis for human participation under the rule of God. Pannenberg's construction of the Son's active relation to the Father in terms of "subordination" (but not vice versa) is, in part, because of his intention to designate the Son as an "archetype of the destiny of created being to achieve communion with God."[60] That is to say, the Son's distinction from the Father in the Spirit reveals a necessary posture inherent to "sonship," that of human "submission" to the rule of God.[61] Thus, Pannenberg concludes that the "incarnation is the fulfilment of the destiny of all human creatures to live in filial relationship with God which is enacted in Jesus' self-distinction from the Father by becoming obedient to him."[62]

This divine ontological foundation for human participation in "sonship" can, however, be successfully maintained through the lens of triune kenotic-enrichment. By nuancing Pannenberg's view, the ontological pattern of God's rule and of human participation in the life of God can be established, not solely through viewing the Son's relating to the Father as mere "submissive" or "subordinated" obedience but as acts of kenotic-enrichment.[63] Augmenting Pannenberg's theology in this manner opens the possibility for an "archetype of the destiny of created being to achieve communion with God" to be found in Christ's Spirit-fuelled movements of kenotic-enrichment.[64] Such a view reorientates human engagement in kenotic acts of other-centered enrichment, not as mere obedience, but as imitation of, and participation in, the divine nature (2 Peter 1:4). Even if one retains the human appropriateness of expressing obedience and submission to God, we do not need to impute semi-homousian hierarchical notions into the triune structure of being to ground Christ's manner of Incarnational activity. We simply need to understand Christ's economic relating to the Father as expression of the ontological archetype of triune kenotic-enrichment, not expression of a hierarchical divinity. Under such a theological construction, the Son's "obedience" is not demonstrative of a lesser or distinct filial attribute, but rather the temporal translation of the pattern of triune kenotic-enrichment. Christ's obedience and deference to the Father is his kenotic yielding that defines the content of his being. A kenotic yielding that likewise constitutes the life of the Father and Spirit. Without the corrective of a theology of Divine Self-Enrichment, theologians unfortunately find themselves cornered by the narrowness of the ontological significance they attach to the economy of triune relating—they have no other manner by which to interpret Christ's so-called "submissive" activity but as an incommunicable characteristic attributable only to the Son. However, imputed with ontic significance, such a categorization cannot but result in imputing asymmetrical hierarchy of will and nature into the Godhead.

Pannenberg and Truncated-Kenosis

Pannenberg has a clear aversion to acknowledging mutual kenosis between the hypostases. He argues that manifestations of the divine self-distinctions do "not mean exactly the same thing for each of the three Persons,"[65] thus he restricts a "kenotic" manifestation to the being of the Son alone. Although he identifies the movement between the divine Persons in terms that amount to giving and receiving, handing over and back, glorifying and praising, he does not (unlike Bulgakov) perceive these movements as kenotic and inherent to each hypostasis. Although Pannenberg recognizes kenosis in the Son, where "Jesus manifests himself to be the Son of God by emptying himself,"[66] of the idea of kenosis inherent to the Father he states, "it is one thing to say that the self-emptying obedience of Christ has its 'origin in God' the Father . . . because after all the Father commissioned the Son with his mission to the world. But it is quite another thing to speak of a self-emptying activity on the part of the Father himself."[67] In another place, on a narrow interpretation of Scripture, Pannenberg polemically asserts that,

> there is not the slightest evidence . . . in any other place in the New Testament . . . that the Father emptied himself . . . Even in connection with the Son, that idea occurs only in the one place of Paul's letter to the Philippians and nowhere else in the entire New Testament . . . Therefore, with regard to the inner-trinitarian life, one should not speak of a mutual kenosis, though there is a mutual devotedness of Father, Son and Spirit in relation to each other as well as a mutual dependence.[68]

One of the reasons Pannenberg eschews a repetition of hypostatic kenosis, particularly for the Father, is because he has in mind an erroneous concept more akin to a *truncated*-kenosis (kenosis devoid of enrichment that amounts to mere depletion), not an *enriching*-kenosis. Yet, this type of truncated-kenosis imputed to paternity is, however, in direct contradiction to Pannenberg's descriptive content regarding the Son's kenosis. Pannenberg identifies a pattern that reflects the notion of an enriching-kenosis in the Son's activity. He says, "The self-emptying of the Preexistent *is not a surrender or negation* of his deity as the Son. *It is its activation*."[69] He highlights that the nature of divinity is expressed through the Son's kenosis in the Incarnation, arguing that "the self-emptying and self-humbling that we find when we compare the eternal deity of the Son to his incarnation must not be seen as a limitation but as an *expression of the eternal deity*."[70] Pannenberg clearly articulates here that the Son's kenosis is an expression and actualization of divinity. Yet, regarding the Father, he rejects kenotic activity on the basis that it amounts to a mere emptying of divinity (truncated-kenosis), saying that an interpretation of the Father's activity in the Son's crucifixion as kenosis "would have been disastrous with regard to the Son, because the Father, if he had emptied himself, could have no longer employed his omnipotence to raise the crucified one from the dead."[71] Here, Pannenberg correlates paternal kenosis with a diminished "emptying" of divinity (truncated-kenosis) but for the Son it is constitutive for divine life (enriching-kenosis). An inconsistency is evident here in Pannenberg's view of the nature of divine kenosis, one that arguably dissolves divine unity. The inconsistency becomes further pronounced when Pannenberg identifies triune love as mutual devotedness but not as mutual kenosis.[72] However, defining divine love in his *Systematics* he imputes triune love with self-giving (kenosis) at its core, saying:

> If, however, the one loves self in the other instead of loving the other as other, then love falls short of the full self-giving . . . and since the self-giving is mutual there is no one-sided dependence . . . The spirit that unites two or more Persons need not always manifest itself as the mutual self-giving of the I and the Thou. But all forms of the fellowship live finally by the power of the love which *manifests itself in its most original and complete form in mutual self-giving*. This applies especially to the trinitarian life of God.[73]

If, on Pannenberg's own interpretation, divine love is manifested in self-giving and "the Trinitarian life of God is an unfolding of this love," then kenosis belongs to the nature of love, in which case it must be a communicable attribute of all three hypostases.[74] If self-giving love is only imputed to the being of the Son, then the divine nature is asymmetrically construed, and Divine essence is not unified.[75] Furthermore, if kenosis is an expression and actualization of deity, why would this expression and actualization be absent from the Father and the Spirit? If, as Pannenberg argues, the Father's deity is commensurate with his kingdom and lordship, would not the act of the Father handing over this kingdom and lordship to the Son be a kenotic act—a self-giving from Father to Son? Which, according to Pannenberg's logic, will accord with the very actualization of the Father's deity as the Son consummates the kingdom. Surely such paternal divine acting evidences the deep patterning of kenotic-enrichment.

While Pannenberg initiates new ground for exploring the dynamism of the triune relations, it is at this point that Divine Self-Enrichment fruitfully augments Pannenberg's interpretation as it advocates *tri*-hypostatic kenosis as constitutive for divinity. Perceiving divinity as characterized by tri-hypostatic expressions of kenotic-enrichment not only gives credence to divine self-distinction but also interprets these distinctions as repetitions of the *One* divine nature as affirmed in the Nicene Creed: "God from God, Light from Light, true God from true God."[76] Contra Pannenberg, and in affinity with Bulgakov, the economic actions of Father, Son and Holy Spirit reflect the unity of the nature of God, where kenosis must be a characteristic inherent to *all three* divine hypostases.

Pannenberg, Crypto-Hegelianism and the Fullness of God

Despite scholarly criticism to the contrary, Pannenberg premises his Trinitarian theology on a fullness, not deficiency, of God's being, while simultaneously taking seriously God's profound relationality with the world. Through the "ec-statically" related triune mutuality (in history) where each hypostasis is the fullness of deity in the fullness of divine unity, Pannenberg argues that God's kingdom is divinely self-realized.[77] Thus, divine fullness is conceptualized as a dynamically achieved "goal." Wary, however, of referring to "goals" of divine action because the concept presupposes a "gulf between the selection of a goal and its attainment,"[78] Pannenberg articulates God's goal of establishing the kingdom as the "self-actualisation of God."[79] Thus, the Father, Son and Holy Spirit are "primarily the subject of the divine action."[80] Unlike human goal setting, where the subject presupposes the goal and the goal refers to a need or deficiency to be achieved incrementally, God achieves his kingdom from an eternal reality: "God actualizes himself in the world by his coming in to it. For this eternal existence in the fellowship of the Father, Son and Holy Spirit is presupposed and his eternal essence needs no completion by his coming into the world."[81] God's deity, therefore, is construed as free and open to the future,[82] but also as an expression of the true God from "eternity to eternity."[83]

Scholars have, however, taken exception with Pannenberg's attempts to connect "the eternal self-identity of God with a becoming time."[84] O'Donnell, Venema and Hunsinger critique in Pannenberg what they view as a Hegelian tendency to posit dependency of God's deity on the world.[85] Others, such as

Westphal, Clayton and Mostert, however, defend Pannenberg's refined position and his explicit rejection of a process-driven deity.[86] The crypto-Hegelian charge is difficult to sustain given Pannenberg's continual refutation of the "idea of a divine becoming in history."[87] Of God, Pannenberg unequivocally argues, that "the manifestation of his lordship over the world of creation, *does not make good a lack* in his eternal being but incorporates his creatures into his eternal fellowship of the Son with the Father through the Spirit."[88] Pannenberg upholds divine fullness (acknowledging the concepts of divine self-sufficiency and simplicity) as God establishes his kingdom in creation.[89] The God of self-sufficient triune fullness is, however, unambiguously engaged with the temporal world. Thus, Pannenberg's views advocate neither "a God who develops in history, nor a God untouched by events in time."[90] Rather, he proposes a harmonizing principle of "retroactive permanence," where the eschatological establishment of "God's rule over creation" reveals that "God's being will turn out to have been eternally what it is then, from the standpoint in time, established to be."[91]

Pannenberg's eschatological construal of the Trinity holds significance for Divine Self-Enrichment. First, it affirms an intratrinitarian dynamic that establishes divine fullness in harmony with classical theistic concepts such as aseity and simplicity (see chapters 2 and 3). Second, divine sufficiency and fullness of being are upheld as congruent with God's relationality with the world without eliding a future eternal dynamism. And third, Pannenberg's notion of God's self-actualized deity also helpfully expresses the difference between divine and human well-being. It demonstrates how human goals are defined by the gulf between the goal and the lack of possession of that end, whereas the divine goal of divine life is self-actualized from eternal accomplishment.[92] This point is important when establishing the ontological correspondence and disparity between divine and human enrichment (see chapter 7 for more detail).

Kenotic-Enrichment: The Goal and Mode of the Kingdom?

Pannenberg advances that the creature's knowledge of God is derived through God's action and goal. He explains that "we know the distinctiveness of his [God's] essence . . . by the characteristics of his working."[93] God's working, on Pannenberg's account, is to achieve the divine goal, which is—the establishment of the eschatological kingdom and the rule of God over creation. These two parameters, divine work and divine goal, not only give us vital information as to where to look for characteristics of the divine nature but raise two pertinent questions relevant to Divine Self-Enrichment. First: What is the telos or purpose of the establishment of the kingdom? And the second: Are there identifiable characteristics inherent to the actualization of this kingdom?

To the first question. Christiaan Mostert clarifies the telos of Pannenberg's "kingdom" as "nothing other than the glory of the Trinity" and, through the Spirit, "the completion and perfection of the creation."[94] In other words, consistent with the matrix of a theology of Divine Self-Enrichment, the goal of the eschatological kingdom is the actualization of the eternal perfection of triune all-blessedness and its impartation to creation. God desires not to retain his glory of well-being for himself alone. The glory of divine rule is graciously shared with those who participate in the kingdom's reign. The nature of kingdom rule, therefore, contextualizes and conditions the well-being of citizens of the kingdom.

To the second consideration—whether there are identifiable characteristics that attend the actualization of the "kingdom." As we have discussed, Pannenberg restricts his interpretation of the mode of the kingdom's actualization to the eschatological event of the Son's *subordinate* self-distinction and the handing back and forth of the kingdom in the Spirit between the Son and Father. Beyond this mutual exchange, Pannenberg is cautious to articulate characteristics of divine relationality that establish the kingdom. However, through the lens of Divine Self-Enrichment, Pannenberg's initial intuition may be further refined. Instead of interpreting the exchange between Father and Son through, what appear to be, anthropological conceptions of power, submission or subordination, we might rather view the exchange that establishes the reign of God as the mutual communicable essence of divine kenotic-enrichment. This does not deny Pannenberg's identification of the obedience of Jesus of Nazareth to the Father. Rather, as I have already argued, it proposes that Jesus' obedience to the Father should be characterized as an act of enriching kenotic love toward the Father, consistent with the divine nature, not as an ontological inference of divine subordination *in se*. Through this nuanced approach we can further interpret the Father giving the Son the kingdom is an affirmation of the Son's greatness and worth, a gift of enrichment that the Son then likewise gifts back to the Father in the Spirit. Through the lens of Divine Self-Enrichment, Pannenberg's consummation of the rule of God via the "handing over" of the kingdom to the Son and its re-gifting back to the Father is not evidence of an asymmetrical divine relating but rather evidences that *the way of the kingdom* and thus *the life of God* are patterned by a mutuality of kenotic-enrichment.

Anticipation of Well-Being: Now and Not Yet

Finally, Pannenberg's theology gives eloquence to the tension between the "now" and the "not-yet" of the divine rule in creation. He advances an anticipation of the future consummated kingdom (not-yet), as well as the proleptic in-breaking of this futurity through the historical event of Jesus (now). These two poles provide important bearings for comprehending the nature of creation's participation in divine life. The anticipation of the eschatological kingdom, where temporal creation participates fully "in God's eternal (Trinitarian) life"[95] reveals an ontology of future wholeness that shapes the present striving toward well-being. Thus, Pannenberg says: "If the future means the future of salvation as the fulfillment of the *whole* person, then knowledge of this future, regardless of its hiddenness, is constitutive for human life as it is now."[96] Yet, this anticipation also locates the disjunction between future wholeness and the current reality of the world's unfulfilled longing. The wholeness of the futurity of the divine kingdom remains a still yet-to-be certain hope. Holding these two perceptions together allows humanity's orientation toward well-being to be affirmed as a right anticipatory activity without the illusion of a concurrent achievable utopia. Pannenberg's theology, thus, provides a further basis for understanding the temporality and contingency of human well-being as the foretaste of future participation in the well-being of the triune God. The well-being of God's all-blessedness is the ontological origination, the context and certain conclusion for the repetitions found in the created order. This is why a theological ontology of triune well-being is of vital significance for the grounding and explication of Christian ethical and doxological contemplations.

CONCLUSION

As we have explored, the theological impulses of Divine Self-Enrichment—*God enriching God in the fullness and perfection of God*—have consonance with Pannenberg's overarching insight that the multi-directional relations of the Divine Persons are constitutive for deity. Pannenberg's Trinitarian interpretation is also a useful starting point that may be extended to identify greater specificity regarding characteristics of divine intra-relatedness. The key aspects of Pannenberg's theology that augment a theology of Divine Self-Enrichment can be summarized as follows:

1. The content of divine being is not exclusively derived from the traditional relations of origin of a one-sided begetting and spirating but from a mutuality of varying relations among the divine Persons.
2. Divine unity is commensurate with self-distinguishing relations between Father, Son and Holy Spirit. In divine self-distinction the hypostases define and depend on each other for the expression and being of deity. Pannenberg's concept of hypostatic self-distinction affirms the first

dynamic relational element of Divine Self-Enrichment's definition—*God* enriching *God*.

3. The Father, Son and Holy Spirit are, through active and passive giving and receiving, establishing the kingdom or rule of God as the goal of their relations. This exegetical interpretation affirms another dynamic element of Divine Self-Enrichment's definition—God *enriching* God. Divine Self-Enrichment or the all-blessed life of divinity, however, provides a broader theological proposition under which Pannenberg's concept of kingdom rule may be categorized. Whereas Pannenberg interprets the intra-relations as establishing the kingdom of God, this in fact serves the ultimate telos of the glory of divine well-being, in which creation participates, proleptically and eschatologically.

4. Pannenberg upholds a distinction between the immanent and economic Trinity, where the economic relations demonstrate the eternal essence of divinity. The immanent and economic Trinity are only conflated eschatologically, with retroactive permanence. In this way, Pannenberg's view of an eschatological eternity affirms the notion of the dynamic fullness and self-sufficiency of God's being. Such a perception clarifies that a simplicity of triune abundance is compatible with divine relationality to the creation. These concepts again affirm the theological logic of the final element of the definition of Divine Self-Enrichment—*in the fullness and perfection of God*.

5. Pannenberg affirms the dynamic nature of gift and receipt among the hypostases through terms such as glorifying, handing over and back, praise and love. While Pannenberg identifies the exegetical facts of these dynamics, he does not, however, systemize their characteristics. Divine Self-Enrichment, thus, augments this gap in his Trinitarian theology.

6. Anticipation of the future reign of God (the triune life of well-being that is self-actualized) and the proleptic in-breaking of this reign in history allows us to perceive the ontological basis for the incremental realization of human well-being without utopian illusions. Pannenberg's theological insight holds together the "now" and "not-yet" tension of the reign of God experienced by creation. The eschaton provides the final horizon of creation's communion in triune life, gifted through the Holy Spirit as a present anticipatory participation. These are important insights for understanding the similarities and differences between the attainment of divine and human well-being.

7. Divine Self-Enrichment posits that *triune* enriching-kenosis is a key characteristic of divine interrelatedness, a concept excluded from Pannenberg's system. Pannenberg attributes kenosis to the Son alone. However, this arguably creates hierarchical difference in the Godhead and dislocates the unity of the divine nature. Positing intra-Trinitarian

relating under the umbrella term of "enriching-kenosis" envisages an authentic ontological mutuality of the self-giving nature of triune love without the inference of semi-homoisian hierarchy.

NOTES

1. Wolfhart Pannenberg, *Systematic Theology*, vols. 1–3, trans. Geoffrey W. Bromiley (Grand Rapids, MI: Eerdmans, 1991–1998). Originally published as *Systematische Theologie*, Band i–iii (Gottingen: Vandenhoeck & Ruprecht, 1988). Herein referred to as *ST1*, *ST2*, and *ST3*.

2. Christoph Schwöbel, "Rational Theology in Trinitarian Perspective: Wolfhart Pannenberg's Systematic Theology," *The Journal of Theological Studies* 47, no. 2 (1996): 499.

3. Pannenberg, *ST1*, 299.

4. Ted Peters, *God as Trinity: Relationality and Temporality in the Divine Life* (Louisville, KY: Westminster Press, 1993), 136.

5. Peters, *God as Trinity*, 136.

6. Pannenberg asserts that the derivation of the plurality of the divine Persons from one essence inevitably leads to the problem of modalism or subordinationism. Pannenberg criticizes Karl Barth for subordinating his doctrine of the Trinity "to a pretrinitarian concept of the unity of God." Pannenberg, *ST1*, 273.

7. Pannenberg, *ST1*, 273, 313.

8. Pannenberg, *ST1*, 319. See also footnote 183 of *ST1* where Pannenberg outlines how Staniloae, Moltmann, Gott, and R. W. Jensen have identified similar conceptions of the divine unity.

9. Pannenberg emphasizes that holding the Father as the origin of deity for the Son and Holy Spirit seems "to rule out genuine mutuality in the relations of the Trinitarian Persons." He therefore rejects that the unity of God is derived solely from the relations of origin, or a single divine mode expressed in three modes, such as found in Augustine's concept of the divine mind. Pannenberg, *ST1*, 311–12.

10. Wolfhart Pannenberg, *Jesus—God and Man*, 2nd ed., trans. Lewis L. Wilkins and Duane A. Priebe (Philadelphia: Westminster, 1977), 180. Originally published as *Grundzuge der Christologie* (Giitersloh: Gerd Mohn, 1964).

11. Pannenberg, *ST1*, 320. Mostert explains that Pannenberg is not opposed to the concept of relations of origin, rather what he opposes is "the exclusive view of the trinitarian relations in terms of relations of origin." Christiaan Mostert, *God and the Future: Wolfhart Pannenberg's Eschatological Doctrine of God* (London: Bloomsbury Publishing Plc, 2002), 229.

12. Pannenberg, *ST1*, 320. My italics. Pannenberg argues that "if, however, we call the Father the fount or principle of the deity of the Son and Spirit in the sense that they are dependent on him for deity but not he on them, then the reciprocity of the self-distinction, and therefore of the trinitarian Persons, along with their equal deity, is not upheld." Pannenberg, *ST1*, 322.

13. Pannenberg, *ST1*, 320.

14. Pannenberg, *ST1*, 321.
15. Pannenberg, *ST1*, 305. Also, "we may [not] reduce their description to the traditional concepts of procession, begetting and breathing." Pannenberg, *ST1*, 307.
16. Pannenberg, *ST1*, 320. My italics.
17. Pannenberg, *ST1*, 299. Pannenberg states "One can know the intertrinitarian distinctions and relations, the inner life of God, only through the revelation of the Son." Pannenberg, *ST1*, 273.
18. Pannenberg, *ST1*, 308.
19. Of triune distinction, Pannenberg argues, "Jesus expressly differentiated God the Father from himself . . . This self-distinction from God finds its clearest expression in the prayer of Jesus to the Father." See Pannenberg, *ST1*, 263. Likewise of the Holy Spirit he also argues "he is clearly distinct from Jesus." Pannenberg, *ST1*, 270.
20. Pannenberg, *ST1*, 309.
21. Pannenberg, *ST1*, 310.
22. Pannenberg, *ST1*, 310–11.
23. Pannenberg, *ST1*, 313. My italics. Pannenberg does not disregard the Holy Spirit in this intratrinitarian activity but maintains that the "Spirit is not just breathed. He also fills the Son and glorifies him in his obedience to the Father, thereby glorifying the Father himself." Pannenberg, *ST1*, 320.
24. Pannenberg, *ST1*, 327. In this way, Pannenberg seeks to connect the economic Trinity with the immanent Trinity and, against Barth, whom he criticizes for removing God from history, he seeks to understand the unity of God through God's revelation in the economy of salvation. But this is quite different from Moltmann or LaCugna who conflates both the economic and immanent.
25. Pannenberg claims that "lordship goes hand in hand with the deity of God. It has its place already in the intratrinitarian life of God, in the reciprocity of the relation between the Son, who freely subjects himself to the lordship of the Father, and the Father, who hands over his lordship to the Son." Pannenberg likewise confirms Moltmann's affirmation of divine lordship as belonging "already to God's intratrinitarian life as an inner work." Pannenberg, *ST1*, 313. See also Jürgen Moltmann, *The Trinity and the Kingdom of God: The Doctrine of God*, trans. Margaret Kohl (Minneapolis: Fortress Press, 1993), 92–93.
26. Pannenberg, *ST1*, 324.
27. Pannenberg, *ST1*, 325.
28. Pannenberg, *ST1*, 325.
29. Pannenberg, *ST1*, 269.
30. Pannenberg, *ST1*, 317.
31. Pannenberg, *ST1*, 309.
32. Pannenberg, *ST1*, 312.
33. Pannenberg, *ST1*, 426.
34. Mostert, *God and the Future*, 4.
35. Wolfhart Pannenberg, *Basic Questions in Theology*, vol. 2, trans. George H. Kehm (London: SCM, 1971), 242. Originally published as *Grundfragen systematischer Theologie*, Bd I (Gottingen: Vandenhoeck & Ruprecht, 1967).
36. Mostert, *God and the Future*, 88.

37. Mostert, *God and the Future*, 94.
38. Mostert, *God and the Future*, 94. See also Pannenberg, *Theology and the Kingdom of God*, ed. Richard J. Neuhaus (Philadelphia: Westminster Press, 1969), 131..
39. Mostert, *God and the Future*, 94.
40. Pannenberg, *Theology and the Kingdom of God*, 133 in Mostert, *God and the Future*, 95.
41. Stanley J. Grenz, *Reason for Hope: The Systematic Theology of Wolfhart Pannenberg* (Oxford: Oxford University Press, 1990), 69.
42. Pannenberg *ST1*, 331.
43. Mostert, *God and the Future*, 217. This connection is both epistemological and ontological. Epistemological—as the eschaton will reveal God to be God, and ontological—because God "is eternally what God is" with history having a bearing on God's being. Mostert, *God and the Future*, 223. Hunsinger finds this construction, present in both Jenson and Pannenberg, problematic, describing it as "dialectic historicism with a teleological contour." George Hunsinger, "Robert Jenson's Systematic Theology: A Review Essay," *Scottish Journal of Theology* 55, no. 2 (2002): 175.
44. See J. O'Donnell, "Pannenberg's Doctrine of God," *Gregorianum* 72, no. 1 (1991): 95–96, www.jstor.org/stable/23578753; Cornelis P. Venema, "History, Human Freedom and the Idea of God in the Theology of Wolfhart Pannenberg," *Calvin Theological Journal* 17, no. 1 (1982): 75.
45. Peters, *God as Trinity*, 141.
46. Pannenberg "The God of History," trans. M. B. Jackson, *Cumberland Seminarian* 19, nos. 2–3 (1981): 28–41. Originally published as "Der Gott der Geschichte: Der trinitarische Gott und die Wahrheit der Geschichte," *Kerygma und Dogma* 23, no. 2, 1977: 76–92.
47. This intuition is expressed by his intention to "define the relational nexus of the *perichoresis* more accurately, and also show how it relates to the unity of the divine life." Pannenberg, *ST1*, 321.
48. Grenz, *Reason for Hope*, 67. Original italics.
49. See for example, Linn Tonstad, "'The Ultimate Consequence of His Self-Distinction from the Father . . . ': Difference and Hierarchy in Pannenberg's Trinity," *Neue Zeitschrift für Systematische Theologie und Religionsphilosophie* 51, no. 4 (2009): 383–99.
50. Pannenberg, *ST1*, 303. See also *ST1*, 299.
51. Yet, there is an inherent problem with this. If, on Pannenberg's argument, the Son's activity is reduced to ontic subordination and obedience to the Father is not a divine characteristic attributed to the Son that has no similar continuity with the Father's being?
52. Pannenberg, *ST1*, 309.
53. Pannenberg, *ST1*, 309. My italics.
54. Linn Tonstad, "Difference and Hierarchy," 390.
55. Tonstad, "Difference and Hierarchy," 391, 392.
56. Miroslav Volf, "The Trinity is our Social Program: The Doctrine of the Trinity and the Shape of Social Engagement," *Modern Theology* 14, no. 3 (July 1998): 407. Volf at footnote 20 of the same paper highlights the difficulty with

harmonizing Pannenberg's notion of "ontological equality" and the "moral subordination" of the Son (*ST1*, 324–25).

57. Pannenberg, *ST1*, 312–13. Pannenberg outlines the activity of the Father, saying "Matthew 28:18 says that *all power is given* to the risen Christ in heaven and on earth. According to Luke 10:22 and Matt. 11:27 even the pre-Easter Jesus can claim that *all things are given* him *by the Father*. John 5:23 (cf. v. 27) says that the *Father has given all judgment* to the Son so that all *might honor him as they do the Father*. Luke 10:22 goes even further than this when it says that all things, not just judgment alone, are given to the Son. The Son is not merely the representative of the rule of God; he executes it. *He is the holder of lordship*." It begs the question as to why deference or submission of the Father in relation to the other hypostases is considered inappropriate to the nature of paternal divinity, especially if self-giving love is considered at the heart of God's expression in Christ. My italics.

58. Pannenberg, *ST1*, 309.
59. Pannenberg, *ST1*, 313. My italics.
60. Schwöbel, "Rational Theology," 509.
61. Schwöbel, "Rational Theology," 511.
62. Schwöbel, "Rational Theology," 512.
63. The unified divine ontology of kenotic-enrichment is enacted though the Son's obedience, praise and worshipful posture of servitude to the Father, where the Son's divine relating demonstrates self-giving to the Father in the Spirit that is symbiotically his own enrichment (divine actualization).
64. Schwöbel, "Rational Theology," 509.
65. Pannenberg, *ST1*, 321.
66. Wolfhart Pannenberg, "God's Love and the Kenosis of the Son: A Response to Masao Abe," in *Divine Emptiness and Historical Fullness: A Buddhist-Jewish-Christian Conversation with Masao Abe*, ed. Christopher Ives (Valley Forge, PA: Trinity Press International, 1995), 247.
67. Pannenberg, "The Kenosis of the Son," 248.
68. Pannenberg, "The Kenosis of the Son," 248. McCormack echoes Pannenberg here when he states, "In truth, it should go without saying that Scripture only knows of one use of the verbal form of kenosis and that this use is applied solely to Christ Jesus." Bruce Lindley McCormack, *The Humility of the Eternal Son: Reformed Kenoticism and the Repair of Chalcedon*, Current Issues in Theology (Cambridge: Cambridge University Press, 2021), 292–93.
69. Pannenberg, *ST3*, 377. My italics.
70. Pannenberg, *ST3*, 320. My italics.
71. Pannenberg, "The Kenosis of the Son," 249.
72. Pannenberg, "The Kenosis of the Son," 249.
73. Pannenberg, *ST1*, 426–27. My italics. In various explications of Pannenberg's theology he equates kenosis with self-denial, self-abnegation, self-emptying but he also links the concept of self-abnegation with self-giving. In *Christian Spirituality and Sacramental Community* Pannenberg argues that Christ prefigures the "path of self-abnegation which the Christian must follow." This path of imitation is "characterised by conformity with Christ on the part of the believer, as it is characterised

on the part of Jesus Christ by the service of *self-giving love*." Wolfhart Pannenberg, *Christian Spirituality and Sacramental Community* (Darton, Longman & Todd: London, 1984), 104. Thus, he equates self-emptying (kenosis) with self-giving. Again, in *ST2* Pannenberg explains the concept of *"self-emptying* and *self-humbling* of the Son" as "primarily an expression of the *self-giving*" (p. 379, my italics). Thus, Pannenberg uses the concepts of self-emptying and self-giving interchangeably. The concept of self-giving can be viewed as part of the constitution of kenosis in the manner of "family resemblances" advocated by Wittgenstein. See Ludwig Wittgenstein, *Philosophical Investigations*, trans. G. E. M. Anscombe. 2nd ed. (Oxford: Blackwell, 1998), 65ff. Recalling Wittgenstein's "family resemblances," Coakley describes the common scholarly usages of kenosis as sliding from "meanings from 'risk' to 'self-limitation' to 'sacrifice' to 'self-giving' to 'self-emptying.'" See Sarah Coakley, "Kenosis: Theological Meanings and Gender Connotations," in *The Work of Love: Creation as Kenosis*, ed. John Polkinghorne (Grand Rapids, MI: Eerdmans, 2001), 203. If the triune life of God is a mutuality of self-giving then it must be considered mutually kenotic.

74. Pannenberg, *ST1*, 447.

75. Tonstad judges that the lack of mutual divine kenosis in Pannenberg's theology undermines an authentic construction of reciprocal mutuality between the divine Persons that is free from hierarchical *taxis*. Tonstad, "Difference and Hierarchy," 395, 398.

76. Nicene Creed, anglicansonline.org/basics/nicene.html.

77. Pannenberg, *ST1*, 428. This fullness of God's being is the fullness of each of the Persons of the Godhead and their mutual reciprocal relations. Peters articulates of Pannenberg's understanding, saying: "the Son is fully himself in relation to the Father; the Father is fully himself in relation to the Son; and the Spirit is fully himself in witness to both." Peters, *God as Trinity*, 139.

78. Pannenberg, *ST1*, 380.

79. Pannenberg, *ST1*, 386.

80. Pannenberg, *ST1*, 388

81. Pannenberg, *ST1*, 390.

82. Venema, "History, Human Freedom," 68. According to Venema, Pannenberg reconceives God's freedom as "openness to the future" because he is "the coming God," not as a "being that already exists," but rather that he is the God of the future (pp. 67–68). Grenz and Olson argue that for Pannenberg, God's rule, identical with his deity, "is not yet revealed, [thus] his being is still in the process of coming to be." However, this view is not process theology but rather an "expression of the idealist notion that the Absolute is self-realized in and through its negation of its would-be limit, the finite non-absolute." Stanley J. Grenz and Roger E. Olson, eds., *Twentieth Century Theology: God and the World in a Transitional Age* (Downers Grove, IL: Intervarsity Press, 1992), 216.

83. Pannenberg, *ST1*, 331.

84. Wolfhart Pannenberg, "Problems of a Trinitarian God," *Dialog* 26, no. 4, (1987): 251. Translated by P. Clayton from '*Probleme einer trinitarischen Gotteslehre*,' in W. Baier, et al., *Weisheit Gottes—Weisheit der Welt*, vol. 1 (St Ottilien, 1987).

85. See O'Donnell, "Pannenberg's Doctrine of God," 95–96. Venema argues that Pannenberg's position is Hegelian in nature, saying: "If God's deity and his reign are so closely identified and this reign is said to be realized at the end of history, it would mean that historical process is necessary to the reality of God, to his 'coming into being.'" C. P. Venema, "History, Human Freedom," 75.

86. Westphal goes as far as to conclude that "Pannenberg may well be the most articulate anti-Hegelian since Kierkegaard." Merold Westphal, "Hegel, Pannenberg, and Hermeneutics," *Man and World* 4, no. 3 (1971): 276. This view is confirmed by Clayton who argues that "Pannenberg has rejected enough of Hegel and incorporated enough of others that the label 'Hegelian' will not stick." Philip Clayton, "Anticipation and Theological Method," in *The Theology of Wolfhart Pannenberg: Twelve American Critiques, with an Autobiographical Essay and Response*, eds. Carl E. Braaten and Philip Clayton (Minneapolis: Augsburg Publishing House, 1988), 133. Mostert also claims "Pannenberg rejects any help that might come from process theology, with its idea that God *becomes* God in the history of the divine action." Mostert, *God and the Future*, 193. However, regarding O' Donnell's criticism that Pannenberg's conceptualization of the immanent and economic Trinity is "dangerously close to process theology with its finite God" (O'Donnell "Pannenberg's Doctrine of God," 95), Mostert argues that the criticism must be that "he falls into this despite his best intentions." Mostert, *God and the Future*, 228.

87. Pannenberg, *ST1*, 331.

88. Pannenberg, *ST1*, 389, 390. Grenz argues that Pannenberg's God is not dependent on the world process for God's being because the Hegelian model is applied "to the mutual relationships of the three trinitarian Persons, not to their relationship to the world." Grenz, *Reason for Hope*, 82.

89. Mostert maintains that "Pannenberg accepts the idea of the simplicity of God; the divine unity is 'absolutely simple, without composition.'" Mostert, *God and the Future*, 210.

90. Mostert, *God and the Future*, 223.

91. Mostert, *God and the Future*, 229. Mostert explains—"where the eschaton becomes the 'place' or time at which what is the case in time coincides with what is the case in eternity." Mostert, *God and the Future*, 220–21.

92. Pannenberg states of human goal setting: "we pursue the goal so as to meet a lack in the totality and autarchy of the subject . . . Because the I is still on the way to becoming itself, in the strict sense there can be no talk of self-actualization on our part. This would demand that from the beginning of its action the acting I would be identical in the full sense with the determination which is to be the result of the action. This condition is met only in the case of the divine action." Pannenberg, *ST1*, 390.

93. Pannenberg, *ST1*, 359.

94. Mostert, *God and the Future*, 234.

95. Mostert, *God and the Future*, 2–3.

96. Pannenberg, *ST3*, 543. Pannenberg does identify that the nature of the eschatological kingdom is the ontological basis and future for created life. Pannenberg, *ST3*, 531.

Chapter 6

Divine Self-Enrichment in Hans Urs von Balthasar

The theology of Han Urs von Balthasar has been received as both inspired and controversial. Never to hold an academic position, Balthasar saw his vocation as one reconnecting theology to spirituality, where theology commences from the posture of worship. His major work, in a fifteen-volume trilogy, envisions leading "the reader to an awareness of the enrapturing power of Being" through an examination of the beautiful (*The Glory of the Lord*), the good (*Theo-Drama*) and the true (*Theo-logic*).[1] Throughout this trilogy, Balthasar outlines his anthropology, Christology, soteriology, ecclesiology, eschatology and, for my specific interest, his Trinitarian convictions (foundational for his theological enterprise). En-route to his various conclusions, Balthasar advances theological insights that affirm and sustain the broader concept and logic of Divine Self-Enrichment—*God enriching God in the perfection and fullness of God.*

Here, I will explore three facets of Balthasar's Trinitarianism that weave "golden threads" consistent with Divine Self-Enrichment. The first draws attention to the affinity of logic between Balthasar's central concept of triune "Difference" and the hypostatic activity inherent to the concept of "*God enriching God*." The second demonstrates that Balthasar's understanding of the kenotic nature of divine life sources the economic manifestations of divine relationality. In this regard, his theological intuition affirms a kenotic nucleus integral to the very concept of "God *enriching* God." The third facet considers Balthasar's construal of the fecundity of intratrinitarian life as necessarily congruent with divine simplicity and aseity (and the derivatives of immutability and impassibility) rather than the loci of a process-driven Hegelianism. Balthasar's commitment to the abundant movement of divine life and to the tradition's classical guardrails affirm a central contention of my overall project's contention: that triune enrichment is located and actualized in *the fullness and perfection of God.*

INTERPRETING THE ETERNAL FROM THE ECONOMIC TRINITY

Alongside Bulgakov and Pannenberg, Balthasar advocates a dynamic and relational view of the Trinity, emphasizing God's infinite abundance, a "super-becoming"[2] in the Trinitarian life, where the reality of God "as Love" is revealed through "the unfolding of the personal relations."[3] While some scholars attempt to reduce Balthasar's Trinitarian elucidations to mere speculation of the transcendent, the interpretative soil for Balthasar's insights are never disconnected from the economic events pertaining to the second person of the Trinity, Jesus the Christ.[4] The intratrinitarian activity that Balthasar deciphers as "eternal movement," in fact, gains its potency from the scriptural revelation of the life of Christ.[5] Thus, Balthasar argues that "it is only on the basis of Jesus Christ's own behaviour and attitude that we can distinguish such a plurality in God. Only in him is the Trinity opened up and made accessible."[6] Significantly, Balthasar uses the Incarnation as a hermeneutic to interpret the characteristics of triune relationality, placing particular emphasis on Jesus' immersive experiences of the Cross and Holy Saturday. Like Barth, Balthasar draws ontological inferences for divine being from the noetic phenomenology of the economic Trinity. For Balthasar, "Jesus' life, death and resurrection become the interpretive key to understanding both who he is . . . and what the condition for the possibility of his appearing is (doctrine of the Trinity)."[7]

On this Christological foundation, Balthasar espouses that "God is Life,"[8] a life constituted by the "eternal activity of self-giving among the Divine Persons," where divine being is "best understood in terms of event and act rather than essence."[9] For Balthasar, divine essence is commensurate with "the eternally constituted event of the free, mutual self-giving of the Divine Persons."[10] This eternal triune dynamism presupposes divine action in creation and is the ontological archetype for human imitation: "In a sense we could say that the universe is, in von Balthasar's view, God's way of dramatizing *God's love for God*. The wonderfully various and freely existing life of creatures is a particular mode of Trinitarian delighting and self-giving."[11] Like the a priori condition for creation, Balthasar considers the dynamism of triune being as the conditioning factor for the nature of the salvific work of God in Christ. In the final analysis, this interpretive position is central for understanding Balthasar's identification of an intra-triune kenosis, wherein God's Incarnational action proffers no change in the eternal divine nature, but rather reveals that God is defined by triune "reciprocal self-surrender."[12] Balthasar's view, once again, emphasizes the legitimacy of resisting a proposition that the self-giving kenotic nature of God is a divine attribute exclusive to the Son. On the contrary, arising within the unity of the divine nature, kenosis emerges as a communicable perfection.

TRINITARIAN KENOSIS: DIVINE DIFFERENCE AND HOLY SATURDAY

In conjunction with orthodox Trinitarianism, Balthasar affirms a unity of hypostatic differentiation commensurate with the essence of divine being. Significantly, he argues that the Incarnation provides evidence for the nature of this essence. As the paramount revelation of divinity to humanity, Christ's assumption of human nature is, for Balthasar, "the heavenly reality itself, translated into earthly language,"[13] where the Christological events in the economy demonstrate God's eternal inner life of intratrinitarian kenosis. This conviction directly results from his presupposition that "whatever takes place in the economy must express a reality that exists eternally within the immanent life of the Trinity."[14] For Balthasar, kenotic relationality, not abstract divine essence, is at the core of God's being.[15] His constructive Trinitarian theology, therefore, extends beyond the mere identification of perichoresis and instead characterizes the primal nature of perichoresis as kenotic. For Balthasar, the radical love of God's being is actualized through a free and mutual kenosis. In the unity of divine life there is a common hypostatic *ekstasis*—an outward, other-centered movement between the triune hypostases. Rowan Williams succinctly encapsulates Balthasar's view here:

> Balthasar appears to argue . . . that we can speak of activity and passivity in God: there is a doing and a being-done-to—though not in any simple way. The Father *gives* to the Son and Son receives and then *gives in return*; thus it is not only that the Father is "active" and the Son "passive"; the Father gives, but also allows himself to be defined by what is given, "becoming" Father through the "consent" of the Son and the Spirit to be given life from his abundance.[16]

In Balthasar's reasoning, divine kenosis, while demonstrated in the economy, does not originate "in the cross or the Incarnation, but in the Father's generation of the Son."[17] The paternal inauguration of an eternal Trinitarian kenosis grounds the subsequent kenotic patterning seen in the Incarnation and Cross.[18] The Father's generative "first kenosis" therefore becomes the "organising principle of the remainder of his theological work."[19] From this principle, Balthasar views Trinitarian life as "both active and receptive; both the bestowing of life and the grateful receiving of life, a letting-be and a being-let-be. It is thus a twofold negation of individual self-assertion, a refusal to be for oneself alone and a refusal to look for the ground of one's being in an individuality divorced from relation."[20] He concludes that the "total 'kenosis' of each [divine person] and thankful ('eucharistic') return to each of himself by the others becomes the ground of Trinitarian unity, being and love."[21]

Here, the overtones with Bulgakov's kenotic Trinitarianism are evident. Yet, while Balthasar, like Bulgakov, commences with the traditional taxonomy of the relations of origin (Father, Son and Holy Spirit), Balthasar differs from Bulgakov by giving prominence to the concept of an infinite distance or difference (*Abstand*) within the Godhead as foundational for the intimate relationality between the hypostases. This difference in God is not akin to self-alienation but "an act of love and freedom that causes real otherness to subsist . . . as a self-emptying, a kenosis."[22] The following passage captures this dynamic view of the mutuality of divine kenosis that accords with *Abstand*:

> The Father strips himself, without remainder, of his Godhead and hands it over to the Son; he "imparts" to the Son all that is his. "All that is thine is mine" (Jn 17:10). The Father must not be thought to exist "prior" to this self-surrender (in an Arian sense): he *is* this movement of self-giving that holds nothing back. This divine act that brings forth the Son, that is, the second way of participating in (and of *being*) the identical Godhead, involves the positing of an absolute, infinite difference [or distance; *Abstand* can mean either] that can contain and embrace all other distances that are possible within the world of finitude, including the distance of sin. Inherent in the Father's love is an absolute renunciation: he will not be God for himself alone . . . The Son's answer to the gift of Godhead (of equal substance with the Father) can only be eternal thanksgiving (*eucharistia*) to the Father, the Source—a thanksgiving as selfless and unreserved as the Father's original self-surrender. Proceeding from both, as their subsistent "We," there breathes the "Spirit" who is common to both: as the essence of love, he maintains the infinite difference between them, seals it and, since he is the one Spirit of them both, bridges it.[23]

Divine difference is integral to his view of divine togetherness, where "the most intimate interpenetration"[24] becomes possible through *mutual* kenosis. The evidential key to this divine eternal reality is, for Balthasar, the economic revelation of the Cross and Christ's descent into Sheol. Balthasar concludes that "otherness" must be part of God's life for God to faithfully and fully be God through crucifixion, death and sheol—"the absolute contradiction of the glory of God."[25] Importantly, and congruent with divine immutability, he emphasizes that the separation of the Father and Son on the Cross and the descent of Christ into sheol introduces no "new" characteristic into God's being "because infinite distance and something like alienation were always already there."[26] Careful of a Hegelian logic that places a divine contingency on creation, Balthasar underscores that God cannot be God without "limitless self-giving" and observes that this reality is "not the result of anything external" to God.[27] He emphasizes that "[w]ithout grasping this there is no escape from the machinery of Hegelian dialectic."[28] For Balthasar, otherness and kenosis are inherent to divine ontology and do not arise through a world process.

From a compressed scriptural interpretation of both the Cross and Holy Saturday as representative of an *abandonment* of the Son by the Father, Balthasar locates his ontologically situated "distance" (*Abstand*) within the divine identity. For Balthasar, the "crucified Son does not simply suffer the hell deserved by sinners; he suffers something below and beyond this, namely, being forsaken by God."[29] In *Theo-Drama* III, Balthasar moves toward the ontological logic undergirding temporal abandonment, saying: "The Son's 'God-forsakenness' on the Cross cannot be interpreted one-sidedly as something felt solely by the dying Jesus; if God is objectively forsaken here, then we must say that *God is forsaken by God*."[30] Ultimately, Balthasar's interpretation of the crucifixion and descent as an abandonment of the Son by the Father propels the ontological substratum of *Abstand* (divine distance) as an eternal feature of triune life. Paternal "abandonment" conditions what he thinks he needs to locate in his doctrine of the Trinity to account for its temporal actuality.[31] In the end, Balthasar construes the hypostatic *separation* of Father and Son as a direct manifestation of divine kenosis. It is at this point, I part ways with Balthasar; questioning whether the kenotic life of divinity is necessarily equated with separation and distance or whether intratrinitarian kenosis is better viewed as the life-giving telos of bountiful unity and intimacy.

Although Balthasar does enlist the Holy Spirit as the continual bond between the Father and Son, even in Christ's descent to Sheol (as the Father withdraws from the Son and the Son descends to hell), his emphasis on hypostatic abandonment arguably strains the unity of the One God.[32] Cecilia Deane-Drummond alludes to this problem: "Balthasar's speculation leads him to think of a drastic separation between Father and Son, epitomised in the death and descent of Christ into hell, but also a separation that seems to be constitutive for the life of the Trinity."[33] There is a certain weight given by Balthasar to a kenosis that gives rise to a divine *separation* rather than a kenosis that primarily articulates divine unity. The kenotic emphasis, thus, appears construed (and read by critics) in a somewhat truncated manner, linked to divine self-loss and self-suffering rather than (on a construal of Divine Self-Enrichment) the mode of divine *life*—an enriching-kenosis that is the patterning of life-giving unity of triune all-blessedness.[34] Somewhat regrettably, Balthasar positions the Son's *abandonment* by the Father as having its precondition in divine kenotic love. Such a reading is, I believe, problematic, not least for its speculative properties, as noted by Bruce McCormack,[35] but also on account of the theological incompatibility of imputing suffering into divine ontology. Karen Kilby emphasizes this point, arguing:

> Balthasar is fundamentally blurring the distinction between love and loss, joy and suffering. If love and renunciation, suffering (or something like it) and joy, are linked, not just in the Christian life, but eternally in God, then ultimately suffering and loss are given a positive valuation; they are eternalised and take on an ultimate ontological status. And then, it seems to me, it becomes hard to understand how Christianity can possibly be "good news."[36]

Alyssa Pitstick likewise reasons that,

> the truth of Christ's descent stands over against any "tragic Christianity," any seeking of redemption in God-abandonment as such . . . Christ has come that we might *have life*, not death, and that we might have it in its fullness (see Jn 10:10). It would be the worst betrayal of this age (not to mention of Christ) to offer it elaborate theological platitudes suggesting its wounds *are* its life, thereby remaking God in its image.[37]

Feminist theologians also resist such a kenotically-wounded interpretation of divinity, expressing concern that it potentially fosters the "glorification of gratuitous suffering" and serves as the foundation for "a justificatory principle for the relegation of women to positions of obedience, self-sacrifice, and silent victimhood, which, when understood as a behavioural model, is perceived to sanction self-evacuation particularly among those whose sense of self may already be compromised."[38]

While Kilby and Pitstick suggest that Balthasar bequeaths "ontological status" to suffering and loss, there is room to argue that Balthasar merely employs analogical language indicative of a divine excess of love that allows for the *possibility* of the Cross and Holy Saturday.[39] Regarding the question of "whether there is suffering in God," Balthasar proposes that "there is something in God that can develop into suffering. This suffering occurs when the recklessness with which the Father gives away himself (and *all* that is his) encounters a freedom that, instead of responding in kind to the magnanimity, changes it into a calculating, cautious self-preservation."[40] Such an understanding resonates with Volf's explication of the epistemic translation of divine love in a sinful world:

> The Trinitarian cycle of perfect self-donations cannot be simply repeated in the world of sin; the engagement with that world entails a process of complex and difficult *translation* . . . In the labor of "taking away the sin," the delight of love is transmuted into the agony of love—the agony of opposition to non-love, the

agony of suffering as the hand of non-love, and the agony of sympathy with non-love's victims. Hence the Cross of Christ.[41]

With these allowances in mind, Balthasar's kenotic view of God perhaps never intends to impute ontological suffering into divine being but to merely ascribe *Abstand*—the ontological explication that gives rise to a separation of the Father and Son. Moreover, Balthasar's writings, far from being preoccupied with scholastic precision, orient toward a theological expression that exceeds a neat and controlled symmetrical balancing of the mystical and the logical. Indeed, Timothy Yoder contends that Karen Kilby's critique of Balthasar "completely misses the mark," as she misinterprets Balthasar's "hymnic . . . almost lyrical description of the depths of God's self-sacrificing and reckless love," reducing it to mere speculation lacking scholastic precision.[42] While McIntosh and Neil Ormerod opine that Pitstick's interpretation of Balthasar suffers from "a sort of genre mistake"[43] that forces "Balthasar's theological aesthetics through a scholastic sieve,"[44] that fails to engage the work as an evocative spiritual invitation to live into the drama of God's being. Certainly, it is not out of the ambit to view Balthasar's construal of Christ's death and suffering as an expression of the almost inconceivable self-giving nature of divine love, exemplified in John 15:13—"Greater love has no one than this, that someone lay down his life for his friends."[45]

However, while I agree with Balthasar that triune kenosis undergirds the nature of divine love demonstrated in the Passion, it is quite a different proposition to infer infinite distance and difference (*Abstand*) into the Trinity as the kenotic condition for the Father's alleged abandonment of the Son. The very proposition that the Father abandons the Son is a perverse rendering of the nature of divinity. Of this inference, Deane-Drummond locates an anthropomorphic center saying, "to take this to the extreme of trinitarian separation and alienation in the way Balthasar attempts seems to me mistaken, for it implies a brokenness in the heart of God *that is a mirror of human despair*."[46] Like in the case of Jürgen Moltmann, Balthasar arguably places a disproportionate emphasis on the "Cry of Dereliction," resulting in a disputable portrayal of divine being. The importance assigned by Balthasar to divine abandonment seems to represent a one-sided emphasis that overlooks the consistent nature of God's being that must condition both the Cross *and* the Resurrection. *Abstand* might ontically account for the actuality of God's action on the Cross but how might it account for Resurrection? Separating divine kenosis (the Cross) and divine life (the Resurrection) as discrete divine events, may indeed undermine an understanding of the unified expression of divine being. The economic expressions of the simple triune God allow us to understand that both the Cross *and* Resurrection reflect a unified divine ontology that is both kenotic and enriching. Indeed,

Jesus's passion is a union of equally contingent parts—Jesus went through (not around) the Friday of the Cross, through the silence of Saturday, and through to Sunday's joy of resurrection. Whiet these events were distinct they should not be theologically dislocated. From the view of Christ prior to his crucifixion, Friday (enduring the cross) and Saturday (silence) were the *sine qua non* of Sunday's potentiality (resurrection joy).[47]

In other words, there is something in the ontology of the divine nature that gives rise to, and conditions, both the Cross and Resurrection. That "something" is not mere *Abstand* but kenotic-enrichment.

Kilby and Deane-Drummond both highlight the exegetical uncertainty surrounding the oft utilized "Cry of Dereliction" as the basis for a theological construction of the Son's literal abandonment by the Father; an abandonment that tends toward a rent-Trinity.[48] Instead of affirming a cry of abandonment as literal and ontological, the first line of Psalm 22 on the lips of Jesus express a shorthand reference to the whole Psalm. In light of the latter verses of the Psalm, the "Cry of Dereliction" is not indicative of a kenosis that culminates in abandonment, but a cry that links the kenosis of Christ with life-giving vindication, salvation, trust and the nearness of the Father.[49] Asle Eikrem, drawing on insights from Ingolf Dalferth[50] and Eberhard Jüngel[51] regarding God's absence as "hidden presence," presents a similar view when he says,

> Jesus's desperate cry was not that of someone who had lost faith in the existence of God, but of someone who reached out to God even in the experience of God's hiddenness. Only a person who believed God to be present to him would address God in this way in that situation . . . it is misleading to speak of Jesus as experiencing the hell of relationlessness in his death on the cross, as many theologians have been prone to do. Jesus' cry of dereliction was his defence *against* relationlessness.[52]

While Balthasar does envision actualization of deity in other-centered self-giving,[53] the enrichment and intimacy of triune life is not his core orchestrating contemplation. Rather, Balthasar emphasizes a nexus between divine abandonment and distance with Trinitarian kenosis. Scriptural revelation, however, persistently links concepts of divine self-giving with the attainment of life and well-being, not desertion.[54] Balthasar himself correlates the richness of divine *life* with the intratrinitarian relations, but there is no escaping his emphasis on divine "abandonment." As discussed, such an emphasis raises concerns for some scholars about the integrity of divine unity and the potential for tritheistic hypostatic separation.[55]

Divine Self-Enrichment attempts, however, to avert this issue by construing that the unity of relations expressed in hypostatic kenosis (understood as divine self-giving and receiving *not* divine separation) is constitutive for divine life. On this basis, the Cross and Holy Saturday are not interpreted as triune abandonment but as the expansive reach of divine life; where God's triune life swallows up death (Is 25:8; 2 Cor 5:4; 2 Tim 1:10). Likewise, under the broader hermeneutic of Divine Self-Enrichment and in contrast to reductive interpretations commonly present in traditional Christological views of kenosis, the self-emptying of the Son on the Cross does not resonate a "truncated-kenosis"; that is, kenosis primarily characterized by suffering and abandonment. Instead, the Son's cruciform kenosis is rather met symbiotically with exaltation through resurrection. Unfortunately, scholarship that focuses on elucidating the meaning of the Cross and Resurrection and its relevance for triune ontology, tends toward divergent emphases, either focusing on Good Friday, Holy Saturday or Resurrection Sunday. Moltmann takes his cue for God's being from the Cross of suffering on Friday.[56] Balthasar emphasizes the "distance" in God's being uttered through Holy Saturday.[57] Robert Jenson has the liveliness of Resurrection as his theological guide.[58] Each of these thoughtful theologians highlight a particular aspect of the three divine moments as foundational for their theology, with each emphases eliciting attractors and detractors. Yet, an overarching theological framework that enables these pivotal acts of God to be considered in a unified harmony is not usually enunciated.

Contrary to some interpretations of the Passion events of Friday, Saturday and Sunday, Divine Self-Enrichment offers a perspective capable of providing a metaphysical account of divine being that symbiotically links both the kenosis and life of these events. Specifically, the ontological patterning of triune kenotic-enrichment offers a harmonizing framework. The Trinitarian perfection of enriching-kenosis unites Friday's self-giving and Saturday's distance and silence with Sunday's glory. The concept allows for the dynamism of God's simple and abundant nature to be ubiquitously sovereign in the movements of the temporal drama (Cross, Sheol, Resurrection); a movement that actualizes the wholeness of redemption commensurate with the wholeness of the God who redeems. The salvific acts of God in Christ should be viewed as a unity of particularity that reveals the glory and perfection of God. Here, is no mere nominalism but *deus revelatus*. Considering Barth's assertion that the "movement of life in which God is God" corresponds "exactly to His revelation of Himself as God," we can interpret the multiplicity of the converging parts of the Passion as the revelation of the simple God who lives kenotic-enrichment. Barth speaks to this idea, saying,

> multiplicity, individuality and diversity of the perfections of God are those of his simple being, which is not therefore divided and then put together again . . . Rather, the very unity of His being consists in the multiplicity, individuality and diversity . . . Every distinction in God can be affirmed only in such a way as

implies at the same time His unity and therefore the lack of essential discrepancy in what is distinguished.[59]

The concept of kenotic-enrichment identifies the simple vibrancy of a triune ontology capable of illuminating the diverse acts of God contiguous with the very being of God. The nature of God demonstrated through the kenosis of the Cross, and the resultant glory and enrichment of Resurrection, are interwoven, together expressing the ontological patterning of triune being. This cohesive unity of kenosis and enrichment, encompassing both the Cross and Resurrection, serves likewise as the ontic ground for the strange interweaving of loss with life expressed in Christ's edict for human discipleship—"whoever *loses his life* for my sake will *find his life*" (Mt 10:39). There is no other mode to an enriched life but to participate in the divinely-ordained pattern.

INTIMATIONS OF DIVINE SELF-ENRICHMENT

Despite the contestable issues that persist in Balthasar's theology, contained within his corpus are threads that affirm theological foundations consistent with Divine Self-Enrichment. Alongside Bulgakov and Pannenberg, Balthasar resists the Hegelian pull and affirms that divine acting in the world expresses the *fullness* of divine being. In concert with his theological defense of divine aseity and simplicity, Balthasar identifies hypostatic distinction in the Godhead as central to a vivacity of divine being; affirming a central plank of this present work—the subsistence of dynamic "enrichment" between the persons of the Godhead. Although Balthasar's identification of divine *Abstand* may impute too much regarding divine separation, it does confirm distinction between the persons of the Godhead—distinction that grounds the logic of advocating enriching activity *between* the divine persons.[60] Moreover, Balthasar's elucidation of the distinctions of hypostatic agency is undertaken in a manner that avoids "absorption of autonomy" by the other hypostases.[61] Thus, while for Balthasar, God's self-giving has no logical boundary, apophatically he maintains that "the self-gift of the Father to the Son does *not* include his paternity."[62] As such, he maintains that divine kenosis occurs within real relations, where the divine "other" and divine "self" are recognized and affirmed. Balthasar's theology correlates with the axiom of Divine Self-Enrichment—*God enriching God in the perfection and fullness of God*—and affirms that active mutuality is contemporaneous with the simplicity of Trinity.

CHARACTERISTICS AND PURPOSE OF TRIUNE KENOSIS

Having now noted the presence of the theological *desiderata* of Divine Self-Enrichment in Balthasar's theology, this final section explores specific dynamics Balthasar regards as innate to triune kenosis. His views here encompass coherent theological structures that not only give weight to kenosis being considered an essential predicate of the replete unity of divine well-being, but also offer clues as to how to understand the purpose and characteristics of such a mode of being. Significantly, Balthasar affirms particular features of tri-hypostatic kenosis that enact the telos of divine Glory.

Intratrinitarian Speech and Worship

A deeply fascinating insight of Balthasar's contemplations is that of regarding intratrinitarian speech and worship. Extrapolating from the economic acts of God, Balthasar articulates a positive theology that validates the dynamically enriching nature of divine being. Not only so, but Balthasar's theology assists in tracing cataphatic characteristics that attend the perichoretic "divine dance." Following Balthasar's cues we can commence a mapping of the choreography of the divine "dance-steps." These "steps" are an interpretative process to distinguish elements of the *how* of divine life. Here, we begin to parse with Balthasar a further articulation of the nature of the perichoretic "dance-steps" not merely discern the triune "dance."

Balthasar interprets the appearance and donation of divine being to both the "other" of the triune persons and the creation as a form of speech. Regarding the appearance of Being (God) Balthasar states, "in giving itself up, it *speaks* itself, it unveils itself: it is true in itself, but in the other to which it reveals itself."[63] Balthasar argues that God's revelation in the creation is speech that is sourced and conditioned by the primal archetype of intratrinitarian speech. Thus, God speaks (or reveals Godself) in creation, not from contingency, but because the triune God eternally speaks. Balthasar derives his understanding of intratrinitarian divine speech from the Word of God, the personal form of Christ, where God has made his love "recognisable" to the world by speaking in human language.[64] The incarnate Word is the "exegesis" of God[65] "spoken" in recognizable and purposeful language.[66] Jenson identifies a similar concept where the divine act of creation utters from the ontological archetype:

> Already *the Word that is a triune person is God's Utterance in his triune life* . . . Now we must further insist: therefore the Word by which God creates is not silent within him but . . . God commands the world to be, this command is

obeyed, and the event of obedience is the existence of the world . . . God creates the world by utterance of a moral intention for other beings than himself.[67]

What is striking in this logic is its immediate resonance with kenotic-enrichment; where divine utterance displays the hallmarks of a self-giving that generates life. Certainly, for Balthasar, the word spoken in Christ is evidence of the kenotic nature of God's life—in Christ we see "nothing other than the earthly representation of the Trinitarian poverty, in which everything is always given away."[68] And yet, Balthasar's kenosis arguably goes well beyond a narrow "Christological category of self-sacrifice," becoming the very basis for "human divinization and full participation with God."[69] Christ, the Word made flesh (Jn 1:14), is kenotically spoken and kenotically speaking in the world because such a way of being is proper to the eternal triune life. The mode of God's speech to humanity (supremely through the Incarnation) also reveals the mode of divine being. In Christ, God engages personally and conversationally with humanity, knowing and being known (Jn 10:14). Divine communication through the Incarnation is the intimacy of personal command that is oriented to life-giving; an economic repetition of the interpersonal active communication and life of the eternal Trinity.

Alongside speech, the intra-divine life is likewise characterized by Balthasar as a vivid dynamic of triune worship: "When God stands before God we can say 'that God shows honour to God' 'in a reciprocal glorifying,' 'in an eternal, reciprocal worship.'"[70] The intratrinitarian worship that Balthasar advances is marked by transparency and trust, not "blind faith" but "faith as it exists in God, it is in harmony with 'irrefragable knowledge' . . . 'From, before all time, the barriers are down.'"[71] This eternal triune "faith" is a constant readiness to "see and encounter each other completely," where there is mutual contemplation of the greatness of the other hypostases, and where, in the "'time' and 'space'" of love, the triune persons reflect, present desire and prepare gifts to one another."[72] Balthasar views this mutuality as the transparent consideration of the "excess" (greatness) of the triune other; the movement of mutual adoration.[73] Here, the divine persons "know" and are "known" in personal reciprocity, where "there is simultaneous growth in intimacy and in respect for the other person's freedom."[74]

Contemporaneous with his insights regarding "the divine Trinitarian super-expressivity" of speech and worship, Balthasar argues for a developing correspondence in the creature, saying that all forms of "human relationality . . . can become apt expressions of the divine relationality."[75] In this manner, Balthasar links "cosmic life and human personhood"; creatures are embraced, not into "a completed, static divine silence" but as a "'part of speech' within the 'speaking' that is God's own life."[76] Thus, in *Theo-Drama* Balthasar views intratrinitarian speech as eternal "conversation" or "God's prayer-dialogue," and therefore the prototype for creaturely prayer.[77] Balthasar draws analogous conclusions for humanity from intratrinitarian trust and transparency (the hallmarks of human faith in God) and from intratrinitarian adoration (repeated by human adoration of God). Thus, of human worship he asserts: "Worship as we know it is a grace that comes from the triune worship. Nothing is more rooted in God than worship."[78] In other words, redeemed human speech, faith and worship are ontologically conditioned by triune reality and, as such, are enlivened to become *imago Trinitatis*.[79]

Balthasar's insights are primed toward the consequent logic that creatures are ultimately, through the salvific work of God, called to kenotic communion and worship as an integration into, and reflection of, the nature of divine life. This is not a worship that completes God but where humanity is enveloped into the replete life of God and participates in the perfecting of perfection—the speaking of glory and the worship of adoration. From this envelopment, human activity oriented toward the well-being of others, likewise, repeats the image of the Creator through acts of enriching-kenosis. The patterns of a divine ontology of well-being echo in temporal and finite expressions—in mutual and interpersonal dialogue and engagement, relationality of being known and knowing, acknowledging and honoring the value of others, and "speaking" in recognizable and purposeful language. Illuminated by the revelation of divine being, the oft-opaque discussions regarding what constitutes the telos and formation of human well-being receive metaphysical and theological re-centering.

Kilby and Criticism of Balthasar

Two final considerations close out the assessment of Balthasar's insights relevant to the theological framing of Divine Self-Enrichment. The first evaluates the legitimacy of Kilby's stance that Balthasar's contentions regarding the "inner workings of the Trinity" amount to little more than dubious speculation.[80] The second aspect delves into Balthasar's account of the telos behind particular instances of intra-divine dialogue and worship.

To the first issue. Kilby negates, as unsubstantiated speculation, Balthasar's advocacy that the "eternal life of the Trinity is . . . characterised by thanksgiving . . . by worship, and even by petitionary prayer . . . references to mutual acknowledgement, adoration, and petition among the Persons of the Trinity."[81] Certainly, Balthasar's work does contain flourishes of excessive language that arguably extend beyond what might simply be a strict literal reading of Scripture.[82] However, if the logic by which Balthasar relates the immanent and economic Trinity is granted, then it is possible to read the scriptural accounts as containing specific instances and inferences of dialogue and worship between the Father, Son and Holy Spirit. For example, we can identify both verbal and non-verbal adoration by the Father and Holy Spirit at the baptism of Jesus (Mt 3:16–17), the Transfiguration's similar adoration of Jesus by the Father (Mt 17:5), the prayer dialogue of Jesus to the Father in John's gospel (chapters 15–17), Jesus' petitioning of the Father in Gethsemane (Mt 26:39, 42), Jesus' request to the Father on the Cross (Lk 23:34), the final worded-breath offered by Jesus to the Father (Lk 23:46), the singing of praise and thanksgiving by Jesus to the Father (Mk 14:26; Heb 2:12; Mt 26:30), the Spirit leading and Jesus following (Lk 4:1), and the Father fulfilling Jesus' request to pour out the Spirit (Jn 14:16, Acts 1:4). These are not random occurrences, but, on Balthasar's reasoning, revelatory. Given these examples, it is difficult to dismiss Balthasar's insights of intratrinitarian life as merely "speculative." Interpretation of the characteristics of divine relationality from Scripture does not amount to mere conjecture but rather represents a legitimate and often overlooked hermeneutic.[83]

Glory: The Telos of Divine Kenosis

To the second consideration. Balthasar suggests that the scriptural movements of intratrinitarian "speech" and "worship" indicate something of the inner workings of God. The crude question is—so what? What does this divine dynamic achieve and why might such a concept be important? Answering this question is, in part, the intention of this book, which contends that the telos, the goal or purpose of divine kenotic relationality is divine *glory*—the utter well-being, enrichment and expression of divine life. Moreover, the desire for the creation to partake in this well-being, is remarkably, also a divine imperative. What is interesting and pertinent about Balthasar's theology at this point is how he identifies specific interactions within the Trinity that contribute toward filling the notion of kenosis with concrete content. For Balthasar, these economic interactions reveal the constitutive elements that actualize the telos of God's *life*. We can also surmise that these divine dynamics also reveal the telos of the embedded ontological patterns foundational to *all* created *life*.

Balthasar's view of the immanent and economic Trinity advances that the fullness of divine life is demonstrated in the mutual kenotic exchanges of the Godhead in the economy.[84] This dynamic life of divinity is pre-eminently revealed in Christ, who is, for Balthasar, the concrete form of the glory of God.[85] In his volume, *The Glory of the Lord*, Balthasar expounds the scriptural development of the notion of God's glory from the "*kabod* of Yahweh"—an "abstract-sensuous *kabod*," for example, the Shekinah glory of the cloud in Exodus 14:19—to the "concrete-personal *kabod* " of "*doxa Christou*" in the New Testament.[86] In this, Balthasar explores how the movement toward perceiving God as "concretely glorious" developed alongside "the fundamental concepts of the covenant reality: as grace, justice, fidelity, mercy . . . love" and not merely through abstract concepts of honor, praise or power or divine epiphanies.[87] The concreteness of divine glory (*Herrlichkeit*) is ultimately revealed through the materiality of the flesh and blood of the Son's multifarious demonstrations of incarnational kenosis.[88] The Incarnation is, however, paradoxically both the simultaneous proleptic anticipation of a further movement of divine glory and a concealment of glory. On this point, Staale Johannes Kristiansen explains that for Balthasar "beauty is an appearance, but at the same time, it is more: it is a sign that always points towards something deeper."[89] That "something deeper" is the ineffable fullness and perfection of divine glory that is the eternal depths of the kenotic life of the triune God. Because Balthasar holds that "all of God's actions *ad extra* must find their basis in a precondition within the divine life to which they point,"[90] God's glory is demonstrated (not derived) through the Cross of Christ because the beauty and glory of God is eternally and dynamically kenotic. Divine glory is, therefore, not an abstraction but an encounter with the true and the good in the flesh and blood of Christ.[91] Expressing the new covenant reality, the divine glory revealed in Jesus and eminently demonstrated in the crescendo of the Paschal events becomes the quintessential articulation of God's kenotically-shaped divine ontology. As Balthasar states, "when God throws himself away . . . he shows not only the principle of all fecundity and all generosity, but also the essence of his glory."[92]

Alongside Bulgakov and Pannenberg, Balthasar's theological logic validates this present work's maxim: that triune glory is demonstrated and achieved through divine self-giving. On this reasoning, Jesus' correlation in John 13:31 of his "now" impending death with glorification illuminates a depth of meaning that reaches into the very patterning of divine being—"*now* is the Son of Man glorified and God is glorified in him." Kenosis is symbiotic with the enriched and enriching glory of God. Moreover, if created humanity is drawn into the divine life of well-being (the glory of God) then this interpretation gives extended meaning to the glorification of human beings. The glorification of humanity is the increased realization of well-being achieved only in consonance with the core orientation symbiotic to life—kenosis. Humanity's proleptic and eschatological glory is patterned on the recognition of, and reorientation to, the patterning of the Lord of glory: "And we all . . . contemplate the Lord's glory, are being transformed into his image *with ever-increasing glory*, which comes from the Lord, who is the Spirit" (2 Cor 3:18).

CONCLUSION

Balthasar's theology affirms and reinforces aspects of the constructive theological logic of Divine Self-Enrichment. Furthermore, his more "vivid" interpretation of the dynamics of the triune relations provide valuable insights into tracing the constitutive features of divine intra-relatedness. The key points from this examination relevant to the construal of Divine Self-Enrichment may be summarized as:

1. Triune life is highly dynamic where the personal relations constitute divine life and love.
2. The dynamism of divine life is prudently upheld as congruent with Christian theistic concepts of simplicity and aseity (and its derivative immutability).
3. Triune life is constituted by gift and receipt between the divine persons. This reciprocity manifests kenosis—the self-giving to the other is constitutive for divine life.
4. The kenotic nature of eternal divine life underscores the economic manifestations of divine expression in the world. The dynamism of triune intra-relatedness conditions the kenotic nature of the salvific work of God in Christ.
5. While criticism persists regarding ontological issues associated with Balthasar's use of *Abstand*, his concept does introduce the notion of distinction and "otherness" in the Godhead. This provides the logic for advocating activity (enrichment) between the divine persons.
6. The life of God characterized by intratrinitarian speech and worship evidences mutual and interpersonal dialogue and engagement, an openness to being known and knowing, acknowledging and honoring the greatness of another, and speech in recognizable and purposeful language.
7. The purpose and the content of triune kenosis is divine glory. Divine glory is commensurate with divine life and is also the dynamic concreteness of divine well-being expressed in, and experienced by, creation. The glory of divine life and well-being is that to which all things move eschatologically.

NOTES

1. Mark McIntosh, "Hans Urs Von Balthasar (1905–88)," in *The Student's Companion to the Theologians*, ed. Ian S. Markham (Chichester: Blackwell-Wiley, 2013), 356.

2. Hans Urs von Balthasar, *Presence and Thought: An Essay on the Religious Philosophy of Gregory of Nyssa*, trans. Mark Sebanc (San Francisco: Ignatius Press,

1995), 153. Super becoming, for Balthasar, is in no way commensurate with contemporary programs advocating divine mutability. Luy insists that Balthasar's commitment to God's unchangeability does not, however, simply repeat "a classical account of divine immutability without his own qualifications." David Luy, "The Aesthetic Collision: Hans Urs von Balthasar on the Trinity and the Cross," *International Journal of Systematic Theology* 13, no. 2 (2011), 159. See also Gerard F. O'Hanlon, *The Immutability of God in the Theology of Hans Urs von Balthasar* (New York: Cambridge University Press, 1990).

3. McIntosh, "Hans Urs Von Balthasar," 361.

4. For criticism that Balthasar engages in a speculative exercise see Karen Kilby, *Balthasar: A (Very) Critical Introduction* (Grand Rapids, MI: William B. Eerdmans Publishing Company, 2012), 107. However, McIntosh argues that "his Trinitarian theology is, however, rooted in his understanding of Christ; it is not speculative." See McIntosh, "Hans Urs Von Balthasar," 359.

5. Balthasar, *Theo-Drama: Theological Dramatic Theory*, trans. Graham Harrison, vol. 5, *The Last Act* (San Francisco: Ignatius, 1998) (herein *ThDrV*), 77–78. Originally published as *Theodramatik: Bd. IV: Das Endspiel* (Einsiedeln: Johannes Verlag, 1983).

6. Balthasar, *Theo-Drama: Theological Dramatic Theory*, trans. Graham Harrison, vol. 3, *The Dramatis Personae: Persons in Christ* (San Francisco: Ignatius, 1992) (herein *ThDrIII*), 508.

7. McIntosh, "Hans Urs Von Balthasar," 359.

8. Balthasar, *Presence and Thought*, 153. Originally published as *Theodramatik: Bd. II: Die Personen des Spiels. Teil II: Die Personen in Christus* (Einsiedeln: Johannes Verlag, 1978).

9. McIntosh, "Hans Urs Von Balthasar," 357.

10. McIntosh, "Hans Urs Von Balthasar," 359.

11. McIntosh, "Hans Urs Von Balthasar," 362. My italics.

12. Balthasar, *Theo-Drama: Theological Dramatic Theory*, trans Graham Harrison, vol. 2, *The Dramatis Personae: Man in God* (San Francisco: Ignatius, 1990) (herein *ThDrII*), 88. Originally published as *Theodramatik. Bd. II: Die Personen des Spiels. Teil 1: Der Mensch in Gott* (Einsiedeln: Johannes Verlag. 1976).

13. Hans Urs von Balthasar, *Heart of the World*, trans. Erasmo S. Leiva (San Francisco: Ignatius, 1979), 50.

14. Luy, "The Aesthetic Collision," 159.

15. McIntosh argues that, based on Balthasar's study of Gregory of Nyssa and Ignatian spirituality, he commits to a view of God as "eternal activity of self-giving among the Divine Persons," where "reality and being are best understood in terms of event and act rather than essence." McIntosh, "Hans Urs Von Balthasar," 357.

16. Rowan Williams, "Balthasar and the Trinity," in *The Cambridge Companion to Hans Urs Von Balthasar*, eds. Edward T. Oakes, SJ and David Moss (Cambridge: Cambridge University Press, 2004), 45, doi:10.1017/CCOL0521814677.004. See also Balthasar, *ThDr III*, 519. My italics.

17. Kilby, *Balthasar: A (Very) Critical Introduction*, 100.

18. Kilby, *Balthasar: A (Very) Critical Introduction*, 100.

19. Jennifer Newsome-Martin, "The 'Whence' and the 'Whither' of Balthasar's Gendered Theology: Rehabilitating Kenosis for Feminist Theology," *Modern Theology* 31, no. 2 (2015): 221.

20. Williams, "Balthasar and the Trinity," 42.

21. Ben Quash, "The theo-drama," in *The Cambridge Companion to Hans Urs Von Balthasar*, eds. Edward T. Oakes, SJ and David Moss (Cambridge: Cambridge University Press, 2004), 151.

22. Williams, "Balthasar and the Trinity," 38.

23. Balthasar, *ThDrIV*, 323–24.

24. Balthasar, *ThDrII*, 258.

25. Hans Urs von Balthasar, *Glory of the Lord: A Theological Aesthetics*, ed. John Riches, trans. Brian McNeil C.R.V., vol. 7, *Theology: The New Covenant* (San Francisco: Ignatius, 1989) (herein *GloryVII*), 17. Originally published as *Herrlichkeit: Eine theologische, Asthetik*, Band III, 2: *Theologie*, Teil 2: *Neuer Bund* (Einsiedeln: Johannes-Verlag, 1969).

26. Kilby, *Balthasar: A (Very) Critical Introduction*, 101.

27. Balthasar, *ThDrII*, 256.

28. Balthasar, *ThDrII*, 256. See also Balthasar's insistence that God is not reliant on the world for God's being—"The immanent Trinity must be understood to be that eternal, absolute self-surrender whereby God is seen to be, in himself, absolute love; this in turn explains his free self-giving to the world as love, without suggesting that God 'needed' the world process and the Cross in order to become himself (to 'mediate' himself)." Balthasar, *ThDrIV*, 323. Thus, Balthasar emphasizes the freedom of God in the "dispensation of salvation" and not a contemporary conflation of the economic and immanent Trinity where God's economic acts are viewed as necessity. In Hans Urs von Balthasar, *'Mysterium Paschale:' The Mystery of Easter*, trans. Aiden Nichols (San Francisco: Ignatius, 1990), 215.

29. Balthasar, *ThDrV*, 277.

30. Balthasar, *ThDrIII*, 530. My italics.

31. Alyssa Lyra Pitstick, *Light in Darkness: Hans Urs Von Balthasar and the Catholic Doctrine of Christ's Descent into Hell* (Grand Rapids, MI: Eerdmans, 2006), 126.

32. Pitstick, *Light in Darkness*, 235–40.

33. Ceclia Deane-Drummond, "The Breadth of Glory: A Trinitarian Eschatology for the Earth through Critical Engagement with Hans Urs von Balthasar," *International Journal of Systematic Theology* 12, no. 1 (2010): 51.

34. This is not to say that Balthasar does not acknowledge the life-giving redemption offered to humanity through the Cross but to highlight that this is not his emphasis.

35. Bruce Lindley McCormack, *The Humility of the Eternal Son: Reformed Kenoticism and the Repair of Chalcedon*, Current Issues in Theology (Cambridge: Cambridge University Press, 2021), 153.

36. Kilby, *Balthasar: A (Very) Critical Introduction*, 120.

37. Pitstick, *Light in Darkness*, 347.

38. Newsome-Martin, "Balthasar's Gendered Theology," 214. Hampson also argues of the common interpretation of kenosis as mere self-emptying, "it may well

be a model which men need to appropriate and which may helpfully be built into the male understanding of God. But . . . *for women, the theme of self-emptying and self-abnegation is far from helpful as a paradigm.*" Daphne Hampson, *Theology and Feminism* (Oxford: Basil Blackwell, 1990), 155.

39. Kilby, *Balthasar: A (Very) Critical Introduction*, 120. Pitstick maintains a similar accusation, saying: "Balthasar seems to ascribe a positive value to suffering and death in themselves in virtue of their likeness to the suffering Redeemer, not to mention the Trinity." Pitstick, *Light in Darkness*, 133.

40. Balthasar, *ThDrIV*, 327–28.

41. Miroslav Volf, "The Trinity Is Our Social Program: The Doctrine of the Trinity and the Shape of Social Engagement," *Modern Theology* 14. no. 3 July (1998): 414.

42. Timothy J. Yoder, "Hans Urs von Balthasar and Kenosis: The Pathway to Human Agency" (PhD Diss., Loyola University Chicago, 2014), 55–56. See Kilby, Karen. "Is an Apophatic Trinitarianism Possible?" *International Journal of Systematic Theology* 12, no. 1 (2010): 65–77. https://doi.org/10.1111/j.1468-2400.2009.00494.x and Kilby, *Balthasar: A (Very) Critical Introduction*.

43. Mark A. McIntosh, "Light in Darkness: Hans Urs von Balthasar and the Catholic Doctrine of Christ's Descent into Hell—by Alyssa Lyra Pitstick," *Modern Theology* 24 (2008): 138.

44. Neil Ormerod, "The Debate Over Light in Darkness and the Catholicity of Hans Urs von Balthasar," *Australian eJournal of Theology* 20, no. 3 (2013): 212.

45. Yoder, "Hans Urs von Balthasar and Kenosis," 70.

46. Deane-Drummond, "The Breadth of Glory," 63. My italics.

47. Jacqueline Service, "Existent Endurance, Vulnerability, and Future Joy," 14 September 2021, blogos.wp.st-andrews.ac.uk/2021/09/14/logia-profile-for-september-existent-endurance-vulnerability-and-future-joy/.

48. Deane-Drummond, "The Breadth of Glory," 52; Kilby, *Balthasar: A (Very) Critical Introduction*, 108. See also John Yocum, "A Cry of Dereliction? Reconsidering a Recent Theological Commonplace," *International Journal of Systematic Theology* 7, no. 1 (2005): 72–80.

49. Kilby, *Balthasar: A (Very) Critical Introduction*, 108. See also Holly J. Carey, *Jesus' Cry from the Cross: Towards a First-Century Understanding of the Intertextual Relationship between Psalm 22 and the Narrative of Mark's Gospel* (London: Bloomsbury Publishing Plc, 2009), 165–67; N. T. Wright, *Jesus and the Victory of God: Christian Origins and the Question of God,* volume 2 (London: SPCK, 1996), 600–601.

50. Ingolf. U. Dalferth, *Becoming Present: An Inquiry into the Christian Sense of the Presence of God* (Leuven: Peeters, 2006), 51.

51. Eberhard Jüngel, *God as the Mystery of the World: On the Foundation of the Theology of the Crucified One in the Dispute between Theism and Atheism* (Grand Rapids, MI: Eerdmans, 1983), 54.

52. Asle Eikrem, *God as Sacrificial Love: A Systematic Exploration of a Controversial Notion* (London: Bloomsbury Academic, 2019), 133.

53. Balthasar, *ThDrV*, 74.

54. The following Scriptures explicate the nexus between life and self-giving: "Whoever want to be my disciple must deny themselves and take up their cross and follow me. For whoever want to save their life will lose it, but whoever loses their life for me and the gospel will save it" (Mk 8:34–36); "We always carry around in our body the death of Jesus, so that the life of Jesus may also be revealed in our body. For we who are alive are always being given over to death for Jesus' sake, so that his life may also be revealed in our mortal body. So then, death is at work in us, but life is at work in you" (2 Cor 4:10–12); "I have come that they may have life and have it to the full. I am the good shepherd. The good shepherd lays down his life for the sheep" (Jn 10:10–11). The Prologue to the Gospel of John also contains the nascent pattern of God's kenotically-enriching life as it connects God's glory with the kenosis of the Incarnation. Of the kenosis of Incarnation the Gospel of John states, "we have seen his glory" (Jn 1:14). Furthermore, Painter understands that the gospel of John similarly equates the glory of God with the self-giving of the Cross, arguing that "the new possibility of eternal life is understood to have come about through the incarnation of the eternal λόγος. His coming made possible the revelation of the glory of God as Father in his Son . . . Paradoxically that glory is revealed in the cross in which the self-giving love of God as Father is seen. The cross is implied by the flesh assumed by the λόγος." John Painter, *The Quest for the Messiah: The History, Literature and Theology of the Johannine Community* (Edinburgh: T&T Clark, 1991), 156.

55. Pitstick, *Light in Darkness*, 291.

56. Moltmann, *The Crucified God*.

57. Balthasar, *ThDrIV*.

58. Robert W. Jenson, *Systematic Theology: The Triune God*, volume 1 (New York: Oxford University Press, 2001), 190.

59. Karl Barth, *Church Dogmatics: The Doctrine of God. Part 1*, vol. 2, eds. G. W. Bromiley and T. F. Torrance (Edinburgh: T. & T. Clark, 1957), 332–33.

60. Balthasar states "Again, we must not see the 'distance' in opposition to, or in conflict with, the 'closeness' . . . at the same time such distance is necessary . . . in order to hold fast to the personal distinctness of each Person both in being and acting." Balthasar, *ThDrV*, 94.

61. Yoder, "Hans Urs von Balthasar and Kenosis," 68.

62. Yoder, "Hans Urs von Balthasar and Kenosis," 68.

63. Hans Urs von Balthasar, *My Work: In Retrospect*, trans. Brian McNeil (San Francisco: Ignatius, 1993), 116.

64. Hans Urs von Balthasar, *Love Alone: The Way of Revelation: A Theological Perspective*, trans. Alexander Dru (London: Burns & Oats Ltd, 1968), 61.

65. Peter, J. Caseralla, "The Expression and Form of the Word: Trinitarian Hermeneutics and the Sacramentality of Language in Hans Urs Von Balthasar's Theology," *Renascence* 48, no. 2 (1996): 111.

66. McIntosh, "Hans Urs Von Balthasar," 362.

67. Robert. W. Jenson, *Systematic Theology: The Works of God*, volume 2 (New York: Oxford University Press, 1999), 7.

68. Balthasar, *ThDrV*, 516.

69. Newsome-Martin, "Balthasar's Gendered Theology," 234.

70. Balthasar, *ThDrV*, 96. Balthasar leans heavily here on the writings of his life-long spiritual colleague Adrienne von Speyr.

71. Balthasar, *ThDrV*, 98.

72. Balthasar, *ThDrV*, 98.

73. Rowan Williams also discusses this briefly in Williams, "Balthasar and the Trinity," 44.

74. Balthasar, *ThDrII*, 120.

75. McIntosh, "Hans Urs Von Balthasar," 357–58.

76. McIntosh, "Hans Urs Von Balthasar," 358.

77. Balthasar, *ThDrV*, 96–97.

78. Balthasar, *ThDrV*, 96.

79. Balthasar, *ThDrV*, 105.

80. Kilby, *Balthasar: A (Very) Critical Introduction*, 105; 112.

81. Kilby, *Balthasar: A (Very) Critical Introduction*, 112–14.

82. Some of Balthasar's vivid depictions of the intratrinitarian life are derived from mystic Adrienne von Speyr's writings. See for example *ThDrV*, 96–98 where he draws heavily from Adrienne von Speyr, *The World of Prayer* (San Francisco: Ignatius Press, 1985).

83. Matthew Bates, in *The Birth of the Trinity*, argues for an exegetical strategy based on reading the biblical text through a hermeneutic of triune relationality; what he calls "prosopological exegesis." Bates discusses how early Christians interpreted the Old Testament dialogues "to provide a panoramic view of the relationship between Father, Son and Spirit," where they perceived "the story of the interior of the divine life." Matthew W. Bates, *The Birth of the Trinity: Jesus, God, and Spirit in New Testament and Early Christian Interpretations of the Old Testament* (Oxford: Oxford University Press, 2015), 2.

84. Balthasar, *ThDrV*, 105.

85. On this interpretation we can understand the kenosis of the Incarnation, articulated in John 1, as the beholding "of his Glory" (Jn 1:14).

86. Hans Urs von Balthasar, *Glory of the Lord: A Theological Aesthetics*, ed. John Riches, trans. Brian McNeil C.R.V., and Erasmo Leiva-Merikakis, vol. 6, *Theology: The Old Covenant* (San Francisco: Ignatius, 1991), 415. Originally published as *Herrlichkeit: Eine theologische, Ästhetik*, Band III, 2: *Theologie*, Teil I: *Alter Bund* (Einsiedeln, Johannes Verlag, 1967) (Herein *GloryVI*), 415.

87. Balthasar, *GloryVI*, 415.

88. Luy, "The Aesthetic Collision," 159.

89. Staale Johannes Kristiansen, "Hans Urs von Balthasar," in *Key Theological Thinkers: From Modern to Postmodern*, eds. Svien Rise and Staale Johannes Kristiansen (New York: Routledge, 2016), 260.

90. Luy, "The Aesthetic Collision," 161.

91. This is why Luy states that Balthasar insists "that theology must never 'move beyond' the humanity of Jesus in a desire to attain knowledge of 'naked divinity.'" Luy, "The Aesthetic Collision," 159.

92. Balthasar, *GloryVII*, 432.

Conclusion to Part II

Thorough the analysis of this part II, it has become clear that theologians across ecumenical lines identify a movement between the triune persons characterized by mutual giving and receipt. Moreover, a striking symmetry resounds in their theological affirmations that this dynamism is, in fact, constitutive for divine *life*. While Bulgakov asserts that triune mutuality is constitutive for "Sophia" (the life of God constituted by divine self-revelation), Pannenberg—that it is constitutive for kingdom rule (the life of God constituted by the rule of God); and Balthasar—constitutive for *Abstand* (the life of God constituted by divine difference); each intuitively identifies and describes nascent logic consistent with the broader theological elements of Divine Self-Enrichment. Significantly, through nuancing the insights from Bulgakov, Pannenberg and Balthasar, a coherent systematic logic of Divine Self-Enrichment is refined to assert that divine *life* is symbiotic with triune relational kenosis—the "enriching-kenosis" or "kenotic-enrichment" of the eternal Trinity. The final part of this book now considers specific triune expressions that attend kenotic-enrichment, parsing the "dance-steps" of the "divine-dance," while also sketching some nascent implications for human well-being.

PART III

The Divine "Dance-Steps"

In light of the critical determinations of part I and II, this part III marks the culmination of our inquiry as it undertakes two final tasks. First, it categorizes broad traits attending the expression of kenotic-enrichment in the economy of triune inter-relationality; that is, it demarcates "dance-*steps*" that attend the "divine-dance." Second, it sketches some embryonic implications for how the constitutive features of divine well-being ground and contextualize a Christian rationale and praxis for human well-being. For this second task I reflect on correspondences that may reasonably be drawn between the characteristics of triune life and human life. Importantly, no mere "model" requiring human imitation is proposed. Rather, creaturely well-being is predicated on the redemptive re-enlivenment toward the ontological conditions that likewise source created existence itself. On this point, Sydney Carter's well-known song lyric is a pertinent analogy: "I am the Lord of the Dance, said he . . . And I'll lead you all in the Dance said he."[1] Carter's song resonates the implications envisioned in this final part III, that for temporal created beings to "dance" the good, the beautiful or the enrichment of life, *communion* with the "Lord of the dance" is primary. That is, the gift of communion with the triune God sources, contextualizes and configures all *life*. As such, the conclusions articulated in this final section resolve with some nuance—human imitation of the divine is an enveloped-imitation into the dynamics of the enriching life of the Trinity, initiated and sustained by the Spirit of God.

Unifying and vivifying humanity with the divine conditions for created well-being involves the redemptive propulsion of God facilitated by the Holy Spirit. Such a concept ultimately heralds the necessity of worship as constitutive for the "good" life. Enrichment is doxologically actualized; for God, in the simplicity of triune being, and for humanity, in the contingent potentiality of a life oriented to the Creator. Through the dynamic working of the Spirit of God, humanity is drawn into worship—the acknowledgment of the nature and being of God with attendant reorientation of life.[2] In this worshipful posture, the divine dynamics of well-being are actualized, with ever-increasing glory for the life of the world. Such an understanding not only defies the enticement of Pelagianistic humanism but affirms divine being as the gracious genesis of, and possibility for, an enriched humanity.

With these ends in mind, and to take stock of our prior reasoning, let me reiterate the logic that ground these final two chapters: (1) Divine kenotic-enrichment patterns God's ways in the world (economic Trinity). (2) The pattern of enriching-kenosis is antecedently operative in the immanent Trinity. (3) The patterning is, accordingly, to be discerned in the dynamic of God's eternal works in creation and in human life. Thus, whenever human life evidences the kind of kenotic-enrichment displayed in the economic Trinity, there we see intimations of the work of God. In this sense, the archetype of divine enrichment is antecedently operative in creation, where kenotic-enrichment is a condition of createdness. (4) The divine pattern, embedded in human life, is not only configured to creaturely contingency but is also disrupted by sin. Instead of kenotic-enrichment bringing life and well-being, egoistic-enrichment or truncated-kenosis deforms the divinely initiated conditions of createdness. (5) Human beings retain, however, the divinely initiated desire for well-being. (6) Advancing well-being and enrichment requires human adaptation to the antecedent pattern of divine kenotic-enrichment that is embedded in createdness and redeemed through God's work in the world. Actualizing such a reorientation requires the transfiguring movement of the life of the Spirit of God.

NOTES

1. Sydney Carter, "Lord of the Dance," 1967.
2. Daniel W. Hardy, *God's Ways with the World: Thinking and Practising Christian Faith* (Edinburgh: T&T Clark, 1996), 14.

Chapter 7

Kenotic-Enrichment

Characteristics and Implications of Divine Self-Enrichment

We are now at the point where the shape and logic of a theology of Divine Self-Enrichment—*God enriching God in the perfection and fullness of God*—has been articulated. At the heart of this concept is that God's all-blessedness is dynamically derived through the triune relationality of Father, Son and Holy Spirit giving and receiving each to the other in unifying oneness. By tracing the pattern of triune relating present in Scripture and canvassed in the theologies of Bulgakov, Pannenberg, and Balthasar, a clarified vision of a broad witness to the nature of God has opened for us. That witness presses toward a wholeness of triune *well*-being that is kenotic in essence and form. "Kenotic-enrichment" or "enriching-kenosis" shapes the actualized pleroma of divine life. Deriving its conceptual quality from the dynamics of the Trinity, the primary characteristic attending divine enrichment—kenosis (typically considered as a self-emptying or self-giving) does not, however, elide self-reception. To "receive" incorporates a self-giving. John Milbank identifies such an interchange, saying: "Even our current word 'give' can slide towards its opposite: 'to give way' means to provide a passage, to allow a certain reception of something, and to say of a tree that 'it gives' with the wind, or has 'give' in it, is to denote a pliability equivalent to a capacity to receive."[1] The mutual kenosis identified between the triune hypostases is both gift *and* receipt, where receipt is also self-giving, a yielding to receive. This allows us to distinguish kenotic-enrichment from (a) egoistic-enrichment (self-enhancement devoid of self-giving) and (b) theological interpretations that reduce the concept of kenosis to a truncated-kenosis (a self-giving severed from enriching receipt).

Examining aspects of Bulgakov's, Pannenberg's, and Balthasar's Trinitarian theologies gives us ecumenical affirmation to construe giving and receiving as constitutive for triune life. That examination also revealed broad theological resources ripe for transposition into the domain of human life and ethical praxis. However, moving from systematic logic to an operative theology requires a further consideration of the traits of divine relationality accompanying triune well-being. This chapter, therefore, moves from the previous higher level "inner logic" regarding divine enrichment to some intermediate categories that help ground the earlier inquiry and align its insights to the "flesh and blood of reality."[2] From this perspective, I agree with Miroslav Volf when he argues that abstract principles alone "are not pure gold" but rather pure gold is "the narrative of the life of the Trinity, at whose heart lies the history of self-donation."[3] It is only when cognitive principles expound the broader kenotic narrative of the life and being of God that dogma becomes usefully *concretissimo*.

CHARACTERISTICS OF TRIUNE ENRICHING-KENOSIS

Synthesizing the inquiry of the preceding chapters, the below particularities emerge as significant conceptual coordinates attending the dynamics of triune kenotic-enrichment.

Free and Volitional Gift and Receipt

- The divine persons operate in free and volitional interrelated agency; such a freedom in divine self-positing is integral to the nature of divine love.
- Triune giving and receiving is neither obliged nor coerced.

Interpersonal Communication

- The divine persons are open to receiving from each other through transparent and intimate knowing and being known.
- There is self-awareness and self-giving present in speech and action.

Symbiotic Speech and Act

- Divine speech (both verbal and non-verbal communication) is purposeful and is attended by substance and materiality of act. Speech is therefore truthful and faithful to God's being.
- Speech is conducted in a mutuality of recognizable "language"; it is thus able to be given and received with meaning.

Equal Being in Mutual Dependency

- As there is no relational hierarchy within God, hypostatic kenosis of gift and receipt has a unified equilibrium. The Father's being is dependent on the Son, the Son's identity dependent on the Father, and without the mutuality of giftedness through the Spirit there is neither Son nor Father. Each divine person is the fullness of God in the Oneness of God; thus, divinity has equality in mutual dependency.
- Triune being is constituted in the distinctive worth of each hypostasis and through the mutual responsibility of Father, Son and Holy Spirit honoring and upholding the hypostatic divine identity.
- The divine persons acknowledge the greatness and worth of the other, the interdependent agency of each divine person is acknowledged and honored.

The diagram in figure 7.1 elucidates the "enriching" (a kenotic-enrichment) components of the overarching concept of Divine Self-Enrichment: God *enriching* God in the perfection and fullness of God. In other words, it clarifies a broad interpretation of the elements that coinhere with the dynamics of triune well-being.

FROM TRINITARIAN WELL-BEING TO HUMAN WELL-BEING

Before discussing the pragmatic implications that kenotic-enrichment has for the constitutive factors of human well-being, it is crucial to consider how

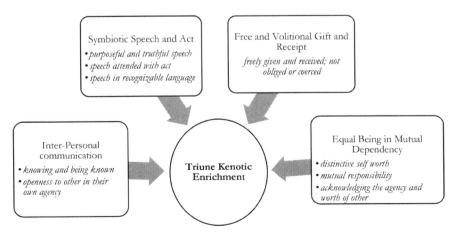

Figure 7.1. The Nature and Characteristics of Divine Self-Enrichment. By the author.

humans may be said to correspond to divine being in any regard. One cannot simply draw a univocal correspondence from God to humanity to conclude— "This is how God is: therefore, this is how humans should be."[4] In the Christian tradition, God is not ontologically commensurate with the creation; "God is not the greater, more replete version of the created order; God is of an utterly different order of Being."[5] And yet, God's ontological distinction does not elide divine relationality and affinity with the creation. There is a compatible harmony between the two.[6] To draw meaningful correspondences between divine well-being and human well-being, similarity and dissimilarity between God and humanity must be acknowledged. Two questions prompt the inquiry here: In light of the ontological divergence between Creator and creation, is it possible for humanity to fulfil the exhortation from Scripture to be "imitators of God" (Eph 5:1)? And, if divine imitation is possible, in what ways can responsible imitation of the triune God (*imitatio Trinitatis*) be exhorted?

ONTOLOGICAL SIMILARITY AND DISSIMILARITY

Although championing the practical relevance of the doctrine of the Trinity, Catherine LaCugna also warns that "the practical nature of the doctrine of the Trinity does not mean it is a pragmatic principle that furnishes an easy solution to war or violence, or yields a blueprint for a catechetical program, or settles vexing disagreements over the church's public prayer."[7] *Imitatio Trinitatis*, this side of the eschaton, will not provide a panacea to the dysfunction of world affairs or usher in the fullness of human well-being. Given this, and other limitations, some may advocate avoiding Trinitarian theology by which to locate the conditions for created well-being. Such an avoidance, I believe, is mistaken. Limitation does not equate to fruitlessness. It means that a considered approach is required to frame the foundation and vision for human well-being beyond quixotic fantasy. The ontological significance of the being of God for creation, despite divine incommensurability, should not be underestimated.

With this in mind, a key position maintained throughout this book is the necessity to resist the temptation to conflate the Creator and the creation. Alongside this position, and central to orthodox Christian doctrine, is, however, the notion that the *incommensurable* God is imaged in humanity (*imago Dei*). Despite the plethora of interpretations of what *imago Dei* ultimately means, central is that humans are constituted in such a way that a gracious affinity exists between the creature and the Creator. This affinity is, however, qualified by ontological difference. Recognizing this "incommensurable-commensurability of God and not-God" is a necessary guardrail when drawing parallels between the Creator and creature.[8] Without this guardrail, one may be tempted to draw inferences from the Trinity open to the type of critique Volf exacts on Nicholas Fedorov's[9] proposed social program of Trinitarian imitation, arguing:

> No arguments need to be wasted on showing that Fedorov's proposal is specious and his vision chimerical. It is one thing to espouse belief that in the resurrection of Christ power is at work "capable of transfiguring nature" . . . But the claim that "God has placed in our hands all the means for regulating cosmic disorders" . . . because we participate in the divine life, is the stuff of which dreams are made.[10]

Without attending to *dissimilarity* between the Creator and creature the pragmatic implications of kenotic-enrichment may well amount to nothing more than an unattainable utopic vision. Yet, in the absence of *similarity* between Creator and creature—the resonance of divine ontology that initiates and animates human well-being—there is little point in reflecting on the divinely-ordered ontic ground for human well-being at all. That humans are made in the image of God and are to imitate God should be affirmed.[11] Acknowledging distinction between the Creator and creature is not to exclude correspondence nor does it subvert human well-being as being derived from the ontology of divine well-being. Pannenberg's insights (chapter 5) are useful here, particularly his measured unity between the tension of the "now" (proleptic in-breaking of God's reign through Christ) and the "not-yet" of the reign of God (anticipatory waiting for the future reign of God). Pannenberg's theology assists in both affirming an impetus for realizing human well-being in the "now"—the kingdom of God that ushers in well-being for the creation is a present reality (similarity of Creator and creature), and the reality of an *incremental* realization of human well-being—where humanity awaits the future consummation of the kingdom (dissimilarity of creature and Creator). Acknowledging ontological similarity and dissimilarity is necessary to maintain both hope for, and gradual actualization of human well-being, without succumbing to illusions of utopia or the despondency of delay.

Limitations on Correspondence: Dissimilarity

A myriad of divergent features exist between Trinity and humanity. I will, however, limit my discussion here to two key differences that significantly alter the human articulation of the divine foundations of well-being. First, unlike divine well-being, human well-being is subject to temporal contingency. And the second is the distorting impact of sin.

Human Well-Being as Temporally Contingent

As I have indicated previously, human well-being is never self-sufficiently and singularly derived (contra triune simplicity).[12] Instead, it is realized through union with the life of the Creator, engagement with other humans and the created context of life. Humanity has no self-derived nor immediate state of well-being, a fact confirmed by Thomas Aquinas, who argues—"God produced many and diverse things so that what was wanting in one expression in the divine goodness might be supplied by another; for goodness, which in God is single and uniform, in creatures is multiplied and diverse."[13] This contingency means that human well-being is attained incrementally, where "*development* is synonymous with life"[14] and the "temporality of becoming is the very nature of creation."[15] Human life, characterized by contingent "becoming," is subject to growth and development. The nature of humanity lives in the interval between what is and what will be. For the creature, therefore, kenosis and enrichment have an *intervallic* symbiosis. However, in accord with simplicity and aseity, divine enrichment actualizes through a symbiotic *immediacy* of kenosis and enrichment. God lives all-blessedness and well-being as an abundance of actualized potential. Humans do not. Creaturely well-being is inscribed with un-actualized potential.[16] For creatures made in the divine image, the pleroma of divine well-being compels the unsatiated human desire toward a "becoming" wholeness.

Sin and the Restriction of Human Well-Being

Unlike divinity, where the symbiotic immediacy of kenotic-enrichment constitutes the fullness of life, contraindications of truncated-kenosis or egoistic-enrichment conspicuously typify human life marred by sin. These contraindications epitomize the nature of sin, the missing of the divine-mark (hamartia), that impede human well-being. Human aversion to the divine ways ultimately restricts the realization of creaturely well-being, as only the triune source substantiates its repetition. Indeed, the very creation of the world receives its life through orientation and obedience to the divine Word—"and God said . . . and it was so" (Gen 1). The being of God speaks the ways of life—"and God said . . . " and with energetic animation creation follows the divine command—" . . . and it was so."[17] Obedient orientation to the divine Word, always commensurate with God's being, is the realization of life. The divine Word propels not only the original creation of well-being but likewise its redemption—"One does not *live* by bread alone, *but by every word* that comes from the mouth of God" (Mt 4:4).[18] It follows then that if the divine Word originates and sustains the patterns that actualize life and well-being, then its abjurement results in death and impoverishment.

Read through the heuristic of divine kenotic-enrichment, the Genesis 3 account of the fall of humanity, with its resultant diminishment of human well-being, reveals the dynamics of both egoistic-enrichment and truncated-kenosis. The human temptation to egoistically-enrich was inherent in the lure of the serpent's inducement to partake of the divinely restricted tree of knowledge—"you will be like God" (Gen 3:5). Humanity sought divine likeness in antithesis to the pattern of a divinely-contoured life; they sought to grasp, not to give. Death ensued. Relations diminished. The created harmony—fractured. The primordial fall also ultimately heralded a giving-of-self to that which could not enrich, that is, knowledge without love (truncated-kenosis).[19] The choice to dislocate enrichment from the kenotic nature of divine life deformed and restricted the actualization of human well-being. The unholy pattern embedded in Genesis 3 continues unceasingly. Refusing to orientate to "the active presence of God and the energetic order," humans experience the consequences of "impoverishment . . . the loss of energy and order."[20] Humans, as desiring creatures, are oriented to either life or death—"I have set before you today life and prosperity, death and adversity" (Deut 30:15).[21] When rightly oriented toward God, a life-giving pattern ensues, but when attraction is disoriented from the divine vision, a self-ordered decay unwinds itself. Hardy poignantly presses such an idea, saying:

> Creatures are created to move towards God. When creatures somehow lose that towardness—becoming obsessive at some point, separating from the whole of things and serving only themselves—then the creation loses its order. To lack attraction to others and to God is to suffer the inertia of self-attraction: in Luther's terms, to be "twisted into self."[22]

Embedded in all layers of personal and communal human structures resides a deep resistance to the divine life of kenotic-enrichment.[23] Marred by a continuing enticement to sin, humanity's correspondence to God necessitates the redeeming ways of the Holy Spirit. When considering the implications of divine ontology for human well-being such recognition is an important caveat to avert a Pelagianistically-styled humanism.

Similarity: Creaturely Correspondence with the Creator's Well-Being

If, as I argue, giving and receiving characterize the ontology of divine being, one would expect to see a repetition of such traits embedded in the movement of created life. Bulgakov's conception of a repetition of divine life (Divine Sophia) in the created life (Creaturely Sophia), without confusion of the two, accords aptly here.[24] Woven from the very life of God (Gen 1:26), kenotic-enrichment is, therefore, not alien to humanity. At the core of human interaction, personally and socially, we find the interchange of giving and receiving. Consider marriage, childbirth, trade, conversation, education, and governing—the exchange of giving and receiving saturates life. An enriching marriage is inculcated through the self-giving and faithful commitment one to the other. Embryonic existence receives its energy and nurture in the interchange of the gifted womb of woman. The give and take of worded-exchange mark relationality in conversation. And yet, a distortion and disruption of the interchange of gift and receipt in all these examples can manifest harm, deprivation or death. The dense layers of social and personal giving and receiving infuse all human endeavor with a capacity to invoke richness or poverty of life. Humanity though, as a result of its "fallen" state, requires a marked alteration in its orientation for the attainment of the divine intention for created well-being. This reorientation requires participation in the divine expressions that attend kenotic-enrichment, a turning away (repentance) from the deformed misalignments of egoistic-enrichment and truncated-kenosis. The Apostle Paul perceives such a restructured orientation when he advocates—"Live by the Spirit . . . and do not gratify the desires of the flesh. For what the flesh desires is opposed to the Spirit, and what the Spirit desires is opposed to the flesh, for these are opposed to each other" (Gal 5:16).

KENOTIC-ENRICHMENT: NASCENT IMPLICATIONS FOR HUMAN WELL-BEING

Cognisant of the above qualifications, let us now turn to some emergent implications for human well-being that transpire from the economic interchanges that attend the actualization of triune well-being (see figure 7.1). These are:

1. Free and Volitional Gift and Receipt
2. Interpersonal Communication
3. Symbiotic Speech and Act
4. Equal Being in Mutual Dependency

Coherent with a theology of Divine Self-Enrichment, these categories call attention to the resonant theological pulse inherent in human existence. It is essential to note, however, that while there is differentiation between these categories it is impossible to silo or separate them. Additionally, the considerations offered here are nascent only, providing preliminary insights for ecclesiology and the broader, complex spectrum of issues impacting human well-being. Among important areas for further research is a deeper consideration of the ecclesial implications of kenotic-enrichment. Insights regarding kenotic ecclesiology already exist, derived from more conventional Christologically-shaped concepts of kenosis.[25] However, investigation into the convergence and divergence of the conceptual parameters between more traditional notions of kenosis and the triune concept of "enriching-kenosis" could yield further insight. My hunch is there would likely be significant continuity between the two, given that the soundings of the triune God resonate in and through Christ. Nevertheless, one notable point of variance doubtless resides in the ecclesial and relational implications that might arise from imputing kenosis in the personal paternity of the Father and the breath of the Spirit.

Free and Volitional Gift and Receipt

A central quality of triune kenotic-enrichment is that it is infused with freedom, not coercion. Yet, the notion of freedom here should not be confused with secular conceptions that exude obvious overtones to English philosopher John Mills' defining parameters as primarily freedom "from" the interference of others or external determiners. In a statement that could be the catchphrase of the contemporary Western milieu, Mills argues the "only freedom which deserves the name, is that of pursuing our own good in our own way, so long as we do not attempt to deprive others of theirs, or impede their efforts to obtain it."[26] Christian freedom is, however, construed in a very different direction. Taking its cue from the divine archetype, creaturely freedom is discerned in the movement "toward" the things of God, as Dietrich Bonhoeffer argues, "the freedom of the Creator demonstrates itself by allowing us to be free, free for the Creator."[27] In the image of the freely-determined God that not only, in freedom, gifts Godself to Godself through tri-hypostatic ecstasy, but also freely gifts Godself to the creation, humans find the definition of freedom. Again, with theological precision, Bonhoeffer espouses such a concept, saying:

> freedom is not a quality that can be uncovered; it is not a possession . . . it is a relation and nothing else. To be more precise . . . Being free means "being-free-for-the-other" . . . because God does not keep God's freedom to God's self, we can think of freedom only as a "being free for . . . " because I am bound to the other. Only by being in relation with the other am I free.[28]

With divine resonance, giving freely also means volitional giving; giving that is neither obliged nor duressed. As Willie James Jennings observes in his commentary on the book of Acts, yielding to the embrace of God's life can never be "compelled"; sacrificial living is "invitation" not "injunction."[29] This is a giving that also does not *demand* return, and yet, remains open to a reciprocity that is integral to well-being. In triune life, the *response* to gift is likewise conditioned by an expression of free agency. A gift unwelcomely imposed arguably ceases to be a "gift." A lack of freedom in giving or receiving may lead either to coercion or condescension, which ultimately, no matter how sufficient the gift, obscures enrichment. Enrichment, as in divine originator, cannot be forced or obliged but is fashioned in the free participation of kenosis. Balthasar, discerning that human self-giving and surrender to God is "the highest of human acts since it passes over into the omnipotence of God,"[30] presses, therefore, that love and freedom must also accompany such self-relinquishment.[31] Balthasar, cognisant of the possibility that human self-giving can degenerate "into dangerous forms of oppression," insists that self-giving requires volitional freedom. Acts of surrender are not, for Balthasar, to be classified by some kind of "passivity that slackly waits on the turn of events or resignation that bows its head."[32] Rather, the human repetition of divine self-giving is activated in freedom. Balthasar emphasizes that human participation, through God's grace, in the divine pattern of self-surrender does not eliminate "personal freedom" but "preserves and intensifies it."[33] The act of yielding oneself to God, and the ensuing divine envelopment, is inseparable from one's "*own*" will and *self*-surrender."[34] God freely receives that which is freely given.[35]

Michael Welker identifies a similar requirement of freedom for self-giving in what he identifies as core dimensions of God's reign. According to Welker, the creature enters into the reign of God in Christ through an "ethos of free, creative *self-withdrawal*."[36] This "self-withdrawal," an extension of Huber's concept of "self-limitation," infers acts done "on behalf of others."[37] Welker highlights that participating in God's reign, as articulated by Christ (Mt 19:16–30), involves freely performing acts of self-withdrawal for others in such a way that it "radically alters a person's life as previously lived."[38] Indeed, the demands of this new way of life in Christ are so radical that it prompts a stunned inquiry—"Then who can be saved?"[39] Importantly, Welker's notion of "self-withdrawal" resonates with the concept of kenotic-enrichment in that it is not only characterized by a radical *volitionality* but also by a definition that includes freedom connected to both giving and *receiving*. Welker emphasizes that it is essential for the human expression of "free, creative self-withdrawal for the sake of others" to not "focus merely on active approaches, that is, on the concrete praxis of self-withdrawal, for access to God's reign is characterised no less by experiences of mercy we have ourselves *received*."[40] The potential for humans to freely self-give emerges in the humble and non-coerced *receipt* of the open gift of God and others.

Alert to these dynamics, an impetus for a Christian fostering of expressions of human well-being (organizational, ecclesial or personal) would do well to consider whether praxis encourages free and voluntary participation or whether coercion, obligation or worse, blatant duress are operative.[41] Ultimately, the question I wish to provoke here is whether mechanisms intended to progress human well-being advance or undermine human agency and freedom. At the very least, Christians need to remain alert to the reality that assumptions regarding human agency exist in all modalities aimed at advancing human well-being. These assumptions will always either realize or restrain enrichment.

Extending our thinking a little further as to the implications of a well-being articulated in freely-gifted giving, another question arises—whether it is appropriate that Christian engagement in professionalized activities for well-being be subject to reporting requirements of "effectiveness"; where "effectiveness" is measured by input (the gift) as well as the output or outcome (receipt of gift). While I acknowledge the desire for transparency and accountability underlying monitoring and evaluation of effectiveness, the parameters established to determine such "effectiveness" may actually conceal expressions of duress and non-voluntary obligation on the beneficiaries of initiatives. Interrogating the prior assumptions of the delivery mechanisms may assist to uncover whether there is a bias against human agency and freedom in an effectiveness agenda. For example, where a program outcome is not achieved: Is it because the program and evaluation design are premised on criteria for "effectiveness" that assumes recipients will respond as humans with limited agency and freedom to participate? In other words: Is the "outcome" contingent on the beneficiaries behaving in a predetermined manner entrenched in the design? Is this assumed beneficiary-behavior volunteered freely or coerced? Or worse, not even sought? Effectiveness perhaps needs to be rethought to give greater weight to the agency of the perceived "beneficiary." An indicator of effectiveness may, in fact, be the ability to advance the *free agency* of beneficiaries in program activities.

Here, a related question is prompted: Are outcome driven "effectiveness" agendas always needed when it comes to enhancing well-being? Could an activity ever simply be given "freely"; designed without conditional requirements of response placed on beneficiaries? In professionalized care modes regulated by governance requirements such a suggestion would indeed be controversial. Holding freedom and reciprocal responsibility of both giver and receiver may be a difficult balance to maintain. Yet, if we fail to even entertain the concept of freely-gifted enrichment, or at least a shift in what we mean by "effectiveness," we may restrict well-being by what "outcomes" we can achieve and measure.[42] We might constrain human enrichment by what "response" the beneficiaries are predetermined to oblige the "giver." This is a significant issue, particularly in light of the reality that human enrichment is subject to delay and yet, in order to justify expenditure, there is usually a requirement to produce evidence of beneficial outcomes on a quick timetable. Often, because the justification of programs addressing well-being are outcome driven, rather than justified on the basis that giving and receiving is integral to all human well-being, an unintended truncation of well-being may, in fact, be fuelled. A praxis of kenotic-enrichment that affirms freedom and non-coercion at the center of relational giving and receiving may assist to unmask an unhealthy nexus between gift, conditional or duressed receipt, and assumptions of effectiveness. Such a notion might allow for expanding other measurements of value when assessing the achievement of human well-being. In this way, a Christian theological rationale may positively contribute to asserting characteristics inherent for well-being that exhibit the nature of the triune God in the world, and supplement deficiencies within dominant secular constructions.

Interpersonal Communication

A further dynamic of triune-being uncovered in our exploration thus far is that the divine persons actualize enrichment through personal engagement and dialogue. Intimate fellowship marks the divine relationality of enrichment. Yet, is such a characteristic imbued in human efforts to extend well-being? Are these qualities prioritized? Or, Are initiatives premised on impersonal knowledge and a disconnection from personal self-giving? When severed from interpersonal engagement, knowledge of the "other" may be reduced to an abstracted "knowledge" open to manipulation, rather than a knowing and being known attendant with enrichment.[43] Emmanuel Levinas intuits the importance of *personal* human interactions; arguing that personal face-to-face exchanges impose the presence of "other" to such an extent that the interaction propels responsibility for the "other."[44] Levinas says: "a face imposes itself upon me without my being able to be deaf to it or to forget it, that is, without my being able to suspend my responsibility for its distress."[45] Personal engagement often discloses the need, vulnerability and capacity of oneself and another. However, within the contours of human well-being, the temptation remains to generalize the "face" for efficiency, define it through algorithm, perceive it as image rather than physical reality, or ignore it as unwelcome imposition. Obviously, impersonal knowledge regarding sizeable populations or communities is useful in delivering various initiatives, but such methods can no doubt dilute the impression of the "face" of the other by reducing interpersonal engagement. The point here is not to undermine administrative efficiencies but rather to highlight the importance of relational drivers for human well-being, and to caution against the mere commodification of the human subject or the reduction of human subjects to a dataset. Certainly, Mark McIntosh locates in the Trinity the grounding of personal engagement, contending that the "inter-personal, trinitarian, ground of truth means that knowing and understanding always include personal involvement and transformation, delight in the illimitable richness of life, and reverence for the humility and availability to the other that marks authentic participation in truth."[46] Balthasar, likewise, places a high importance on the actual materiality of human individuals when it comes to defining the constituent factors of a *personal* encounter, saying:

> If I bump against a fellow human being, I discover two things especially: the border of my freedom and the reality of his [or her] freedom, for his [her] freedom only becomes real to me when two bodies encounter each other. And precisely because I can experience this reality as real, I realise that I cannot do anything about it. It is simply true, and I am forced to let it be true; and *only because of this hard experience of the not-I can human community arise*. This collision reveals the juxtaposition of freedoms that become present to each other, and so collision of freedoms becomes the presupposition for life together . . . only when we discover the mystery of the other, as mediated by the body, can true community arise. And, therefore, *community can never be organised from some neutral height (sociologically or politically) without eventually turning Persons into a number and without the living individual body becoming a piece of manipulable matter*. But where the clash of bodies is transformed into a mutual facing of one another—and it will do so because the physical senses are the occasion for mutual cognition and recognition—there and only there will arise that "between word"—or as we say, following the Greek term, "dia-logue."[47]

If we take the divine ontological parameters of well-being seriously, interpersonal communication and material interaction with the "other" may be far more necessary to genuine human enrichment than we might wish to admit. Enrichment between humans necessitates an imposition of responsibility for others that, while at times elicits joy, will also entail the relinquishment of comfortable detachment. In understanding the divine dynamic, Christians should exercise caution toward correlating reductive and impersonal knowledge with the enactment of another's enrichment. The quest to achieve a *breadth* of well-being (outcomes for as many as possible) may ironically undermine human well-being. Breadth of reach, made possible through impersonal mechanisms, might, in fact, be at the expense of a *depth* of enrichment. If well-being is not stimulated through mechanisms that encourage personal and mutual engagement, mechanisms may appear productive but fail to deliver authentic human enrichment.

Symbiotic Speech and Act

One of the more intriguing concepts of the intratrinitarian relations is the permeation of speech.[48] Scripture is replete with instances where the triune persons nourish and authenticate, through word and act, the other divine persons. The divine persons never engage in self-hypostatic praise but ecstatically affirm the worthy identity of the divine other. This affirmation coalesces with intratrinitarian responsibility and trust. The Father affirms the worth and righteous identity of the Son as "all things" are gifted to him (Mt 11:27; Jn 3:35; Eph 1:20–21). The Spirit is honored as the one sent to speak the word of the Father (Jn 16:13) and give glory to the Son (Jn 16:14). The Son trusts his spirit into the Father's hands at Golgotha (Lk 23:46), declaring the Father's faithful and constant love that would indeed "receive" the precious offering. In the economy, God demonstrates that the eternal nature of intratrinitarian speech is configured by both verbal and non-verbal kenotically-enriching communications.[49]

Karl Barth's interrogation of the Word of God leads him to state the simple fact that "God's Word means that God speaks."[50] Christ, as the incarnate Word of God (*logos*), is the pre-eminent exegesis of the divine identity in recognizable human grammar. For Barth, God's Word is therefore not mere random utterance, or "only talk"[51] but is directed speech for a purpose.[52] That purpose, according to the logic of Divine Self-Enrichment is the "life" of animated triune well-*being*. Divine speaking is not only a personal self-revelation of the truth of being—"what God speaks is never known anywhere in abstraction from God himself," but is commensurate with a divine act un-differentiated from God's Word—"That this revelation happened and how it happened is no accident . . . He is completely himself in this That and How."[53] God's purposeful speech, in the simplicity of God, means that God's speech is God's act, with no secondary movement abstracted from the speech.[54] Divine-word commensurate with divine-being saturates God's acts in the immanent and economic Trinity. As such, Barth says, "God always speaks a *concretissimum*."[55] That is to say, that God's Word is not something other than Godself; it is not abstracted from what God does but concretely expresses God's nature. The New and Old Testaments show a direct connection between Word and Creation, Word and Calling, Word and remission of sins, Word and miracle, Word and blessing.[56] As such, the nature of divine speech becomes highly relevant to the nature of human well-being; it reconfigures speech as an important proponent for advancing human enrichment. Shaped by ontic precedence, human speech should be considered as an external expression of inner content, as Peter Caseralla attests:

The highest function of an image appears in a word, for the insubstantiality of the image is fully overcome in a word. A word is a sensible sign filled with meaning in which signification emanates not from the sensible sign but from an interior and hidden act. Speech is therefore the outward expression of this dynamic inner word.[57]

From this standpoint, like its divinely predicated origin, human speech may be understood as exegesis of the individual, the community, or the organization. Resonant with the divine archetype, human speech is not extraneous to the person or organization; it is never mere speech. Instead, it represents the expression of the content of that which is speaking—the signification of an interior word. Such an idea is, however, not a call to an unattainable divine imitation. As I have already argued, God's simplicity ensures a symbiotic unity between speech and action. Not so for humans. Rather, what I intend to highlight here is that human participation in the divine conditions for well-being necessitates a closer intentional alignment between content and speech, word and act. This encapsulates the concept of "truth" in human speech, wherein words are consistent with content, not "mere talk" devoid of substance.[58] Truthful "speech," whether verbal or non-verbal, is the external and demonstrable communicative act consistent with inner content. Such a nexus is indeed evoked by Jesus when he says:

No good tree bears bad fruit, nor again does a bad tree bear good fruit; for each tree is known by its own fruit. Figs are not gathered from thorns, nor are grapes picked from a bramble bush. The good person out of the good treasure of the heart produces good, and the evil person out of evil treasure produces evil; for it is out of the abundance of the heart that the mouth speaks. (Luke 6:43–45)

Lies or hypocrisy represent a divergence of essence and form, content and act. Again, Jesus adumbrates the discord: "Woe to you, scribes and Pharisees, hypocrites! For you are like whitewashed tombs, which on the outside look beautiful but inside are full of the bones of the dead and of all kinds of uncleanness" (Mt 23:27). As a divine repetition, the nature of *enriching*-speech becomes not only characterized by truth but also by kenotic gift and receipt.[59] Indeed, the very concept of conversation in the English vernacular has gift and receipt at its center. Milbank explains:

The phrase "giffe-gaffe" is equivalent to our "give and take," and suggests that taking differs from giving merely by a single vowel. In an equally old variation, "the giffes and the gaffes," meaning "the gains and the losses," it is the gifts that are the takings. It is clear that there is some confusion here as to where giving ends and taking begins, and that what is crucial is not a distinction of actor and respondent, but the shuttling process of to-and-fro itself. This is confirmed by later uses of "giffe-gaffe" to mean uninhibited conversational interchange.[60]

Understanding speech, therefore, as a movement of giving and receiving allows us to perceive that effective and enriching speech requires a mechanism to give (the tongue, the pen, the gesture) and a mechanism to receive.[61] For meaning to be conveyed and received, these mechanisms need to have resonance and affinity. Put differently, speech needs to be in recognizable and receivable form. Following Jennings, for speech to be receivable it needs to be spoken kenotically, where it humbly learns and loves the language of those to whom it speaks. Jennings condenses this idea in beautiful rawness in relation to the Incarnation, saying, "Speak a language, speak a people. God speaks people, fluently. And God, with all the urgency that is with the Holy Spirit, wants the disciples of his only begotten Son to speak people fluently too."[62] Echoing the divine archetype, human speech should be considered as integral, not merely functional, to the purpose of enrichment. There is great power in word. However, too often human word becomes disconnected from purpose or power, shrivelled to a sound bite or a Tweet devoid of substance. And yet, both verbal and non-verbal speech should be harnessed for the expansion of well-being. Not only the content of communications, but its delivery, its wordedness, can either enrich or diminish well-being. For the Christian, what is communicated (content) and how it is communicated (form) should be understood as witnessing to the very nature of God, the God who is faithfully content, word and act.

These nascent reflections provoke challenging questions as to whether Churches, para-Church "faith" organizations or Christian individuals exude "mere talk" or substantival speech (truth) in the content and delivery of human well-being. Do "mission" statements exhibit a genuine connection between speech (exterior expression) and theological belief (interior content)? Does the content and delivery of well-being signify "Christian" theology or mimic secular cosmology? For the Church, the content of God's being should contour the content and pragmatics of its sociality both within the community and as witness to world. Encounters with the triune God should shape the interior dynamics of human well-being, as well as mold the exterior manifestation. In the absence of "speech" reflecting theological content, the notion of a specific "Christian" expression of well-being may merely exhibit an emptied-out notion; where there is no significant difference in the content of its "speech" compared to non-Christian expressions. The challenge here is to bring a closer symbiosis between the *content* of speech and its outward expression; where Christians derive the dynamics of progressing human enrichment from the revelation of who and *how* God is.

Christians should be alert to oft-hidden content or philosophical foundations of actions designed to promote "well-being" that are, in fact, contra to the expressed being of God. Replete with theological content, the torch of kenotic-enrichment might be shone upon the modes accompanying well-being (from scoping and design, policy and strategy, delivery, establishment of partnerships, and measurements of effectiveness) to reassess the nexus of content and praxis. A reassessment that advances well-being through speech and act that is permeated with the characteristics of triune *life*. The question prompted in the end is this: Do verbal and non-verbal "speech" express an exteriorized correspondence with the divine conditions for created well-being? If not, this may be an indicator that theological characteristics for well-being are being negotiated away in the face of a competing cultural or cosmological paradigm. And the challenge: to move from "mere talk" to radical revisioning of praxis; where Christians involved in advancing human well-being can offer a distinguished "Christian" witness to the world, contoured by divine dynamics.

Equal Being in Mutual Dependency

A documented problem plaguing the delivery of human well-being involves the asymmetry often present between those considered "donors" and "recipients"; between those with differing expressions of power.[63] Asymmetry between "givers" and "recipients" can precipitate the deforming of relational dynamics into manipulation or un-enriching domination or passivity. Similarly, potential imbalance can arise from a self-sufficient mindset that expresses itself toward the "other" in a manner that restricts mutuality; where a one-way direction from the "giver" to "recipient" regulates the relation.[64] Social and political scientist, Karl Deutsch, argues that this type of mentality construes power in a "narrow sense" where "output over intake, the ability to talk instead of listen" is prioritized; a power that is ultimately expressed as the "ability to afford not to learn."[65] Such a relational engagement arguably has greater correspondence with a divine ontology espoused in semi-homousian Trinitarian theologies, where a one-way paternal "sending" and a functionally subordinated Son to Father determines the eternal triune relations of origin.[66] In such theology, the Father is the active agent with primary authority regarding the triune relations—sending, giving, and generating—reflecting a hypostatic nature that essentially requires no receptivity for paternal being.[67] A theology of Divine Self-Enrichment, however, espouses a mutuality of tri-hypostatic dependence, where the worth of each divine person as giver *and receiver* is confirmed. In triune life, both giving and receiving echoes through the shared equality of hypostatic being.

However, cognisant of the ontological distinction between God and humanity, positing a divine replication of shared mutual engagement for humanity is not intended to elide the reality of asymmetry between classes of persons. Think, for instance, of parent and child, teacher and student, or carer and caree. Asymmetry in temporal relations is often quite unavoidable and, indeed, necessitated. Yet, the relevance of mutual engagement for an enriching interaction still holds. Indeed, the mutual need of the "other" is a necessity for self—"self is itself only by being in a state of flux stemming from 'incursions' of the other into the self and of the self into the other. The self is shaped by making space for the other and by giving space to the other."[68] While human differences in relational power exist, consistent with a theology of *imago Dei*, the inherent equal value of being human is never elided. This is quite different from neo-liberal definitions of human value, where people are generally valued on the basis of capacity and productivity, "for *what they are worth* rather than for *who they are*."[69] Yet, the intractable divine encryption of the mutual necessity of an "I" and a "thou" for personhood, meaning and enrichment is the ultimate signifier of true human value.[70] The significance of each human individual for the communal substance of existence remains true regardless of the capacity of the subjective "I" or "thou." Here, I am reminded of Joanna Leidenhag's consideration of autism and her subsequent rebuke of theologies that conflate personhood and human value with relational capacity.[71] In the "I-Thou" nature of personalized humanity relationality is a "given" quality, not merely an enacted capacity. Humans are intrinsically immersed in the shared nature of "I-Thou" relations simply by virtue of their existence. One does not become "more" or "less" human on account of capacities. The givenness of human relationality in their myriad forms (whether relatedness to God, to other humans, to the temporal world) are all embedded with the seen and unseen rhythms of the ontic nature of kenotic-enrichment, which includes not only giving but receiving. This rhythm is something that is lived and discovered, not conferred by mere ability or capacity.[72]

Brian Brock's contemplations in *Wondrously Wounded*, regarding the necessity of mutual relationality for the actualization of the Body of Christ (1 Cor 12), are helpful in extending an understanding of the requisite personal interchange integral to human well-being.[73] Brock alerts us to the fact that the healthy functioning of the body of Christ (actualized through gift and receipt between Spirit-infused persons) depends not on social status or some inherent individual "ability" but on what might be interpreted as a kenotic posture of humility. Brock notes, however, that humans often conflate the ability to receive enrichment with the appearance of a person's ability to affect such an outcome (i.e., their status or social capacity). Confusing appearance with ability may result, however, in a deprivation of the enrichment God intends.[74] Brock, using disability as an example, expresses it like this:

> The gift that someone with a disability might bring . . . cannot simply be said to rest with that individual (his or her disability), nor is it appropriate to say that it rests with those who receive it . . . *Gifts need to be discovered "in between" the bearer and recipient.* This in between is the particular theatre of operations of the Spirit who does not only *originate* the gifts but needs actively to *donate* them right into the middle of interpersonal relational space . . . Relinquishing the status markers that are everything to competitive and pecking order–attuned humans is the condition for the gifts God gives to become visible. The gift given by the disabled person, the poor person, the recovering addict, all those of low esteem *to the world*, emerges only through the *spiritual discernment* that is utterly certain that in the places where the eyes of fallen humanity expects nothing there is a *charisma* to be received.[75]

Unfortunately, it is not uncommon for initiatives promoting well-being to fail to recognize that "recipients" are humans endowed with intrinsic worth, able (whatever their bodily or psychological state) to enrich others including the so-called "beneficiary." Arguably, recognizing and integrating the value of both recipient and giver into Christian paradigms of well-being is to submit to a new phroneō (φρονέω), a new way of thinking, a divine way that is reconfigured for temporal life (Phil 2:5). In the temporality of creaturely existence, the inclination to express mutual dependence among equal beings does not mystically rescind the societal markers of relational asymmetry. What it does alter is the perspective on how "status markers" are no longer deemed the exclusive or predominant factors regulating the realization of human enrichment. Instead, the mere fact that another "is" holds the ineffable possibility of the gift or receipt of enriched being.

These embryonic reflections raise various questions for those oriented to enacting well-being, for example: How might we allow ourselves to be shaped by those we seek to serve? What might a "giver" (in a posture of self-giving receipt) receive or learn from a "beneficiary"? Are interactions of well-being based on erroneous and unacknowledged self-sufficiency of either participant? These questions seek to provoke praxis that inherently affirms the worth of the "other"; where gift and receipt moves toward equally configured mutuality. Without such mutuality of dependence, a danger to both identities may imperil well-being, where either human agency is reduced by the overwhelming encroachment of another or inflated by a self-sufficiency that refuses to receive.[76] Yet, it is also important to note the reality that integrating dependence and free agency in mutual responsibility often translates into a giving-of-self that is open to vulnerability and risk.[77] Such is the demonstrative revelation in the life-giving kenotic engagement of Christ at Calvary, where the nexus of vulnerability, self-giving and enrichment was expressed as "power-in-vulnerability."[78] In the shadows of a sinful world, commitment to mutuality and dependence for the sake of human well-being will be difficult, require personal effort, and, most likely, yield disappointment. However, it also holds the potential to be life-giving.[79] As in divinity, the human possibility for an enriched life erupts in the vulnerability of self-giving and receipt.

NOTES

1. John Milbank, "Can a Gift Be Given? Prolegomena to a Future Trinitarian Metaphysic," *Modern Theology* 11, no. 1 (1995): 120.

2. Thomas. F. Torrance, *Incarnation: The Person and Life of Christ*, ed. Robert T. Walker (Downers Grove, IL: IVP Academic, 2008), 233.

3. Miroslav Volf, "The Trinity Is Our Social Program: The Doctrine of the Trinity and the Shape of Social Engagement," *Modern Theology* 14, no. 3, (July 1998): 412.

4. Miroslav Volf, "Being as God Is," in *God's Life in Trinity*, eds. Miroslav Volf and Michael Welker (Minneapolis: Fortress Press, 2006), 5. Aquinas identifies three types of possible correspondences between God and humanity—equivocal, analogous and univocal. Thomas Aquinas, *Summa Theologica*, trans. Fathers of the English Dominican Province (Westminster: Christian Classics, 1981), www.corpusthomisticum.org/sth0000.html, 1.13.10. R Obj 3. See also John. M. Frame, *A History of Western Philosophy and Theology*, 1st ed. (Phillipsburg, NJ: P&R Publishing, 2015, 153.

5. Jacqueline Service, "Trinity, Aseity, and the Commensurability of the Incommensurate One," *St. Mark's Review*, no. 250 (2019): 63–76.

6. Sonderegger refers to this as "compatibilism." Katherine Sonderegger, *Systematic Theology: The Doctrine of God*, vol. 1 (Minneapolis: Fortress Press, 2015), xix.

7. LaCugna, *God for Us*, 379. A similar caution is presaged in Miroslav Volf's classic article "The Trinity Is Our Social Program."

8. Service, "Trinity, Aseity, and the Commensurability of the Incommensurate One," 73.

9. Fedorov's proposal is outlined in Paul Evdokimov, *Le Christ dans la pensée Rusee* (Paris: Cerf, 1970) and is discussed in Volf, "The Trinity Is Our Social Program," 401–7.

10. Volf, "The Trinity Is Our Social Program," 404.

11. There are some who may question whether humanity should be imitating Christ (*imitatio Christi*) or the Trinity (*imitatio Trinitatis*). I argue these are not mutually opposing concepts. Rather, it is through Christ that revelation of the immanent Trinity is provided. We cannot simply carve away examples of Jesus' life from its antecedent reality in the immanent Trinity. For example, Keith E. Johnson, "Imitatio Trinitatis: How Should We Imitate the Trinity," *Westminster Theological Journal* 75, no. 2 (2013): 317–34 contends that "we are also called to imitate the servant-leadership of Christ. Rather than imitating . . . a supposedly 'non-hierarchical' Trinity . . . Jesus instructs his disciples to emulate *his* leadership" (p. 329). On this basis, Johnson concludes that "the pattern for Christian humility is not some kind of intra-trinitarian kenosis (contra Hans Urs von Balthasar) but the *economic* self-emptying of the Son on the cross" (p. 329). What Johnson fails to comprehend is that in Christ, in the economic works of God, the immanent Trinity is revealed. If non-hierarchy can be

evidenced in Christ's leadership, it is because non-hierarchy is a feature of the triune God. Christ's example of self-emptying on the Cross is, likewise, the economic manifestation of the immanent reality and life of divine self-emptying among the triune persons. To argue otherwise runs the risk of tritheism and the dissolution of the unity of God. Furthermore, Johnson suggests that humanity "imitates God under the condition of sin" and that "we see God's love displayed *in the context of human rebellion and suffering*" (p. 324). Thus, he concludes, that human imitation should not be made of the triune relations (as no sin or rebellion exists *in se*) but rather of God's mode of relating to the world. We forgive, he says, because we see God's forgiveness toward humanity. Although, in one sense this is true, it is important to understand that the economic works of God are a "translation" of the immanent Trinity in the world (Volf, "The Trinity Is Our Social Program," 414). One could characterize the forgiveness and grace extended to humanity as manifestations of triune kenotic-enrichment in God's encounter with the world of not-God. Forgiveness and grace are the manifestation of divine giving for the enrichment of humanity.

12. Kathryn Tanner and Keith E. Johnson both note the substantial difference between God's simple perichoretic intra-relationality and humanity's non-simple relationality. Johnson argues that, unlike God, humans do not "indwell one another such that their subjectivities overlap." Johnson, "Imitatio Trinitatis," 322. Tanner also clarifies that "unlike the divine Persons, we exist apart from our relations with others." Kathryn Tanner, *Christ the Key* (Cambridge: Cambridge University Press, 2010), 244–25.

13. Thomas Aquinas, *Summa Theologiae*, trans. Fathers of the English Dominican Province (Westminster: Christian Classics, 1981), corpusthomisticum.org/sth0000.html, 1a.47.1.

14. Sergeĭ Bulgakov, *The Comforter*, trans Boris Jakim (Grand Rapids: Eerdmans, 2004), 207. Originally published as *Uteshitel'* [The Comforter]. Pt 2. of *O bogochelovechestve* (Paris: YMCA-Press, 1936). Original italics.

15. Sergiĭ Bulgakov, *The Bride of the Lamb*, trans. Boris Jakim (Grand Rapids, MI: Eerdmans, 2002), 58. Originally published as *Nevesta agntsa* [The Bride of the Lamb]. Pt 3 of *O bogochelovechestve* (Paris: YMCA-Press, 1945).

16. Bulgakov insists, "The becoming world . . . is only in a state of *potentiality*, which the world must actualize in itself." Bulgakov, *The Lamb of God*, 127.

17. Robert W. Jenson, *Systematic Theology: The Works of God*, volume 2 (New York: Oxford University Press, 1999), 7–8.

18. Athanasius, likewise, connects creation and salvation to the same divine Word, saying: "it is first necessary to speak about the creation of the universe and its maker, God, so that one may thus worthily reflect that its recreation was accomplished by the Word who created it in the beginning. For it will appear not all contradictory if the Father works its salvation in the same one by whom he created it." Athanasius, *On the Incarnation*, §2, 53.

19. 1 Corinthians 13:2.

20. Daniel W. Hardy, *God's Ways with the World: Thinking and Practising Christian Faith* (Edinburgh: T&T Clark, 1996), 84.

21. See also, for example, Proverbs 18:21 that affirms the dual possibilities resulting from a conversation when it says, "Death and life are in the power of the tongue, and those who love it will eat its fruits."

22. Daniel W. Hardy et al., *Wording a Radiance: Parting Conversations on God and the Church* (London: SCM, 2010), 47.

23. Zizioluas refers to a similar concept when he explicates sin as the resistance to communion. See John Zizioulas, *Being as Communion: Studies in Personhood and the Church* (London: Darton, Longman & Todd, 1985), 101–3.

24. Bulgakov, *Lamb of God*, 159; Bulgakov, *Bride of the Lamb*, 50–51; 60.

25. Donald MacKinnon, *The Stripping of the Altars* (London: Fontana, 1969); John C. McDowell, Scott A. Kirkland and Ashley John Moyse, eds., *Kenotic Ecclesiology: Select Writings of Donald M. MacKinnon* (Minneapolis: Fortress Press, 2016); Samuel Youngs, *Making Christ Real: The Peril and Promise of Kenosis* (Eugene, OR: Pickwick Publishing, 2022); Martyn Percy, "Kenotic Ecclesiology and the Disestablishment of the Church of England under the Reign of Charles III," *Journal of Anglican Studies*, 2023, 1–17; Gyrid Kristine Gunnes, "An Ecclesiology of a Queer Kenosis? Risk and Ambivalence at Our Lady, Trondheim, in Light of the Queer Theology on Kenosis of Marcella Althaus-Reid," *Feminist Theology* 28, no. 2 (2020): 216–30; Timothy G. Connor, *The Kenotic Trajectory of the Church in Donald MacKinnon's Theology: From Galilee to Jerusalem to Galilee* (London: T&T Clark, 2013); Michael J. Gorman, *Inhabiting the Cruciform God: Kenosis, Justification, and Theosis in Paul's Narrative Soteriology* (Grand Rapids, MI: William B. Eerdmans Publishing, 2009); and Michael J. Gorman, *Cruciformity: Paul's Narrative Spirituality of the Cross* (Grand Rapids, MI: W.B. Eerdmans Pub, 2001).

26. J. S. Mill, *On Liberty, Considerations on Representative Government*, ed. J. M. Dent (London: Everyman, 1993), 81. Mill argues that even in a democracy we can find ourselves under a kind of tyranny and therefore what is needed is the protection of liberty in the following terms—"protection also against the tyranny of the prevailing opinion and feeling; against the tendency of society to impose . . . its own ideas and practices as rules of conduct on those who dissent from them." See page 73 of the same work.

27. Dietrich Bonhoeffer, *Dietrich Bonhoeffer Works: Creation and Fall: A Theological Exposition of Genesis 1–3*, vol. 3, eds. John W. De Gruchy, and Douglas S. Bax (Minneapolis: Fortress Press, 2004), 63.

28. Bonhoeffer, *Creation and Fall*, 63.

29. Willie James Jennings, *Acts: A Theological Commentary on the Bible* (Louisville, KY: Presbyterian Publishing Corporation, 2017), 193.

30. Hans Urs von Balthasar, *Two Sisters in the Spirit: Thérèse of Lisieux and Elizabeth of the Trinity* (San Francisco: Ignatius, 1992), 323.

31. McIntosh, "Hans Urs Von Balthasar," 363. As noted previously, alert to the danger of a theologically-induced coercive servility, feminist theologians have continued to contest and reject the legitimacy of kenosis as a beneficial theological category. Daphne Hampson, grappling with the theme of kenosis from Philippians 2, fails to see how "self-emptying and self-abnegation is . . . helpful as a paradigm" to women oppressed by enforced hierarchy and domination. Daphne Hampson, *Theology and*

Feminism (Oxford: Basil Blackwell, 1990), 155. The revised and invigorated vision of the features of kenosis through the lens of kenotic-enrichment may yet go some way to revive kenosis with positive legitimacy.

32. Balthasar, *Two Sisters in the Spirit*, 323.

33. Balthasar, *Two Sisters in the Spirit*, 253.

34. Balthasar, *Two Sisters in the Spirit*, 253. My italics. See also Oliver Davies who notes that human compassion is activated through a kenotically contoured "dispossessive intentionality" that accords with voluntary choice. Oliver Davies, *A Theology of Compassion* (London: SCM Press, 2001), 16–18.

35. 2 Cor 9:7.

36. Michael Welker, *God the Revealed: Christology*, translated by Douglas W. Stott (Grand Rapids, MI: William B. Eerdmans Publishing, 2013), 223–24. Original italics.

37. Welker extends Wolfgang Huber's original idea that defines the content of both the "law and the reign of God" as an orientation to an *"ethos of free self-limitation."* Wolfgang Huber, *Konflikt und Konsens. Studien zur Ethik der Verantwortung* (München: Kaiser, 1990), 205ff, in Welker, *God the Revealed*, 223–24.

38. Welker, *God the Revealed*, 224.

39. Welker, *God the Revealed*, 225.

40. Welker, *God the Revealed*, 225. My italics.

41. In cases of human incapacity, such as extreme cognitive or physical impairment, further nuancing of this general affirmation would be required.

42. Stirrat and Henkel raise the issue of freely-gifted giving, saying "the problem with the pure gift is . . . the seemingly lack of reciprocity: that the receiver is left in a position of indebtedness and powerlessness." See R. L. Stirrat, and H. Henkel, "The Development Gift: The Problem of Reciprocity in the NGO world," *The Annals of the American Academy of Political and Social Science* 554, no. 1 (1997), 73.

43. McIntosh advocates that the "world's own tendencies to reductive and impersonal knowledge need to be immersed in the habit of self-giving love." McIntosh, "Hans Urs Von Balthasar," 364.

44. Emmanuel Levinas, *Ethics and Infinity: Conversations with Philippe Nemo* (Pittsburgh: Duquesne University Press, 1985), 97–99.

45. Emmanuel Levinas, *Basic Philosophical Writings*, ed. Adriaan R. Peperzak, Simon Critchley and Robert Bernasconi (Bloomington: Indiana University Press, 1996), 54.

46. McIntosh, "Hans Urs Von Balthasar," 364.

47. Hans Urs von Balthasar, *Epilogue*, trans. Edward T. Oakes, SJ (San Francisco: Ignatius Press, 1991), 104. First italics are original. The second italics are mine.

48. When I refer to speech I am referring to both verbal and non-verbal communication.

49. Hans Urs von Balthasar, *My Work: In Retrospect*, trans. Brian McNeil (San Francisco: Ignatius, 1993), 116; McIntosh, "Hans Urs Von Balthasar," 356.

50. Karl Barth, *Church Dogmatics: The Doctrine of the Word of God. Part* 1, vol. 1, eds. G. W. Bromiley and T. F. Torrance (Edinburgh: T&T Clark, 1975), 132. Hereafter *CD I/1*.

51. Barth, *CD I/1*, 143.

52. Barth, *CD I/1*, 139.
53. Barth, *CD I/1*, 137, 297.
54. Barth, *CD I/1*, 143.
55. Barth, *CD I/1*, 137.
56. Barth, *CD I/1*, 144.
57. Peter. J. Caseralla, "The Expression and Form of the Word: Trinitarian Hermeneutics and the Sacramentality of Language in Hans Urs Von Balthasar's Theology," *Renascence* 48, no. 2 (1996): 123.
58. Barth, *CD I/1*, 143.
59. This is not to elide the ethical tensions that may arise where the strict obfuscation of truth may, in fact, elicit another's well-being. For example, where lying to protect the whereabouts of a vulnerable person from a perpetrator may, in fact, secure a future enrichment.
60. Milbank, "Can a Gift Be Given?" 119–20.
61. Barth, *CD I/1*, 151.
62. Jennings, *Acts*, 29–30.
63. This is borne out in the aid and development industry in the delivery of programs for the alleviation of poverty and the well-being of humanity. Stirrat and Henkel identify that the donor/donee relationship is tainted by an "asymmetry between givers and receivers" where even "acts of pure giving" seemingly free of reciprocal obligation "may become a form of patronage and a means of control." Stirrat and Henkel, "The Development Gift," 72–75. Moore, likewise, identifies a problematic inequality in sponsor-child relationships in Alana Moore, "'Whatever You Did for One of the Least of These Brothers and Sisters of Mine': Christianity and the Dilemmas of Child Sponsorship," *St Mark's Review*, no. 261 (2022): 23–40.
64. Williams says, "for created being to reflect divine being, it does not have to aspire to some illusion of self-sufficiency." Rowan Williams, "Balthasar and the Trinity" in *The Cambridge Companion to Hans Urs Von Balthasar*, eds. Edward T. Oakes, SJ and David Moss (Cambridge Companions to Religion. Cambridge: Cambridge University Press, 2004), 42.
65. Karl Wolfgang Deutsch, *The Nerves of Government: Models of Political Communication and Control* (New York: The Free Press, 1966).
66. For examples of this type of Trinitarian theology see Wayne Grudem, *Systematic Theology: An Introduction to Biblical Doctrine* (Grand Rapids, MI: Zondervan, 1994), 250; and Bruce A. Ware, *Father, Son and Holy Spirit: Relationships, Roles, and Relevance* (Wheaton, IL: Crossway, 2005), 71.
67. *Inter alia* the human implications drawn from such a triune ontology is one of female subordination to a male counterpart with a correlated asymmetry of authority and function. See for an example of this type of correlation in Bruce A. Ware, "How Shall We Think about the Trinity?" in *God under Fire*, eds. Douglas S. Huffman and Eric L. Johnson (Grand Rapids, MI: Zondervan, 2002), 270. For a contestation of Ware's views see Scott D. Harrower, "Bruce Ware's Trinitarian Methodology," in *Trinity without Hierarchy: Reclaiming Nicene Orthodoxy in Evangelical Theology*, eds. Michael F. Bird and Scott D. Harrower (Grand Rapids, MI: 2019), 207–23.
68. Volf, "The Trinity Is Our Social Program," 410.

69. Emanuel De Kadt, "Should God Play a Role in Development?" *Journal of International Development* 21, no. 6 (2009): 783. Original italics.

70. Macmurray emphasizes how "the personal relations of persons is constitutive of personal existence; that there can be no man until there are at least two men in communion." John Macmurray, *Persons in Relation: Being the Gifford Lectures Delivered in the University of Glasgow in 1954* (London: Faber and Faber, 1970), 12.

71. Joanna Leidenhag, "The Challenge of Autism for Relational Approaches to Theological Anthropology," *International Journal of Systematic Theology* 23, no. 1 (2021), 109–34. For Ledienhag's reference to Spaemann's essay, "Are All Human Being Persons?" see Robert Spaemann, *Persons: The Difference between "Someone" and "Something,"* trans. Oliver O'Donovan (Oxford: Oxford University Press, 2017).

72. Oliver O'Donovan. "Again, Who Is a Person?" in *On Moral Medicine: Theological Perspectives in Medical Ethics*, 3rd ed., edited by M. Therese Lysaught et al. (Grand Rapids, MI: William B. Eerdmans Publishing Company, 2012), 609.

73. Brian Brock, *Wondrously Wounded: Theology, Disability, and the Body of Christ* (Waco, TX: Baylor University Press, 2019), 202ff.

74. Brian Brock, *Wondrously Wounded*, 220.

75. Brian Brock, *Wondrously Wounded*, 220–21. Original italics.

76. Volf expresses a similar notion when he argues, "Non-assertiveness of the self in the presence of the other puts the self in danger either of dissolving into the other or being smothered by the other; non-deference of the other before the self, puts weak selves who are unable to assert themselves in danger of being either manipulated or violated." Volf, "The Trinity Is Our Social Program," 410. Original italics.

77. Donald Mackinnon states in a chapter entitled "Kenosis and Establishment" in *The Stripping of the Altars*, that a Christologically contoured kenosis requires the Christian to "live an exposed life . . . to be stripped of the kind of security that tradition, whether ecclesiological or institutional, easily bestows." See also John C. McDowell, Scott A. Kirkland and Ashley John Moyse, eds., *Kenotic Ecclesiology: Select Writings of Donald M. MacKinnon* (Minneapolis: Fortress Press, 2016), 190.

78. Coakley, *Powers and Submissions*, 5.

79. The temporal delay or disconnect between kenosis and enrichment has continuity with Welker's noting of a similar twofold reality attending his concept of "self-withdrawal." Welker states, that "creative self-withdrawal . . . can often seemingly lead nowhere . . . elicit no discernible mutual interplay or interaction of any tangible life transformation" and yet "even in the midst of the inconspicuousness of its concrete activity God's power is nonetheless discerned—there one can indeed anticipate that the good seed will eventually be enormously fruitful." Welker, *God the Revealed*, 232–33.

Chapter 8

Epilogue

The Doxological Posture of Enrichment

As I have pressed with some emphasis, the recognition of the divine context and contours for creaturely well-being is not advocacy for a Pelagian notion that situates the attainment of well-being as a self-enclosed human achievement. Instead, the enriching purposes of God for humanity are premised on the eternal self-giving of the life of God. Godself, as the one who *is life*, confers "on the world the conditions *for life*."[1] While the eschaton provides the final horizon of creation's communion with the triune God, the Holy Spirit moves to envelop human creatures in the "now" of proleptic participation. The Spirit draws humanity toward the fullness of life by "re-orienting the human will and habitude . . . *back to God*."[2] Saying this is not, however, to restrict the divine impetus for creaturely well-being to the domain of the "sacred" or the confines of the Church, where Christians consider themselves to have a monopoly over actualizing human well-being. Inklings of well-being that intimate divine content, wherever found, might best be acknowledged as creaturely repetitions of the contours of divine life, albeit deprived of the truthful increase through the Christ-directed work of the Spirit (2 Cor 3:18). Such a thought might well reflect the difference between the universal imaging of God in all humanity and the particular reconfiguring into the *likeness* of God for believers through worship.[3] Simply put, divine orientation precedes human transformation.

The enrichment of humanity, as a creaturely reiteration of divine ontology, is dependent on the transformative movement of the Spirit toward the kenotic pattern of the ways of God. Oliver Davies espouses a similar idea when he argues that faith leads to the intertwining of human existence with the kenotic patterning displayed in the Incarnation. Davies says, "Jesus is the kenosis of God, given to us as love, whom *we receive in a parallel motion* of kenotic love as recognition-affirmation and obedient following, or discipleship."[4] Only in harmony with the kenotically-enriching pattern of

God's being is human life transformed. As David Bentley Hart insists, "only God can join us to God" and only God's ways can bring about an enriched life.[5] The Spirit invites humanity into the life of God in a manner consistent with the nature of God. That is, human interaction with God is an envelopment in the ways of God such that enriching-kenosis is manifest. In early church Trinitarian theology, the Holy Spirit is not only referred to as the "bond of love" (*vinculum caritatis*) between the Father and the Son but also as the "perfector" of the love within the immanent Trinity.[6] As the "perfector," the Spirit resounds in *ekstasis*—that movement of love which is outwards and toward the other. The Spirit is "that other in whom Father and Son meet 'again,' in the commonality of their love for another."[7] In the works of God *ad extra* the Spirit, who opens divine joy of love within the Trinity, is the same one that "makes the divine joy open to the otherness of what is not divine, of creation."[8] And so, just as the Spirit completes and perfects the Trinity's life immanently, the Spirit draws humanity into the enriching-kenosis of divine life and "refashions humanity after the likeness of God."[9] This refashioning, experienced with startling power at Pentecost, is, according to Willie James Jennings, "the revolution of the intimate. This is the beginning of a community broken open . . . turned out by the Spirit."[10] This Spirit-filled community is, like its Creator, called into the movement of kenotic-enrichment that unfolds outwards as a blessings of life. Without the Spirit, humanity senses the contours of well-being, but the unveiling of the Creator's work remains restricted, bound by intellectual narrowness or self-sufficient works devoid of divine propulsion. Pope Paul VI in *Populorum Progressio* hints at such a notion, saying a

> narrow humanism, closed in on itself and not open to the values of the spirit and to God *who is their source*, could achieve apparent success, for man can set about organising terrestrial realities without God. But closed off from God, they will end up being directed against man. A humanism closed off from other realities becomes inhuman.[11]

Indeed, apart from the Spirit, who is "the amniotic fluid in which our knowledge of God takes form," human efforts to actualize enrichment will remain well-intentioned but inadequate.[12]

Resembling triune life, worshipful self-giving is symbiotic with communion in, and reception of, enrichment. Creaturely participation *in* God's life is only possible when it mirrors the manner *of* God's life; it requires a giving of oneself and the voluntary receipt of God's gift of Godself. Mary, *Theotokos*, is a prototype for such a way. She is, according to Elizabeth Behr-Seigel, the "eschatological sign" preceding Pentecost, demonstrating how life is attained in the surrender of a participatory response to the Holy Spirit.[13] The mode of

Epilogue 171

God's life, that Mary embodies, is the only mode able to materialize divinely-orchestrated life in the world. The Annunciation narrative is demonstrative here. Mary freely participates in the pattern of the kenotically-enriching life of God as she consents to being God's "favoured one" and agrees to the Spirit's closeness (Lk 1:38). The prophetic utterances of her enrichment, her "blessedness" (Lk 1:42, 48), come as she gives herself to receive divinely initiated pregnancy. In the freedom of volunteered agency, Mary kenotically declares herself "the slave of the Lord" (Lk 1:38). This self-referential is, though, no truncated-kenosis. Just as the persons of the Trinity give and receive through free self-positing to the other divine persons, so Mary *gifts herself* to divine purpose for the life of the world. The nature of Mary's agreement to God's purposes is located in the use of the word δούλη—"slave." It is Mary who renders herself as "slave." This—a designation, a posture of being—is self-given and not imposed, and resolutely oriented to the beauty, truth and goodness of the life of God for enrichment to be realized. Interestingly, Acts 2:18 (one other of the only three occurrences of δούλη in Luke-Acts) mirrors the same pattern that connects freely-entered "slavery" with enrichment—"Even upon my slaves, both men and women, in those days I will pour out my Spirit." Again, human participation *in* God's life reflects the manner *of* God's life. Receiving the Holy Spirit occurs in the synchronous giving-of-self to the freedom of the divine master. The utter relinquishment of self to God is symbiotic with the receipt of life and being.[14] Mary's engagement with the divine act of Incarnation is prototypical for human union with God.[15] That is, she demonstrates that the mode of human participation *in* God's life is premised on the eternal divine pattern; it requires a relinquishment of self—a kenosis. As Klaus Hemmerle envisages—"Trinitarian ontology is not only something thought contains, but something thought carries out . . . with one's thinking and speaking—but also, therefore, with one's very exist-ence—*to enter into its rhythm oneself.*"[16] The nature of Mary's cooperation with the divine purpose of the Son's Incarnation is her entering into the rhythm, into the pattern of God's life; a patterning that continues in the economy of the Son's life and is the ontological context for the possibility of humanity's enrichment.

The "I am" sayings of Jesus in John's Gospel, likewise, evidence that communion *in* the life of God requires an alignment *to* the life of God. In other words, the gift of divine life is only received through a divinely-contoured kenotic response. In each of the "I am" sayings, concrete features of the human response to receive divinely enriched life and well-being are elucidated[17]—"I am the bread of life. Whoever *comes to me* will never be hungry, and whoever *believes in me* will never be thirsty" (Jn 6:35); "I am the light of the world. Whoever *follows me* will never walk in darkness but will have the light of life" (Jn 8:12); "I am the gate. Whoever *enters by me* will be saved and will . . . find pasture" (Jn 10:9); "I am the good shepherd . . .

they will *listen to my voice*" (Jn 10:11, 16); "I am the resurrection and the life. Those who *believe in me* . . . will live" (Jn 11:25); "I am the way, the truth and the life. No one *comes* to the Father except *through me*" (Jn 14:6); "I am the vine . . . Those who *abide in me* and I in them bear much fruit" (Jn 15:5). The participatory verbs in each of these sayings is a responsive choice of self-giving to divinity. "Believe," "follow," "enter," "listen," "come," "abide"—each response expresses the relinquishing of self-determination and yields to the divine offer. These kenotic responses are congruent with the pattern of the divine ontology in which life and well-being is realized.

The kenotic movement that inheres with triune life echoes through the economic work of God, and, in turn, is the deep patterning through which humanity enters into a life of communion with God. Like *Theotokos*, humanity is called to a life that voluntarily gives itself to the living God—"Here I am, the servant of the Lord" (Lk 1:38). The way of kenotic-enrichment is likewise woven into the very markers of ecclesial reality, where the finite giving of oneself to baptismal waters, eucharistic participation, scriptural formation and the sacrifice of praise reprises the infinite life of God. Each a movement of kenosis, a yielding and receipt, that simultaneously partakes in and proclaims the life of God. The performative proclamation and reorientation to God's ways pulses in doxology. Enacting well-being is ultimately an act of *worship*, defined perceptively by Hardy as "ontological recognition with its correlative orientation of life."[18] The fullness of life opens itself as a vibrant potentiality through worship that recognizes the dynamics of the all-blessed Trinity and lives surrendered into this truth. Again, Hardy articulates this well, saying: "The ontological recognition of well-being, and the reorientation which accompanies it, are the characteristic activities which occur in worship, where well-being is ascribed to God as his perfection and human beings thereby find the possibility of well-being for themselves."[19]

In construing a systematic ontology of triune well-being, I have endeavored to explore the complex contouring that undergirds that which, on face value, appears as self-evident—that God enjoys all-blessedness. In so doing I have attempted, in some measure, to undertake what Donald MacKinnon encourages for the shaping of the theological task—to unify "a fusion of intellectual and scholarly honesty with practical, personal commitment, of metaphysical thought both rigorous and questioning with sense of human frailty and limitation."[20] This book also provisionally answers what has been a long-term personal question for me: Why does the experience of the "fullness of life" promised by Jesus in John 10:10 tend to elude us? The burgeoning riposte that I have arrived at is that we inherently resist its mode of actualization—as Jesus said, "those who *lose their life* for my sake *will find it*" (Mt 16:25). In considering the interior life of the triune God of well-being, the all-blessed Trinity, we glimpse, emergently, how *life* is dialectically but not oppositionally actualized through self-giving. To experience creaturely well-being is ultimately an invitation to be swathed in the worshipful echo of the "movement which *agape* itself is,"[21] to be enveloped into the ways of the triune Creator, the Creator who gives *life* to the world by *Being* the life of the world.

NOTES

1. Daniel W. Hardy, *Jubilate: Theology in Praise,* ed. David F. Ford (London: Darton, Longman & Todd, 1984), 214. My italics.

2. Daniel Hayes, "The Metaphysics of Christian Ethics: Radical Orthodoxy and Theosis," *Heythrop Journal* 52, no. 4 (2011): 669.

3. Daniela C. Augustine, "Image, Spirit and Theosis: Imaging God in an Image-Distorting World," in *The Image of God in an Image Driven Age: Explorations in Theological Anthropology*, eds. Beth Felker-Jones and Jefferey Barbeau (Downers Grove, IL: InterVarsity Press, 2016), 173. Nonna Verna Harrison and Elizabeth Theokritoff, "The Human Person as Image and Likeness of God," in *The Cambridge Companion to Orthodox Christian Theology*, ed. Mary B. Cunningham (Cambridge: Cambridge University Press, 2008), 78–92.

4. Oliver Davies, *A Theology of Compassion* (London: SCM Press, 2001), 223. My italics.

5. David Bentley Hart, *The Beauty of the Infinite: The Aesthetics of Christian Truth* (Grand Rapids, IL: Eerdmans, 2003), 179.

6. Hart, *The Beauty of the Infinite*, 175–76.

7. Dumitru Staniloae, *Theology and the Church*, trans. Robert Barringer (Crestwood: St. Vladimir's Seminary Press, 1980), 93–94. See Hart, *The Beauty of the Infinite*, 176.

8. Hart, *The Beauty of the Infinite*, 177.

9. Hart, *The Beauty of the Infinite*, 179.

10. Jennings, *Acts*, 27–28.

11. Paul VI, *Populorum Progressio* [On the Development of Peoples], Vatican Website, March 26, 1967, sec. 42, w2.vatican.va/content/paul-vi/en/encyclicals/documents/hf_p-vi_enc_26031967_populorum.html. My italics.

12. Andrew Louth, *Discerning the Mystery: An Essay on the Nature of Theology* (Oxford: Clarendon Press, 1983), 65. Using the phrase "amniotic fluid" is not to suggest that the Holy Spirit is an impersonal agent.

13. Elizabeth Behr-Sigel, *The Ministry of Women in the Church*, trans. Steven Bigham (New York: St Vladimir's Seminary Press, 1991), 202.

14. "Being" here does not infer the givenness of existent being of human biological necessity, the kind that Zizioulas refers to as "hypostasis of biological existence," but is the notion of a fullness of true being more akin to Zizioulas' "hypostasis of ecclesial

existence." See John D. Zizioulas, *Being as Communion: Studies in Personhood and the Church* (London: Darton, Longman & Todd, 1985), 50–56.

15. Behr-Sigel, referring to Mary's complicity with the Holy Spirit, speaks of her as "eschatological sign: she is walking ahead of [humankind] and indicating the end toward which everyone is moving." Behr-Sigel, *The Ministry of Women in the Church*, 202.

16. Klaus Hemmerle, *Theses towards a Trinitarian Ontology*, trans. Stephen Churchyard (Brooklyn, NY: Angelico Press, 2020), 61.

17. These sayings are not merely heralding a realized eschatology, but a "futurist eschatology" with eternal spiritual consequences, particularly in the case of John 11. See D. A. Carson, *The Gospel According to John* (Leicester, England: InterVarsity Press, 1991), 413–14.

18. Daniel. W. Hardy, *God's Ways with the World: Thinking and Practising Christian Faith* (Edinburgh: T&T Clark, 1996), 21.

19. Hardy, *God's Ways with the World*, 23.

20. Donald MacKinnon, *Themes in Theology: The Three-Fold Cord: Essays in Philosophy, Politics, and Theology* (Edinburgh: T. & T. Clark, 1987), 14.

21. Hemmerle, *Theses towards a Trinitarian Ontology*, 35.

Bibliography

Anselm. *Incarnation of the Word*. Vol. 7 of *The Complete Philosophical and Theological Treatises of Anselm of Canterbury*. Translated by Jasper Hopkins and Herbert Richardson. Minneapolis: Arthur J. Banning Press, 2000.

Aquinas, Thomas. *Summa Theologiae*. Translated by Fathers of the English Dominican Province. Westminster: Christian Classics, 1981. www.corpusthomisticum.org/sth0000.html.

Aristotle. *Nicomachean Ethics*. Translated by Robert C. Bartlett and Susan D. Collins. *Aristotle's Nicomachean Ethics: A New Translation*. Chicago: University of Chicago Press, 2011.

Aristotle. *Rhetoric*. Translated by George A. Kennedy. *Aristotle: On Rhetoric: A Theory of Civic Discourse*. 2nd ed. New York: Oxford University Press, 2007.

Arjakovsky, Antoine. "The Sophiology of Father Sergius Bulgakov and Contemporary Western Theology." *St Vladimir's Theological Quarterly*, 49, nos. 1–2 (2005): 219–35.

Arndt, William. F., Frederick. W. Danker, and Walter Bauer. *A Greek-English Lexicon of the New Testament and Other Early Christian Literature*. 3rd ed. Chicago: University of Chicago Press, 2000.

Athanasius, *On the Incarnation*. Translated by John Behr. Yonkers, NY: St Vladimir's Seminary Press, 2011.

Augustine. "The Confessions of Saint Augustine." In *A Select Library of Nicene and Post-Nicene Fathers of the Christian Church: 1886–1889*, 28 vols. in 2 series, eds. Philip Schaff and H. Wace. Reprinted Grand Rapids, MI: Eerdmans, 1956.

Augustine, Daniela C. "Image, Spirit and Theosis: Imaging God in an Image-Distorting World." In *The Image of God in an Image Driven Age: Explorations in Theological Anthropology,* edited by Beth Felker-Jones and Jefferey Barbeau, 173–88. Downers Grove, IL: InterVarsity Press, 2016.

Ayres, Lewis. *Augustine and the Trinity*. Cambridge: Cambridge University Press, 2010.

Ayres, Lewis. "The Fundamental Grammar of Augustine's Trinitarian Theology." In *Augustine and His Critics*, edited by Robert Dodaro and George Lawless, 51–75. London: Routledge, 2000.

Ayres, Lewis. *Nicaea and Its Legacy: An Approach to Fourth-Century Trinitarian Theology.* Oxford: Oxford University Press, 2004.

Ayres, Lewis. "Remember That You Are Catholic (Serm. 52.2): Augustine on the Unity of the Triune God." *Journal of Early Christian Studies* 8, no. 1 (2000): 39–82.

Baillie, D. M. *God Was in Christ.* London: Faber and Faber Ltd, 1955.

Balthasar, Hans Urs von. *Epilogue.* Translated by Edward T. Oakes, SJ. San Francisco: Ignatius Press, 1991.

Balthasar, Hans Urs von. *Glory of the Lord: A Theological Aesthetics*, ed. John Riches, vol. 6, *Theology: The Old Covenant.* Translated by Brian McNeil C.R.V and Erasmo Leiva-Merikakis. San Francisco: Ignatius, 1991. Originally published as *Herrlichkeit: Eine theologische, Ästhetik*, Band III, 2: *Theologie*, Teil I: *Alter Bund.* Einsiedeln: Johannes Verlag, 1967.

Balthasar, Hans Urs von. *Glory of the Lord: A Theological Aesthetics*, ed. John Riches, vol. 7, *Theology: The New Covenant.* Translated by Brian McNeil C.R.V. San Francisco: Ignatius, 1989. Originally published as *Herrlichkeit: Eine theologische, Asthetik*, Band III, 2: *Theologie*, Teil 2: *Neuer Bund.* Einsiedeln: Johannes-Verlag, 1969.

Balthasar, Hans Urs von. *Heart of the World.* Translated by Erasmo S. Leiva. San Francisco: Ignatius, 1979.

Balthasar, Hans Urs von. *Love Alone: The Way of Revelation: A Theological Perspective.* Translated by Alexander Dru. London: Burns & Oats Ltd, 1968.

Balthasar, Hans Urs von. *"Mysterium Paschale": The Mystery of Easter.* Translated by Aiden Nichols. San Francisco: Ignatius, 1990.

Balthasar, Hans Urs von. *My Work: In Retrospect.* Translated by Brian McNeil. San Francisco: Ignatius, 1993.

Balthasar, Hans Urs von. *Presence and Thought: An Essay on the Religious Philosophy of Gregory of Nyssa.* Translated by Mark Sebanc. San Francisco: Ignatius Press. 1995.

Balthasar, Hans Urs von, *Theo-Drama: Theological Dramatic Theory.* Translated by Graham Harrison. *Vol 2. The Dramatis Personae: Man in God.* San Francisco: Ignatius, 1990. Originally published as *Theodramatik. Bd. II: Die Personen des Spiels. Teil 1: Der Mensch in Gott.* Einsiedeln: Johannes Verlag. 1976.

Balthasar, Hans Urs von. *Theo-Drama: Theological Dramatic Theory.* Translated by Graham Harrison. *Vol 3. The Dramatis Personae: Persons in Christ.* San Francisco: Ignatius, 1992. Originally published as *Theodramatik: Bd. II: Die Personen des Spiels. Teil II: Die Personen in Christus.* Einsiedeln: Johannes Verlag, 1978.

Balthasar, Hans Urs von. *Theo-Drama: Theological Dramatic Theory.* Translated by Graham Harrison. *Vol 4. The Action.* San Francisco: Ignatius, 1994. Originally published as *Theodramatik: Bd. III: Die Handlung.* Einsiedeln: Johannes Verlag, 1980.

Balthasar, Hans Urs von. *Theo-Drama: Theological Dramatic Theory.* Translated by Graham Harrison. *Vol 5. The Last Act.* San Francisco: Ignatius, 1998. Originally published as *Theodramatik: Bd. IV: Das Endspiel.* Einsiedeln: Johannes Verlag, 1983.

Balthasar, Hans Urs von. *Two Sisters in the Spirit: Thérèse of Lisieux and Elizabeth of the Trinity.* San Francisco, Ignatius, 1992.

Barnes, Michel. "De Régnon Reconsidered." *Augustinian Studies* 26, no. 2 (1995): 51–79.
Barth, Karl. *Church Dogmatics: The Doctrine of the Word of God. Part 1, vol. 1.* Edited by G. W. Bromiley and T. F. Torrance. Edinburgh: T&T Clark, 1975.
Barth, Karl. *Church Dogmatics: The Doctrine of God, Part 2, volume 2*; *The Doctrine of Reconciliation, Part 2*, volume 4. English translations edited by G. W. Bromiley and T. F. Torrance. Edinburgh: T&T Clark, 1959.
Barth, Karl, *Church Dogmatics: The Doctrine of God. Part 1, vol. 2.* Edited by G. W. Bromiley and T. F. Torrance. Edinburgh: T. & T. Clark, 1957.
Barth, Karl. *The Humanity of God.* Translated by Thomas Wieser and John Newton Thomas. Richmond, VA: John Knox Press, 1968.
Basil. *On the Holy Spirit.* Translated by David Anderson. New York: St Vladimir's Seminary Press, 1980.
Bates, Matthew W. *The Birth of the Trinity: Jesus, God, and Spirit in New Testament and Early Christian Interpretations of the Old Testament.* Oxford: Oxford University Press, 2015.
Bayer, Oswald. *Theology the Lutheran Way.* Translated and edited by Jeffrey Silcock and Mark Mattes. Grand Rapids, MI: Eerdmans, 2007.
Behr-Sigel, Elisabeth. *The Ministry of Women in the Church.* Translated by Steven Bigham. New York: St Vladimir's Seminary Press, 1991.
Bird, Michael F., and Scott D. Harrower, eds. *Trinity without Hierarchy: Reclaiming Nicene Orthodoxy in Evangelical Theology.* Grand Rapids, MI: Kregel Academic, 2019.
Blaising, Craig A. "Creedal Formulation as Hermeneutical Development: A Re-examination of Nicea." *Pro Ecclesia* 19, no. 4 (2010): 371–88.
Boff, Leonardo. *Trinity and Society.* Tunbridge Wells: Burns & Oates, 1988.
Bond H. Lawrence, ed. *Nicholas of Cusa: Selected Spiritual Writings.* Mahwah, NJ: Paulist Press, 1997.
Bonhoeffer, Dietrich, *Dietrich Bonhoeffer Works: Creation and Fall; A Theological Exposition of Genesis. Vol. 3, 1-3.* Edited by John W. De Gruchy, and Douglas S. Bax. Minneapolis: Fortress Press, 2004.
Brock, Brian. *Wondrously Wounded: Theology, Disability, and the Body of Christ.* Waco, TX: Baylor University Press, 2019.
Bromiley, Geoffrey W. *Introduction to the Theology of Karl Barth.* Edinburgh: T&T Clark, 2001.
Brown, Brené. *Daring Greatly: How the Courage to Be Vulnerable Transforms the Way We Live, Love, Parent, and Lead.* New York: Gotham Books, 2012.
Brown, David. *Divine Humanity: Kenosis Explored and Defended.* London: SCM, 2011.
Bulgakov, Sergiĭ. *The Bride of the Lamb.* Translated by Boris Jakim. Grand Rapids, MI: Eerdmans, 2002. Originally published as *Nevesta agntsa* [The Bride of the Lamb]. Pt 3 of *O bogochelovechestve*. Paris: YMCA-Press, 1945.
Bulgakov, Sergiĭ. *The Burning Bush: On the Orthodox Veneration of the Mother of God.* Edited by T. Allan Smith. Grand Rapids, MI: Eerdmans, 2009. Originally published as *Kupina neopalimaia: opyt dogmaticheskogo istolkovaniia nekotorykh chert v pravoslavnom pochitanii Bogomateri*. Paris: YMCA-Press, 1927.

Bulgakov, Sergeĭ. *The Comforter*. Translated by Boris Jakim. Grand Rapids, MI: Eerdmans, 2004. Originally published as *Uteshitel'* [The Comforter]. Pt 2 of *O bogochelovechestve*. Paris: YMCA-Press, 1936.

Bulgakov, Sergiĭ. *Glavy o Troichnosti in Trudy o Troichnosti*. Edited by M. A. Kolerov. Moscow: OGI, 2001.

Bulgakov, Sergeĭ. *The Lamb of God*. Translated by Boris Jakim. Grand Rapids, MI: Eerdmans, 2002. Originally published as *Agnets bozhii* [The Lamb of God]. Pt 1 of *O bogochelovechestve*. Paris: YMCA-Press, 1933.

Bulgakov, Sergeĭ. "Osnovnye problem teorii progressa." *Problemy idealizma: sbornik statei*, edited by P. I. Novgorodtsev. Moscow: Moskovskoe Psikhologicheskoe Obshchestvo, 1902.

Bulgakov, Sergeĭ. *Sophia: The Wisdom of God: An Outline of Sophiology*. Translated by Patrick Thompson, O. Fielding Clarke, and Xenia Braikevitc. Lindisfarne Press: New York, 1993.

Carey, Holly J. *Jesus' Cry from the Cross: Towards a First-Century Understanding of the Intertextual Relationship between Psalm 22 and the Narrative of Mark's Gospel*. London: Bloomsbury Publishing Plc, 2009.

Carson, D. A. *The Gospel According to John*. Leicester, England: Inter-Varsity Press, 1991.

Caseralla, Peter J. "The Expression and Form of the Word: Trinitarian Hermeneutics and the Sacramentality of Language in Hans Urs Von Balthasar's Theology." *Renascence* 48, no. 2 (1996): 110–35.

Castelo, Daniel. "Moltmann's Dismissal of Divine Impassibility: Warranted?" *Scottish Journal of Theology* 61, no. 4 (2008): 396–407.

Charry, Ellen T. *God and the Art of Happiness*. Grand Rapids, MI: Eerdmans, 2010.

Clark, Jacqueline [Jacqueline Service]. "'A Disabled Trinity': Help or Hindrance to Disability Theology?" *St Mark's Review*, no. 232 (2015): 50–64.

Clarke, Matthew, and Mark McGillivray, eds. *Understanding Human Well-Being*. New York: United Nations University Press, 2006.

Clayton, Philip. "Anticipation and Theological Method." In *The Theology of Wolfhart Pannenberg: Twelve American Critiques, with an Autobiographical Essay and Response*, edited by Carl E. Braaten and Philip Clayton, 122–51. Minneapolis: Augsburg Publishing House, 1988.

Coakley, Sarah. *Powers and Submissions: Spirituality, Philosophy and Gender*. Oxford: Blackwell Publishing, 2002.

Coakley, Sarah. "Kenosis: Theological Meanings and Gender Connotations." In *The Work of Love: Creation as Kenosis*, edited by John Polkinghorne, 192–209. Grand Rapids, MI: Eerdmans, 2001.

Cobb, John, and David Griffin. *Process Theology: An Introductory Exposition*. Philadelphia: Westminster Press, 1976.

Congar, Yves. *I Believe in the Holy Spirit*. Vol. 3. Translated by David Smith. New York: Seabury Press, 1983.

Connor, Timothy G. *The Kenotic Trajectory of the Church in Donald MacKinnon's Theology: From Galilee to Jerusalem to Galilee*. London: T&T Clark, 2013.

Cooper. John W. *Panentheism, the Other God of the Philosophers: From Plato to the Present*. Grand Rapids, MI: Baker Academic, 2006.

Coxe, A. Cleveland, Alexander Roberts, and James Donaldson, eds. *The Ante-Nicene Fathers: Translations of the Writings of the Fathers Down to A.D. 325*. 10 vols. 1885–1887. Reprinted. Grand Rapids, MI: Eerdmans, 1987.

Craig, William Lane. "The Kurtz/Craig Debate: Is Goodness without God Good Enough?" In *Is Goodness without God Good Enough? A Debate on Faith, Secularism, and Ethics*, edited by Robert K. Garcia and Nathan L. King, 24–41. Lanham, MD: Rowman & Littlefield Publishers, 2009.

Creel, R. E. *Divine Impassibility*. Cambridge: Cambridge University Press, 1986.

Creel, Richard E. "Immutability and Impassibility." In *A Companion to Philosophy of Religion*, edited by Philip L. Quinn and Charles Taliaferro. Oxford: Blackwell Publishing, 1997.

Crisp, Oliver D. Review of *The Untamed God*, by J. W. Richards, Downers Grove, IL: Intervarsity Press, 2003. *Scottish Journal of Theology* 58, no. 4 (2005): 493–96.

Dahl, Nils Alstrup. "Trinitarian Baptismal Creeds and New Testament Christology." In *Jesus the Christ: The Historical Origins of Christological Doctrine*, edited by Donald H. Juel, 165–86. Minneapolis: Fortress Press, 1991.

Dalferth, Ingolf U. *Becoming Present: An Inquiry into the Christian Sense of the Presence of God*. Leuven: Peeters, 2006.

Davies, Oliver. *A Theology of Compassion*. London: SCM Press, 2001.

Deane-Drummond, Ceclia. "The Breadth of Glory: A Trinitarian Eschatology for the Earth through Critical Engagement with Hans Urs von Balthasar." *International Journal of Systematic Theology* 12, no. 1 (2010): 46–64.

De Kadt, Emanuel. "Should God Play a Role in Development?" *Journal of International Development* 21, no. 6 (2009): 781–86.

Deutsch, Karl Wolfgang. *The Nerves of Government: Models of Political Communication and Control*. New York: The Free Press, 1966.

Dolezal, James E. *God without Parts: Divine Simplicity and the Metaphysics of God's Absoluteness*. Eugene, OR: Wipf and Stock Publishers, 2011.

Dolezal, James E. "Trinity, Simplicity and the Status of God." *International Journal of Systematic Theology* 16, no. 1 (Jan 2014): 79–98.

Dupre. Louis, and Nancy Hudson. *Nicholas of Cusa*. In *A Companion to Philosophy in the Middle Ages*, edited by Jorge J. E. Gracia and Timothy B. Noone, 466–74. Malden, MA: Blackwell, 2002.

Eiesland, Nancy. *The Disabled God: Toward a Liberatory Theology of Disability*. Nashville, TN: Abingdon Press, 1994.

Eikrem, Asle. *God as Sacrificial Love: A Systematic Exploration of a Controversial Notion*. London: Bloomsbury T&T Clark, 2018.

Emery, Gilles. *The Trinity: An Introduction to Catholic Doctrine on the Triune God*. Translated by Matthew Levering. Washington D.C.: Catholic University Press, 2011.

Emery, Gilles. *Trinity in Aquinas*, 2nd ed. Ann Arbor, MI: Sapientia Press, 2006.

Epperly. Bruce G. *Process Theology: Guide for the Perplexed*. London: T & T Clark International, 2011.

Erickson, Millard J. *Who Is Tampering with the Trinity? An Assessment of the Subordination Debate*. Grand Rapids, MI: Kregel, 2009.

Evans. Stephen C, ed. *Exploring Kenotic Christology: The Self-Emptying of God*. Oxford UK: Oxford University Press, 2006.

Farley, Margaret. "New Patterns of Relationships: Beginning of a Moral Revolution." *Theological Studies* 36, no. 4 (1975): 627–46.

Farrow, Douglas B. "Review Essay: In the End Is the Beginning: A Review of Jürgen Moltmann's Systematic Contributions." *Modern Theology* 14, no. 3 (1998): 425–47.

Fiddes, Paul S. *Participating in God: A Pastoral Doctrine of the Trinity*. London: Darton, Longman & Todd, 2000.

Ford, David F., and Daniel W. Hardy. *Living in Praise: Worshipping and Knowing God*. Rev. ed. London: Darton, Longman & Todd, 2005.

Forsyth, P. T. *The Person and Place of Jesus Christ*. London: Independent Press, 1948.

Frame, John M. *A History of Western Philosophy and Theology*. 1st ed. Phillipsburg, NJ: P&R Publishing, 2015.

Franks, Christopher. "The Simplicity of the Living God: Aquinas, Barth and Some Philosophers." *Modern Theology* 21, no. 2 (2005): 275–300.

Gavrilyuk, Paul. "The Kenotic Theology of Sergius Bulgakov." *Scottish Journal of Theology* 58, no. 3 (2005): 251–69.

Gavrilyuk, Paul. *The Suffering of the Impassible God*. Oxford: Oxford University Press, 2004.

Giles, Kevin. *The Headship of Men and the Abuse of Women: Are They Related in Any Way?* Eugene, OR: Cascade Books, 2020.

Giles, Kevin. *Jesus and the Father: Modern Evangelicals Reinvent the Doctrine of the Trinity*. Grand Rapids, MI: Zondervan, 2006.

Giles, Kevin. *The Trinity & Subordinationism: The Doctrine of God and the Contemporary Gender Debate*. Downers Grove, IL: InterVarsity Press, 2002.

Goad, Keith. "Simplicity and Trinity in Harmony." *Eusebeia* 8, no. 1 (2007): 97–118.

Goetz. R. "The Suffering God: The Rise of a New Orthodoxy." *Christian Century* 103, no. 13 (1986): 385–89. EBSCOhost ATLA Serials.

Gorman, Michael J. *Cruciformity: Paul's Narrative Spirituality of the Cross*. Grand Rapids, MI: W.B. Eerdmans Pub. 2001.

Gorman, Michael J. *Inhabiting the Cruciform God: Kenosis, Justification, and Theosis in Paul's Narrative Soteriology*. Grand Rapids, MI: William B. Eerdmans Publishing, 2009.

Gray, John. *Straw Dogs: Thoughts on Humans and Other Animals*. London: Granta Books, 2002.

Gregersen, Niels Henrik. "Deep Incarnation and Kenosis: In, With, Under, and As; A Response to Ted Peters." *Dialog: A Journal of Theology* 52, no. 3 (2013): 251–62.

Gregory of Nazianzus, *Festal Orations*. Translated by Nonna Verna Harrison. New York: St Vladimir's Press, 2008.

Gregory of Nazianzus, *The Oration on Holy Baptism, XL.41*. Accessed 15 July 2023. www.newadvent.org/fathers/310240.htm.

Grenz, Stanley J. *Reason for Hope: The Systematic Theology of Wolfhart Pannenberg*. Oxford: Oxford University Press, 1990.

Grenz, Stanley J., and Roger E. Olson, eds. *Twentieth Century Theology: God and the World in a Transitional Age*. Downers Grove, IL: Intervarsity Press, 1992.

Grudem, Wayne. *Biblical Foundation for Manhood and Womanhood*. Wheaton, IL: Crossway, 2002.

Grudem, Wayne. *Systematic Theology: An Introduction to Biblical Doctrine*. Grand Rapids, MI: Zondervan, 1994.

Gunnes, Gyrid Kristine. "An Ecclesiology of a Queer Kenosis? Risk and Ambivalence at Our Lady, Trondheim, in Light of the Queer Theology on Kenosis of Marcella Althaus-Reid." *Feminist Theology* 28, no. 2 (2020): 216–30.

Gunton, Colin. *Act and Being: Towards a Theology of The Divine Attributes*. Grand Rapids, MI: Eerdmans, 2002.

Gunton, Colin E. *The Actuality of Atonement a Study of Metaphor, Rationality and the Christian Tradition*. London: T & T Clark, 1998.

Gunton, Colin. *The One, the Three and the Many: God, Creation and the Culture of Modernity—The Brampton Lectures 1992*. Cambridge: Cambridge University Press, 1993.

Gunton, Colin. *The Promise of Trinitarian Theology*. Edinburgh: T&T Clark, 1991.

Gunton. Colin. *The Triune Creator: A Historical and Systematic Study*. Grand Rapids, MI: Eerdmans, 1998.

Gunton, C., and C. Schwöbel. *Persons, Divine and Human: King's College Essays in Theological Anthropology*. Edinburgh: T&T Clark, 1991.

Hampson, Daphne. "On Power and Gender." *Modern Theology* 4, no. 3 (1988): 234–50.

Hampson, Daphne. *Theology and Feminism*. Oxford: Basil Blackwell, 1990.

Hanson, R. P. C. *The Search for the Christian Doctrine of God: The Arian Controversy 318–381 AD*. Edinburgh: T&T Clark, 1988.

Hardy, Daniel. W. *God's Ways with the World: Thinking and Practising Christian Faith*. Edinburgh: T&T Clark, 1996.

Hardy, Daniel W. *Jubilate: Theology in Praise*. Edited by David F. Ford. London: Darton, Longman & Todd, 1984.

Hardy, Daniel W., and David F. Ford. *Praising and Knowing God*. Philadelphia: Westminster, 1985.

Hardy, Daniel. W., Deborah Hardy Ford, Peter Ochs, and David F. Ford. *Wording a Radiance: Parting Conversations on God and the Church*. London: SCM Press, 2010.

Harnack von, Adolf. *What Is Christianity?* Philadelphia: Fortress, 1986.

Harrison, Nonna Verna, and Elizabeth Theokritoff. "The Human Person as Image and Likeness of God." In *The Cambridge Companion to Orthodox Christian Theology*, edited by Mary B. Cunningham, 78–92. Cambridge: Cambridge University Press, 2008.

Harrison, Verna. "Perichoresis in the Greek Fathers." *St. Vladimir's Theological Quarterly* 35 (1991): 53–65.

Harrower, Scott. *Trinitarian Self and Salvation: An Evangelical Engagement with Rahner's Rule*. Eugene, OR: Pickwick, 2012.

Harrower, Scott D. "Bruce Ware's Trinitarian Methodology." In *Trinity without Hierarchy: Reclaiming Nicene Orthodoxy in Evangelical Theology*, edited by Michael F. Bird and Scott D. Harrower, 207–23. Grand Rapids, MI: Kregel Academic, 2019.

Hart, David Bentley. *The Beauty of the Infinite: The Aesthetics of Christian Truth*. Grand Rapids, MI: Eerdmans, 2003.

Hart, David Bentley. *The Hidden and the Manifest: Essays in Theology and Metaphysics*. Grand Rapids, MI: Eerdmans, 2017.

Hasker, William. "Objections to Social Trinitarianism." *Religious Studies* 46, no. 1 (2010): 421–39.

Hayes, Daniel. "The Metaphysics of Christian Ethics: Radical Orthodoxy and Theosis." *Heythrop Journal* 52, no. 4 (2011): 659–71.

Hegel, G. W. F. *Phenomenology of Spirit*. Translated by A. V. Miller. Oxford: Oxford University Press, 1977.

Hemmerle, Klaus. *Theses towards a Trinitarian Ontology*. Translated by Stephen Churchyard. Brooklyn, NY: Angelico Press, 2020.

Herbert, T. D. *Kenosis and Priesthood: Towards a Protestant Re-evaluation of the Ordained Ministry*. Carlisle, UK: Paternoster, 2009.

Hill, Wesley. *Paul and the Trinity: Persons, Relations and the Pauline Letters*. Grand Rapids, MI: William B. Eerdmans Publishing Company, 2015.

Himes, Michael J., and Kenneth R. Himes. *Fullness of Faith: The Public Significance of Theology*. New York: Paulist Press, 1993.

Holmes, Stephen R. "Classical Trinity: Evangelical Perspective." In *Two Views on the Doctrine of the Trinity*. Edited by Jason S. Sexton, 25–48. Grand Rapid, MI: Zondervan Academic, 2014.

Holmes, Stephen R. "'Something Much Too Plain to Say': Towards a Defence of the Doctrine of Divine Simplicity." *Neue Zeitschrift für systematische Theologie und Religionsphilosophie* 43, no. 1 (2001): 137–54.

Huber, Wolfgang. *Konflikt und Konsens. Studien zur Ethik der Verantwortung*. München: Kaiser, 1990.

Hunsinger, George. "Election and Trinity: Twenty-Five Theses on the Theology of Karl Barth." *Modern Theology* 24, no. 2 (2008): 179–98.

Hunsinger, George. "Robert Jenson's Systematic Theology: A Review Essay." *Scottish Journal of Theology* 55, no. 2 (2002): 161–200.

Irenaeus. "Against Heresies Part 11, Chpt XIII, 3." In *The Ante-Nicene Fathers: Translations of the Writings of the Fathers Down to A.D. 325. 10 vols. 1885–1887*, eds. A. Cleveland Coxe, Alexander Roberts and James Donaldson. Reprinted. Grand Rapids, MI: Eerdmans, 1987.

Jennings, Willie James. *Acts: A Theological Commentary on the Bible*. Louisville, KY: Presbyterian Publishing Corporation, 2017.

Jenson, Robert W. *Systematic Theology: The Triune God*. Vol. 1. New York: Oxford University Press, 2001.

Jenson, Robert W. *Systematic Theology: The Works of God*. Vol. 2. New York: Oxford University Press, 1999.

Johnson, Elizabeth. *She Who Is: The Mystery of God in Feminist Theological Discourse*. New York: Crossroad Publishing Company, 1993.

Johnson, Keith E. "Imitatio Trinitatis: How Should We Imitate the Trinity." *Westminster Theological Journal* 75, no. 2 (2013): 317–34.

Jüngel, Eberhard. *God as the Mystery of the World: On the Foundation of the Theology of the Crucified One in the Dispute between Theism and Atheism*. Grand Rapids, MI: Eerdmans, 1983.

Kant, Immanuel. *The Critique of Pure Reason*. Auckland: The Floating Press, 1969.

Kärkkäinen, Veli-Matti. "The Trinitarian Doctrines of Jürgen Moltmann and Wolfhart Pannenberg in the Context of Contemporary Discussion." In *The Cambridge Companion to Trinity*, edited by Peter Phan, 223–42. Cambridge: Cambridge University Press, 2011.

Kaufman, Gordon D. *Systematic Theology: A Historicist Perspective*. New York: Scribner, 1968.

Kilby, Karen. *Balthasar: A (Very) Critical Introduction*. Grand Rapids, MI: William B. Eerdmans Publishing Company, 2012.

Kilby, Karen. *God, Evil and the Limits of Theology*. London: T&T Clark Bloomsbury, 2020.

Kilby, Karen. "Is an Apophatic Trinitarianism Possible?" *International Journal of Systematic Theology* 12, no. 1 (2010): 65–77. https://doi.org/10.1111/j.1468-2400.2009.00494.x.

Kilby, Karen. "Perichoresis and Projection: Problems with Social Doctrines of the Trinity." *New Blackfriars* 81, no. 957 (2000): 432–45.

Kornblatt, J. D. *Divine Sophia: The Wisdom Writings of Vladimir Solovyov*. New York: Cornell University Press, 2009.

Kraay. Klaas J. "Theism and Modal Collapse." *American Philosophical Quarterly* 48 (2011): 361–72.

Kristiansen, Staale Johannes. "Hans Urs von Balthasar." In *Key Theological Thinkers: From Modern to Postmodern*, edited by Svien Rise and Staale Johannes Kristiansen, 249–66. New York: Routledge, 2016.

Küng, H. *The Incarnation of God: An Introduction to Hegel's Theological Thought as Prolegomena to a Future Christology*. Edinburgh: T. & T. Clark, 1987.

LaCugna, Catherine Mowry. *God for Us: The Trinity and Christian Life*. San Francisco: HarperSan Francisco, 1991.

LaCugna, Catherine Mowry. "The Relational God: Aquinas and Beyond." *Theological Studies* 46, no. 4 (1985): 647–63.

Law, David R. "Kenotic Christology." In *Blackwell Companion to Nineteenth Century Theology*, edited by David Fergusson, 259–79. Oxford: Wiley-Blackwell, 2010.

Leamy, Katy. *The Holy Trinity: Hans Urs Von Balthasar and His Sources*. Eugene, OR: Pickwick Publishing, 2015.

Letham, Robert, and Kevin Giles. "Is the Son Eternally Submissive to the Father? An Egalitarian/Complementarian Debate." Christian Research Institute, 2009.

Leidenhag, Joanna. "The Challenge of Autism for Relational Approaches to Theological Anthropology." *International Journal of Systematic Theology* 23, no. 1 (2021): 109–34.

Leighton, J. A. "Hegel's Conception of God." *The Philosophical Review* 5, no. 6 (1896): 601–18.

Levinas, Emmanuel. *Basic Philosophical Writings*. Edited by Adriaan R. Peperzak, Simon Critchley and Robert Bernasconi. Bloomington: Indiana University Press, 1996.

Levinas, Emmanuel. *Ethics and infinity: Conversations with Philippe Nemo*. Pittsburgh: Duquesne University Press, 1985.

Liebner, K. T. A. *Die christliche Dogmatik aus dem christologischen Princip dargestellt*, Vol. I/1: *Christologie oder die christologische Einheit des dogmatischen Systems*. Göttingen: Vandenhoeck und Ruprecht, 1849.

Lombard, Peter. *Sentences 1. Distinction VIII*. Accessed September 18, 2016. www.franciscan-archive.org/lombardus/I-Sent.html.

Louth, Andrew. *Discerning the Mystery: An Essay on the Nature of Theology*. Oxford: Clarendon Press, 1983.

Luy, David. "The Aesthetic Collision: Hans Urs von Balthasar on the Trinity and the Cross." *International Journal of Systematic Theology* 13, no. 2 (2011): 154–69.

MacKinnon, Donald. "Reflections on Donald Baillie's Treatment of the Atonement." In *Christ, Church and Society: Essays on John Baillie and Donald Baillie*. Edited by David Fergusson. Edinburgh: T&T Clark, 1993.

MacKinnon, Donald. *The Stripping of the Altars*. London: Fontana, 1969.

MacKinnon, Donald. *Themes in Theology: The Three-Fold Cord: Essays in Philosophy, Politics, and Theology*. Edinburgh: T. & T. Clark, 1987.

Macmurray, John. *Persons in Relation: Being the Gifford Lectures Delivered in the University of Glasgow in 1954*. Gifford Lectures 1954. London: Faber and Faber, 1970.

Manastireanu, Danut. "Perichoresis and the Early Church Doctrine," *ARCHÆVS XI–XII* (2007–2008): 61–93. www.academia.edu/4794642/Perichoresis_and_the_Early_Christian_Doctrine_of_God.

Martin, Michael, ed. *The Heavenly Country: An Anthology of Primary Sources, Poetry, and Critical Essays on Sophiology*. Kettering: Angelico Press, 2016.

McCall, Thomas H. *Forsaken: The Trinity and the Cross, and Why it Matters*. Downers Grove, IL: IVP Academic, 2012.

McCall, Thomas H. "Trinity Doctrine, Plain and Simple." In *Advancing Trinitarian Theology: Explorations in Constructive Dogmatics*, edited by Oliver D. Crisp and Fred Sanders, 42–59. Grand Rapids, MI: Zondervan, 2014.

McCall, Tom. "Holy Love and Divine Aseity in the Theology of John Zizioulas." *Scottish Journal of Theology*, no. 61 (2008): 191–205. doi:10.1017/S0036930608003955.

McCormack, Bruce Lindley. *The Humility of the Eternal Son: Reformed Kenoticism and the Repair of Chalcedon*. Current Issues in Theology. Cambridge: Cambridge University Press, 2021.

McDowell, John C., Scott A. Kirkland, and Ashley John Moyse. *Kenotic Ecclesiology: Select Writings of Donald M. MacKinnon*. Minneapolis: Fortress Press, 2016.

McGuckin, John A., ed. *St. Cyril of Alexandria: The Christological Controversy: Its History, Theology & Texts*. Leiden: E.J. Brill, 1994.

McInerny, Ralph. "Ethics." In *The Cambridge Companion to Aquinas*, edited by Norman Kretzmann and Eleonore Stump, 196–216. Cambridge: Cambridge University Press, 1993.

McIntosh, Mark. "Hans Urs Von Balthasar (1905–88)." In *The Student's Companion to the Theologians*, edited by Ian S. Markham, 353–66: Chichester: Blackwell-Wiley, 2013.

McIntosh, Mark. "Light in Darkness: Hans Urs von Balthasar and the Catholic Doctrine of Christ's Descent into Hell—by Alyssa Lyra Pitstick." *Modern Theology* 24 (2008): 137–39.

Meyers, Bryant. *Walking with the Poor: Principles and Practices of Transformational Development*. New York: Orbis Books, 2011.

Migliore, Daniel L. "The Communion of the Triune God: Towards a Trinitarian Ecclesiology in Reformed Perspective." In *Reformed Theology: Identity and Ecumenicity*, edited by Wallace. M. Alston Jr., and Michael Welker, 140–54. Grand Rapids, MI: Eerdmans, 2003.

Milbank, John. "Can a Gift Be Given? Prolegomena to a Future Trinitarian Metaphysic." *Modern Theology* 11, no. 1 (1995): 119–61.

Mill, J. S. *On Liberty, Considerations on Representative Government*. Edited by J. M. Dent. London: Everyman, 1993.

Molnar, Paul. *Divine Freedom and the Doctrine of the Immanent Trinity*. London: T&T Clark, 2002.

Molnar, Paul. *Faith, Freedom and the Spirit: The Economic Trinity in Barth, Torrance and Contemporary Theology*. Downers Grove, IL: InterVarsity Press, 2015.

Moltmann Jürgen. *A Broad Place: An Autobiography*. Minneapolis: Fortress Press, 2008.

Moltmann, Jürgen. *The Crucified God: The Cross of Christ as the Foundation and Criticism of Christian Theology*. Translated by R. A. Wilson and John Bowden. London: SCM Press, 1974. Originally published as *Der gekreuzigte Gott*, 2nd edn. Munich: Chr. Kaiser Verlag, 1973.

Moltmann, Jürgen. *God in Creation: A New Theology of Creation and the Spirit of God*. Translated by Margaret Kohl. New York: Harper & Row, 1985.

Moltmann, Jürgen. "The Reconciling Power of the Trinity in the Life of the Church and the World." *Triune God: Love, Justice, Peace,* edited by K. M. Tharakan, 32–50. Mavelikkara: Youth Movement of Indian Orthodox Church, 1989.

Moltmann, Jürgen. *The Trinity and the Kingdom of God: The Doctrine of God*. Translated by Margaret Kohl. Minneapolis: Fortress Press, 1993. Originally published as *Trinität und Reich Gottes*. Munich: Chr. Kaiser Verlag, 1980.

Moore, Alana. "'Whatever You Did for One of the Least of These Brothers and Sisters of Mine': Christianity and the Dilemmas of Child Sponsorship." *St Mark's Review*, no. 261 (2022): 23–40. doi/10.3316/informit.769386981164251.

Morris, T. *Our Idea of God: An Introduction to Philosophical Theology*. Notre Dame: University of Notre Dame Press, 1991.

Mostert, Christiaan. *God and the Future: Wolfhart Pannenberg's Eschatological Doctrine of God*. London: Bloomsbury Publishing Plc, 2002. doi.org/10.5040/9780567660756.

Mostert, Christiaan. "Moltmann's Crucified God." *Journal of Reformed Theology* 7, no. 2 (2013): 160–80.

Muller, Richard A. *Post-Reformation Reformed Dogmatics: The Rise and Development of Reformed Orthodoxy, ca. 1520–1725*. Vol. 4. Grand Rapids, MI: Baker Academic, 2003.

Mullins, R. T. "In Search of a Timeless God." PhD diss., University of St. Andrews, 2013.

Mullins, R. T. "Simply Impossible: A Case against Divine Simplicity." *Journal of Reformed Theology* 7, no. 2 (2013): 181–203.

Mullins, Ryan and Shannon Byrd. "Divine Simplicity and Modal Collapse: A Persistent Problem." *European Journal for Philosophy of Religion* 14, no 3 (2022): 21–52.

Newsome-Martin, Jennifer. "The 'Whence' and the 'Whither' of Balthasar's Gendered Theology: Rehabilitating Kenosis for Feminist Theology." *Modern Theology* 31, no. 2 (2015): 211–34.

Nicene Creed. Accessed 26 July 2017. anglicansonline.org/basics/nicene.html.

Nicholas of Cusa, *Nicholas of Cusa's Debate with John Wenck: A Translation and an Appraisal of De Ignota Litteratura and Apologia Doctae Ignorantiae*. Edited by Jasper Hopkins. Minneapolis: Arthur J. Banning Press, 1981.

Nichols, Aiden. "Wisdom from Above? The Sophiology of Father Sergius Bulgakov." *New Blackfriars* 85, no. 1000 (2004): 598–613.

Nimmo, Paul T., and Keith L. Johnson, *Kenosis: The Self-Emptying of Christ in Scripture and Theology*. Chicago: Wm. B. Eerdmans Publishing Co, 2022.

O'Donnell, J. "Pannenberg's Doctrine of God." *Gregorianum* 72, no. 1 (1991): 73–98. www.jstor.org/stable/23578753.

O'Donovan, Oliver. "Again, Who Is a Person?" In *On Moral Medicine: Theological Perspectives in Medical Ethics.* 3rd ed. Edited by M. Therese Lysaught, Joseph Kotva, Stephen E. Lammers, and Allen M. Verhey, 608–16. 3rd ed. Grand Rapids, MI: William B. Eerdmans Publishing Company, 2012.

O'Hanlon, Gerard. *The Immutability of God in the Theology of Hans Urs von Balthasar*. New York: Cambridge University Press, 1990.

O'Regan, Cyril. "The Trinity in Kant, Hegel and Schelling." In *The Oxford Handbook of the Trinity*, edited by Gilles Emery, and Matthew Levering, 254–66. Oxford: Oxford University Press, 2011.

Ormerod, Neil. "The Debate Over Light in Darkness and the Catholicity of Hans Urs von Balthasar." *Australian eJournal of Theology* 20, no. 3 (2013): 207–20.

Padilla, Elaine. *Divine Enjoyment: A Theology of Passion and Exuberance*. New York: Fordham University Press, 2014.

Painter, John. *The Quest for the Messiah: The History, Literature and Theology of the Johannine Community*. Edinburgh: T&T Clark, 1991.

Pannenberg, Wolfhart. *Basic Questions in Theology.* Vol. 2. Translated by George H. Kehm. London: SCM, 1971. Originally published as *Grundfragen systematischer Theologie*, Bd i. Gottingen: Vandenhoeck & Ruprecht, 1967.

Pannenberg, Wolfhart. *Christian Spirituality and Sacramental Community.* Darton, Longman & Todd: London, 1984.

Pannenberg, Wolfhart. "The God of History." Translated by M. B. Jackson, *Cumberland Seminarian* 19, nos. 2–3 (1981): 28–41. Originally published as 'Der Gott der Geschichte: Der trinitarische Gott und die Wahrheit der Geschichte,' *Kerygma und Dogma* 23, no. 2, 1977: 76–92.

Pannenberg, Wolfhart. "God's Love and The Kenosis of the Son: A Response to Masao Abe." In *Divine Emptiness and Historical Fullness: A Buddhist-Jewish-Christian Conversation with Masao Abe*, edited by Christopher Ives, 244–50. Valley Forge, PA: Trinity Press International, 1995.

Pannenberg, Wolfhart. *Jesus—God and Man*. 2nd ed. Translated by Lewis L. Wilkins and Duane A. Priebe. Philadelphia: Westminster, 1977. Originally published as *Grundzuge der Christologie*. Giitersloh: Gerd Mohn, 1964. The 2nd English ed. of 1976 is a translation of the 5th German ed.

Pannenberg, Wolfhart. "Problems of a Trinitarian God," *Dialog* 26, no. 4 (1987): 250–57. Translated by P. Clayton from '*Probleme einer trinitarischen Gotteslehre,*' in W. Baier, et al., *Weisheit Gottes - Weisheit der Welt*. Vol. 1, St Ottilien, 1987.

Pannenberg, Wolfhart. *Systematic Theology*. Vols.1–3. Translated by Geoffrey W. Bromiley. Grand Rapids, MI: Eerdmans, 1991–1998. Originally published as *Systematische Theologie*, Band i–iii. Gottingen: Vandenhoeck & Ruprecht, 1988.

Pannenberg, Wolfhart. *Theology and the Kingdom of God*. Edited by Richard J. Neuhaus. Philadelphia: Westminster Press, 1969.

Papanikolaou, Aristotle. *Being with God: Trinity, Apophaticism and Divine-Human Communion*. Notre Dame: Notre Dame University, 2006.

Papanikolaou, Aristotle. "Person, Kenosis, and Abuse: Hans Urs von Balthasar and Feminist Theologies in Conversation." *Modern Theology* 19, no. 1 (2003): 41–65.

Papanikolaou, Aristotle. "Sophia, Apophasis, and Communion: The Trinity in Contemporary Orthodox Theology." In *The Cambridge Companion to the Trinity*, edited by Peter Phan, 243–58. Cambridge: Cambridge University Press, 2011.

Paul VI. *Populorum Progressio* [On the Development of Peoples]. Vatican Website. March 26, 1967. Accessed February 12, 2023. w2.vatican.va/content/paul-vi/en/encyclicals/documents/hf_p-vi_enc_26031967_populorum.html.

Percy, Martyn. "Kenotic Ecclesiology and the Disestablishment of the Church of England under the Reign of Charles III." *Journal of Anglican Studies*, 2023: 1–17.

Peters, Ted. *God as Trinity: Relationality and Temporality in the Divine Life*. Louisville, KY: Westminster Press, 1993.

Pickard, Stephen. *In-Between God: Theology, Community and Discipleship*. Hindmarsh: ATF Press, 2011.

Pitstick, Alyssa Lyra. *Light in Darkness: Hans Urs Von Balthasar and the Catholic Doctrine of Christ's Descent into Hell*. Grand Rapids, MI: Eerdmans, 2006.

Plantinga, Cornelius, Jr., "Gregory of Nyssa and the Social Analogy of the Trinity." *The Thomist* 50 (1986): 325–52.

Plantinga, Cornelius, Jr., "Social Trinity and Tritheism." In *Trinity, Incarnation and Atonement*, edited by R. J. Feenstra and C. Plantinga, 21–47. Notre Dame: University of Notre Dame, 1989.

Polkinghorne, John, ed. *The Work of Love: Creation as Kenosis*. Grand Rapids, MI: Eerdmans Publishing Co, 2001.

Pugliese, Marc A. "How Important Is the Filioque for Reformed Orthodoxy?" *The Westminster Theological Journal* 66, no. 1 (Spring 2004): 159–77.

Quash, Ben. "The Theo-Drama." In *The Cambridge Companion to Hans Urs Von Balthasar*, edited by Edward T. Oakes, SJ and David Moss: 143–57. Cambridge: Cambridge University Press, 2004.

Rahner, Karl. *The Trinity*. Translated by Joseph Donceel. London: Herder and Herder, 1970.

Richards, J. W. *The Untamed God: A Philosophical Exploration of Divine Perfection, Simplicity and Immutability*. Downers Grove, IL: Intervarsity Press, 2003.

Rogers, Eugene F. *Sexuality and the Christian Body: Their Way into the Triune God*. Malden, MA: Blackwell, 1999.

Rowe, Kavin C. "The Trinity in the Letters of St Paul and Hebrews." In *The Oxford Handbook of The Trinity*, edited by Gilles Emery and Matthew Levering, 41–54. Oxford University Press: Oxford 2011.

Sanders, Fred. *The Image of the Immanent Trinity: Rahner's Rule and the Theological Interpretation of Scripture*. Issues in Systematic Theology 12. New York: Peter Lang, 2005.

Sanders, Fred. "Redefining Progress in Trinitarian Theology: Stephen R. Holmes on the Trinity." *Evangelical Quarterly* 86, no. 1 (2014): 6–20.

Sanders, Fred. *The Triune God*, New Studies in Dogmatics. Grand Rapids, MI: Zondervan, 2016.

Sanders, John. "Historical Considerations." In *The Openness of God: A Biblical Challenge to the Traditional Understanding of God*, edited by Clark H. Pinnock, 59–100. Downers Grove, IL: Intervarsity Press, 1994.

Schaff, Philip and Henry Wace, eds. *A Select Library of the Nicene and Post-Nicene Fathers of the Christian Church, 1886–1889. 28 vols. in 2 series.* Reprinted. Grand Rapids, MI: Eerdmans, 1952–1956.

Schmid, Joseph C. "The Fruitful Death of Modal Collapse Arguments." *International Journal for Philosophy of Religion* 91, no. 1 (2, 2022): 3–22.

Schoonenberg, Piet. "Trinity—the Consummated Covenant: Theses on the Doctrine of the Trinitarian God." *Studies in Religion* 5, no. 2 (1975): 111–16.

Schwöbel, Christoph. "The Generosity of the Triune God and the Humility of the Son." In *Kenosis: The Self-Emptying of Christ in Scripture and Theology*, edited by Paul T. Nimmo, and Keith L. Johnson, 210–26. Chicago: Wm. B. Eerdmans Publishing Co., 2022.

Schwöbel, Christoph. "Rational Theology in Trinitarian Perspective: Wolfhart Pannenberg's Systematic Theology." *The Journal of Theological Studies* 47, no. 2 (1996): 498–527.

Schwöbel, Christoph. "'Taking the Form of a Servant': Kenosis and Divine Self-Giving in Thomas Aquinas and Martin Luther." *Angelicum* 98, no. 1 (2021), 41–64.

Sergeev, Mikhail. *Sophiology in Russian Orthodoxy: Solov'ev, Bulgakov, Losskii, and Berdiaev*. Lewiston: Edwin Mellen Press, 2006.

Service, Jacqueline. "*Divine Self-Enrichment and Human Well-Being: A Systematic Theological Inquiry, with Special Reference to Development and Humanitarian Aid*." PhD diss., Charles Sturt University, Australia, 2018.

Service, Jacqueline. "Existent Endurance, Vulnerability, and Future Joy," 14 September 2021. blogos.wp.st-andrews.ac.uk/2021/09/14/logia-profile-for-september-existent-endurance-vulnerability-and-future-joy/.

Service, Jacqueline. "Trinity, Aseity, and the Commensurability of the Incommensurate One." *St Mark's Review*, no. 250 (2019): 63–76.

Smith, Barry D. *The Oneness and Simplicity of God*. Eugene, OR: Wipf and Stock Publishers, 2014.

Sonderegger, Katherine. "The God We Worship; the Worship We Owe God," *St Mark's Review*, no. 250 (2019): 6–19.

Sonderegger, Katherine. "The Perfection of Divine Love." In *Systematic Theology: The Doctrine of God, volume 1*. Minneapolis: Fortress Press, 2015.

Sonderegger, Katherine. *Systematic Theology: The Doctrine of God*. Vol. 1. Minneapolis: Fortress Press, 2015.

Sontag, Frederick. *Divine Perfections: Possible Ideas of God*. New York: Harper & Brothers: 1962.

Spaemann, Robert. *Persons: The Difference between "Someone" and "Something."* Translated by Oliver O'Donovan. Oxford: Oxford University Press, 2017.

Speyr, Adrienne von. *The World of Prayer*. San Francisco: Ignatius Press, 1985.

Stamatović, Slobodan. "The Meaning of Perichoresis." *Open Theology* 2, no. 1 (2016): 303–23. doi.org/10.1515/opth-2016-0026.

Staniloae, Dumitru. *Theology and the Church*. Translated by Robert Barringer. Crestwood: St. Vladimir's Seminary Press, 1980.

Stirrat, R. L, and H, Henkel. "The Development Gift: The Problem of Reciprocity in the NGO world." *The Annals of the American Academy of Political and Social Science* 554, no. 1 (1997): 66–80.

Stramara, Daniel F. "Gregory of Nyssa's Terminology for Trinitarian Perichoresis." *Vigiliae Christianae* 52, no. 3 (1998): 257–63. doi:10.2307/1584502.

Stratis, Justin. "Speculating about Divinity? God's Immanent Life and Actualistic Ontology." *International Journal of Systematic Theology* 12, no. 1 (2010): 20–32.

Strawn, Brent. A. "The Bible and . . . Happiness?" In *The Bible and the Pursuit of Happiness: What the Old and New Testaments Teach Us about the Good Life*, edited by Brent. A. Strawn, 1–34. Oxford: Oxford University Press, 2012. DOI:10.1093/acprof:oso/9780199795734.003.0000.

Swinburne, Richard. "The Social Theory of the Trinity." *Religious Studies* (2018): 1–19.

Tanner, Kathryn. *Christ the Key*. Cambridge: Cambridge University Press, 2010.

Tanner, Kathryn. *Jesus, Humanity and the Trinity: A Brief Systematic Theology*. Edinburgh: T&T Clark, 2001.

Tataryn, Myroslaw. "History Matters: Bulgakov's Sophianic Key." *St Vladimir's Theological Quarterly* 49, nos. 1–2 (2005): 203–18.

Tataryn, Myroslaw, and Maria Truchan-Tataryn. *Discovering Trinity in Disability: A Theology for Embracing Difference*. Maryknoll, NY: Orbis Books, 2013.

Thuesen, Peter J., ed. *The Works of Jonathan Edwards 26 vols*. New Haven, CT: Yale University Press, 1957–2008.

Tonstad, Linn. "'The Ultimate Consequence of His Self-Distinction from the Father . . .': Difference and Hierarchy in Pannenberg's Trinity." *Neue Zeitschrift für Systematische Theologie und Religionsphilosophie* 51, no. 4 (2009): 383–99.

Torrance, T. F. *Belief in Science and in Christian Life: The Relevance of Michael Polanyi's Thought for Christian Faith and Life*. Edinburgh: The Handsel Press, 1980.

Torrance, T. F. *The Christian Doctrine of God: One Being Three Persons*. Edinburgh: T&T Clark, 1996.

Torrance, T. F. *Incarnation: The Person and Life of Christ*, ed. Robert T. Walker. Downers Grove, IL: IVP Academic, 2008.

Torrance, T. F. *Transformation and Convergence in the Frame of Knowledge*. Grand Rapids, MI: Wm. B. Eerdmans Publishing Company, 1984.

Valliere, Paul. *Modern Russian Theology: Bukharev, Soloviev, Bulgakov: Orthodox Theology in a New Key*. Grand Rapids, MI: Eerdmans, 2000.

Vanhoozer. Kevin. J. *Nothing Greater, Nothing Better: Theological Essays on the Love of God*. Grand Rapids, MI: Eerdmans, 2001.

Vanhoozer, Kevin. J., and Daniel J. Treier. *Theology and the Mirror of Scripture: A Mere Evangelical Account*. Downers Grove, IL: IVP, 2015.

Venema, Cornelis P. "History, Human Freedom and the Idea of God in the Theology of Wolfhart Pannenberg." *Calvin Theological Journal* 17, no. 1 (1982): 53–77.

Volf, Miroslav. *After Our Likeness: The Church as the Image of the Trinity*. Grand Rapids, MI: Eerdmans, 1998.

Volf, Miroslav. "Apophatic Social Trinitarianism: Why I Continue to Espouse 'a Kind of' Social Trinitarianism." *Political Theology: The Journal of Christian Socialism* 22, no. 5 (2021): 407–22.

Volf. Miroslav. "Being As God Is." In *God's Life in Trinity*, edited by Miroslav Volf and Michael Welker, 3–12. Minneapolis: Fortress Press, 2006.

Volf, Miroslav. *Exclusion and Embrace, Revised and Updated: A Theological Exploration of Identity, Otherness, and Reconciliation*. Nashville, TN: Abingdon Press, 2019.

Volf, Miroslav. "The Trinity Is Our Social Program: The Doctrine of the Trinity and the Shape of Social Engagement." *Modern Theology* 14, no. 3 (July 1998): 404–23.

Wainwright, Arthur W. *The Trinity in the New Testament*. London: SPCK 1975.

Ware, Bruce. A. *Father, Son and Holy Spirit: Relationships, Roles, and Relevance*. Wheaton, IL: Crossway, 2005.

Ware, Bruce A. "How Shall We Think about the Trinity?" In *God Under Fire*, edited by Douglas S. Huffman and Eric L. Johnson, 254–77. Grand Rapids, MI: Zondervan, 2002.

Webster, John. "God's Perfect Life." In *God's Life in Trinity*, edited by Miroslav Volf and Michael Welker, 143–52. Minneapolis: Fortress Press, 2006.

Webster, John. "Non ex aequo: God's Relation to Creatures." In *Within the Love of God: Essays on the Doctrine of God in Honour of Paul S. Fiddes*, edited by Anthony Clarke and Andrew Moore, 96–108. Oxford: Oxford University Press, 2014.

Webster, John. "Trinity and Creation." *International Journal of Systematic Theology*, 12, no. 1 (2010): 4–19.

Weinandy, Thomas, G. "Cyril and the Mystery of the Incarnation." In *The Theology of St. Cyril of Alexandria: A Critical Appreciation*, edited by Thomas G. Weinandy and Daniel A. Keating, 55–74. London: T&T Clark, 2003.

Weinandy, Thomas G. *Does God Suffer?* T&T Clark: Edinburgh: 2000.

Weinandy, Thomas G. "Does God Suffer?" *First Things: A Monthly Journal of Religion & Public Life*, no. 117 (2001): 35–41.

Weinandy, Thomas G. *The Father's Spirit of Sonship: Reconceiving the Trinity*. Edinburgh: T. & T. Clark, 1995.

Welker, Michael. *God the Revealed: Christology*. Translated by Douglas W. Stott. Grand Rapids, MI: William B. Eerdmans Publishing, 2013.

Westphal, Merold. "Hegel, Pannenberg, and Hermeneutics." *Man and World* 4, no. 3 (1971): 276–93.

Whitehead, Alfred North. *Process and Reality: An Essay in Cosmology*. Gifford Lectures 1927–28. Edited by David Ray Griffin and Donald W. Sherburne. New York: Free Press, 1978.

Wiarda, Timothy. "Theological Exegesis and Internal Trinitarian Relations." *Scottish Journal of Theology* 76, no. 2 (2023): 99–111.

Williams, Rowan. *Arius: Heresy and Tradition*. London: Darton, Longman & Todd, 1987.

Williams, Rowan. "Balthasar and the Trinity." In *The Cambridge Companion to Hans Urs Von Balthasar*, edited by Edward T. Oakes, SJ and David Moss, 37–50. Cambridge Companions to Religion. Cambridge: Cambridge University Press, 2004. doi:10.1017/CCOL0521814677.004.

Williams, Rowan. *A Margin of Silence: The Holy Spirit in Russian Orthodox Theology*. Éditions du Lys Vert, Québec, 2008.

Williams, Rowan. "*Sapientia* and the Trinity: Reflections on the De Trinitate." In *Collectanea Augustiniana*, edited by B. Bruning, M, Lamberigts, and J. Van Houtem, 317–20. Leuven: Leuven University Press, 1990.

Williams, Rowan. *Sergei Bulgakov: Towards a Russian Political Theology*. Edinburgh: T&T Clark, 1999.

Wittgenstein, Ludwig. *Philosophical Investigations*. Translated by G. E. M. Anscombe. 2nd edition. Oxford: Blackwell, 1998.

Wright. N. T. *Jesus and the Victory of God: Christian Origins and the Question of God*. London: SPCK, 1996.

Yocum, John. "A Cry of Dereliction? Reconsidering a Recent Theological Commonplace." *International Journal of Systematic Theology* 7, no. 1 (2005): 72–80.

Yoder, Timothy J. "Hans Urs von Balthasar and Kenosis: The Pathway to Human Agency." PhD Diss., Loyola University Chicago, 2014.

Young, Frances M., and Andrew Teal. *From Nicaea to Chalcedon: A Guide to the Literature and Its Background*. 2nd ed. London: SCM Press, 2010.

Youngs, Samuel. *Making Christ Real: The Peril and Promise of Kenosis*. Eugene, OR: Pickwick Publishing, 2022.

Youngs, Samuel. "Rehabilitating Kenotic Christology: A Critically Constructive Examination and Strategic Systematization of Jürgen Moltmann's Doctrine of Christ." PhD diss., King's College London, 2017.

Youngs, Samuel J. "Wounds of the Emptied God: The Role of Kenosis at the Cross in the Christologies of Jürgen Moltmann and Sergius Bulgakov." *American Theological Inquiry* 4, no. 2 (2011): 45–58.

Zizioulas, John D. *Being as Communion: Studies in Personhood and the Church.* London: Darton, Longman & Todd, 1985.

Zizioulas, John D. "The Doctrine of the Holy Trinity: The Significance of the Cappadocian Contribution." In *Trinitarian Theology Today: Essays on Divine Act and Being*, edited by Christoph Schwöbel, 51–52. Edinburgh: T&T Clark, 1995.

Index

actus purus, 8, 37
annunciation, 169
Arian, 5, 22n9, 18. *See also* semi-homoisian; subordination
Aristotle, ix, 32, 69n48
aseity, xxii, xxvn15, xxxn78, 10–12, 44, 55, 56–58, 60–65, 66n2, 115, 130; in Bulgakov, 76–77. *See also* fullness; perfection
attributes, divine: communicable, 79, 81, 100–101, 103, 106, 117; incommunicable, 102. *See also* biblical; perfection

Baillie, Donald, xix–xx
Balthasar, Hans urs, 115; abandonment of Son, 119–22; cry of dereliction, 121–22; triune difference, 117–18. *See also* Christology; the Cross; Hegel; Holy Saturday; immanent and economic Trinity
baptism, xii–xiv, xxviin38, 128, 170
Barth, Karl: divine perfections, 21, 37, 51n49, 123; relationality with world, 57, 61–62, 68n34; revelation, xiii, 15–16, 27n67, 27n70, 27n72, 154; simplicity, 41–42, 51n56
begetting, 61, 78–79, 80–81, 95–96, 107
begotten, 4, 78, 80, 82, 156

biblical: attributes of God, 3, 33–34, 36–38, 45, 56; depictions of Trinity, xii–xiii, xv, xvi, xxviin30, xxviin45, 7, 14–15, 19–21. *See also* Scripture
breathes, 74, 110n23, 118
Bulgakov, Sergeĭ, 73; Divine Self-Positing, 4, 7–8, 75–76, 86; diving suffering, 84–85; kenosis 78–80, 82–84. *See also* aseity; Christology; the Cross; Hegel; immanent and economic Trinity; sophiology

Cappadocians, x, 6, 23n17
Christology: xix–xx;, xvii; 73; 87n2; kenotic, xix–xx, xviiin60, xxixnn63–64; 165n77; 87n2, 115–17, 126. *See also* Jesus Christ.
Church, the, 158, 167; early Trinitarian theology of, 5–6, 35–36, 39; hierarchical relations, 18–19, 90n74; kenosis and, 148–49, 165n77, 170; praxis, 139–40, 150–52, 156–57, 159; triune God and, xvii, 156. *See also* creeds
classical theism, 31–33; basis of Divine Self-Enrichment, xviii, xxi–xxii, 37, 77, 105, 115; early church and, 35–36; rejection of, xxivn15, 10,

34–35, 43–48, 48n2, 56, 63; support for, 48n2, 105, 115
communication, xiii, xix, 10, 14, 16, 17, 21, 126, 142, 152–57. *See also* revelation; speech
community: divine, 6, 42, 67n25, 94, 99; human, 152–53, 155, 156, 168
creation: correspondence to God, 127, 144–45, 147–48; distinct from God, 4, 9, 11–14, 36, 43, 68n44, 144–46; fallenness of, 146–47; God's relation to, xiii, xviii, xxii, xxx, 44–46, 56, 60–61, 63–65, 105–7, 116, 168; God's revelation in, xiii, 8, 14–18, 27n67, 57, 125; kenosis and, xxixn63, 65, 85, 125–26, 140; potentiality of, 74–75; well-being of, x, xii, xxiii, 55, 84, 108, 128, 130; *See also* God; love; Sophia
creeds: Chalcedon, 73, 76, 80; Nicene, 4–5, 23n10, 39–40, 104
the Cross, xiv, xx, 45, 47, 65, 84–85; Balthasar's views, 116–18, 132n28, 132n34, 120–24, 129; Bulgakov's views, 91n92; Moltmann's view, 58–62, 67n20
Cusa, Nicholas, 41, 53n82

Damascus, John of, 39–40
death, 134n54, 146–47, 148, 162n21. *See also* Jesus Christ
disability, xi, xxvn23, 57, 158–59
Divine Self-Enrichment, xi, xxi–xxiii, 71, 98, 107–8, 115, 130; aseity and, 55, 62, 76–77, 104–5, 124; axiom of, xvii–xviii, 3; characteristics of, 141–44; as foundation for human enrichment, 56; Hegelianism and, xviii; International Aid and Development and, xxvin25; kenosis and, 78–79, 81, 84–85, 102–4, 106, 123; logic of, 3–4; not as deficiency, xi–xii, 55, 65–66; objections to, xxii, 33, 37, 55, 56; perichoresis and, 6–7, 40; revelation and, 14–21;

simplicity and, xviii, xxi, xxxn78, 33–35, 37–38, 40, 42–43, 48; triune relations and, 6–7, 75, 93, 95–96, 100–101. *See also* classical theism; kenotic-enrichment; immanent and economic Trinity; Paul, Apostle
divine: all-blessedness, 3, 33, 47, 56, 64, 71, 76–77, 78–79, 82–86, 106, 107, 119, 146, 170; distinctions, 110n19; imitation of, 126; *ousia*, 5, 40, 74, 79, 87n8. *See also* attributes, divine; freedom; narcisscism; perfection; Trinity
Divine-Dance, xi, xxvn16, xxviin37, 7, 71, 97, 125, 137, 139
doxology, 139, 170

ecclesiology, xvii, 148–49
enriching-kenosis. *See* kenotic-enrichment
enrichment: actualised in worship, 139–40, 167–71; communal, 7–8, 86, 158; definition of, xi–xii, xxii; delayed, 83, 84, 86, 91n90, 151, 165n79; egoistical, xxiii, xxxn78, 61, 79–80, 140, 141, 146–48; symbiotic with kenosis, xvii, xxviiin60, 61, 78–80, 82–83, 86, 112n63, 123, 129, 137
equality: humans, 157–59; of divine persons, xvi, 5, 18, 19–20, 80–81, 109n12, 118, 143
eschatology, 14, 106–7, 108, 145, 167, 168, 172n17; kingdom, 84, 85, 114n96, 106–8. *See also* future; Pannenberg, Wolfhart
Eternal Functional Subordination (EFS), 18–19
eternal kenosis, xix, xxixn65, 60, 83
evil, xxx, 46, 47, 155
exegesis, xii, 19, 102, 135n83. *See also* hermeneutics

Father: abandonment of son, 59–60, 119–24; activity of, 112n57; deity of, 4–5, 7, 78, 109n12, 113n77,

117, 143; kenosis of, xx, xxixn65, 79, 82–83, 89n37, 102–4, 112n57, 117–18, 124, 149; monarchy of, 66n2, 80–81, 96, 99, 157; perfection of, 3; relation to Trinity, xiii–xiv, xix, 39, 61–62, 75, 78, 94–96, 100–101, 109n9; self-revelation of, 74
freedom, 149; divine, 11–13, 24n34, 34–35, 45–46, 50n23, 57, 68n34, 88n27, 132n28, 142, 149; human, 46, 150–51, 153; of self-giving, 150, 169; restriction of, 9, 48
fullness: divine, xvii–xviii, 38, 41, 55–56, 58, 61–62, 65, 74, 76, 98, 104–5, 108, 113n77, 115, 124; kenosis and, xx, 82, 84, 86, 129; of well-being, 55, 86, 144, 167, 170. *See also* pleroma

generation and procession, 78, 82, 94, 110n15, 118. *See also* Relations of Origin
gift and receipt: freedom of, 142, 149–52; intratrinitarian, xiii, xiv, xvii, xxiii, 9, 20, 75, 82, 108, 130, 141; within human relations, 147–48, 149–52, 155, 158
glorification, xii, xiv, 79, 82–84, 98, 120, 129
God, 26n61; contingent on creation, 10–12, 47, 119; distinct from creation, 3–4, 11–14; and the future, 93, 97, 104; oneness of, xxii, xxvin31, 3–5, 6, 22, 39, 40, 42, 141, 143. *See also* divine; monotheism; Trinitarian; Trinity

Hegel, 25n49, 43, 98; Balthasar and, 118–19, 124; Bulgakov and, 76; Pannenberg and, 97–98, 104–5, 114nn85–86, 114n88
heresies, 22nn9–10, 48n2
hermeneutics, xiii–xiv; xvi. *See also* Scripture
Holy Saturday, 116, 117–24

the Holy Spirit, 4; as bond, 78, 89n45, 119, 168; deity of, 5, 39, 42; divine person, 5, 74, 75; humanity and, 63–64, 108, 147, 156, 167, 168–69, 172n15; kenosis of, 79–80, 104; passivity, 81–82; procession of, 4, 74, 78–79, 89n45, 80–82; Son and, xiv, 80
homoousios, 22, 51n56, 39
hypostases, 40, 22n7. *See also* persons

image of God, 6, 8, 14, 46, 47, 60, 127, 144, 145, 149, 158
immanent and economic Trinity, xiii, xxviin37, 4, 25n41, 25n49, 27n72, 27n81, 16–17, 21, 60, 140, 154;
immutability, xviii, 11, 31–32, 33, 34, 36, 43, 48n1, 115, 118, 130, 131n2
impassibililty, xviii, 31–34, 36, 48nn1–2, 50n23, 50n32, 85, 115; *ad extra* and *ad intra*; xxi, 9, 10, 17–18, 36; Balthasar and, 116–17, 127–28, 132n28; Bulgakov and, 74–75, 77, 91n92; conflation of, 44–45, 57; logic of Divine Self-Enrichment and, 9–12, 14, 77; Pannenberg and, 97, 108, 110n24, 114n86; rejection of, 34–35, 48n2 62–63, 68n44. *See also* passibility
inseparable operations, xvii, 5, 51n55, 52n62, 39–40
Intratrinitarian: dialogue, 127–28, 135n83, 154; movement, x, xvii, xxi, xxviiin58, 6, 43, 56, 57, 94, 96, 116, 117, 123, 168, 171. *See also* perfection; perichoresis
Irenaeus, 39

Jesus Christ: ascension of, 84; death of, 59, 60, 85, 116, 118, 119–21, 122, 123, 129, 133n39; divinity of, xx, 4, 21, 116; forsakenness, 58–60, 119, 122–23; imitation of, 160n11, 101, 112n73; Incarnation, xix–xx, xxi, xxviiin60, 5, 36, 38, 85, 101, 103,

169; obedience of, 106, 112n63; as revelation of God, 16, 38, 93, 123, 125–26. *See also* baptism; the Cross; Father; Holy Spirit; resurrection; the Son

kenosis: communicable attribute, as, 22, 82, 103–4, 116–17; dangers of 150, 159, 162n31, 165n76, 120; enriching-kenosis, xviii, xxiii, 78, 82–85, 103, 108–9, 123, 127, 137, 140, 141; feminist objections, xxiii, xxxin80, 81, 90n69, 120, 133; Incarnation and, xxixn63, 60, 62, 83–84, 91n90, 117, 129, 134n54, 135n85, 167; kenotic theologies, xxixn63–64; meaning, 113n73; Philippians 2, xxviiin60, 22, 78, 83, 96, 102, 159, 162n31; as receipt, 141, 157–59; suffering and, 84–85, 86; Trinity and, 73, 78–84, 121–22, 130; truncated-kenosis, xxiii, xxxn78, 79, 80, 85, 91, 101, 102–3, 119, 123, 140, 141, 146–48, 169; voluntary, 64, 81, 82–84, 142, 149–52, 163n34, 168; vulnerability in, 159–60. *See also* Christology; the Church; Divine Self-Enrichment; Father; Holy Spirit; kenotic-enrichment; love; Moltmann, Jürgen; perichoresis; power; the Son

kenotic-enrichment, xvii–xviii, xxiii; characteristics of, 142–43, 148–49; as equal being in mutual dependency, 157–60; as free and volitional gift and receipt, 149–52; as interpersonal communication, 152–53; as symbiotic speech and act, 154–57

kingdom, xiii, 7, 93, 100–101, 103–4, 137; goal of, 105–6, 108. *See also* eschatology; reign

knowing: epistemological constraints, xvi, 15, 16–17; epistemological mystery, xvi, 10; God, x, xvi, 9, 14, 21, 51n49, 53n82, 105, 110n17, 135n91; inter-personal, 127, 152–53; within Trinity, xiii, 42, 76, 83, 126, 130, 142

Lacugna, Catherine, 10–14, 16–18, 56–57
Liebner, Albert, xix–xx
logos, xxixn63, 64, 76, 79, 154. *See also* Word
lordship, 93, 95–96, 100, 103, 105, 110n25, 112n57
love: divine nature, 11, 13, 26, 81, 88n27, 116, 142; humanity, 64, 147, 163n43, 167; kenosis and, xix, 61, 79, 81, 103, 112n57, 112n73, 117–18; suffering and, 34, 47, 58–61, 68n44, 84–85, 91n95, 119–21; towards creation, xxii, xxviin37, 13, 56–57, 58, 61–62, 125, 132n28, 168; triune, xiii, xiv, xxviin37, 6, 40, 42, 57, 62, 74, 76, 79, 83, 87n1, 97, 126

MacKinnon, Donald, xix, 165n77, 170
Mary, mother of Jesus, 168–69. *See also* annunciation; Theotokos
metaphysics, xxi; absolute necessity, 44, 45, 57; accident, 6, 22, 32, 38, 39, 55, 58, 66; Greek, 31–41, 44–45, 50n32, 54n99, 69n48, 77; Hegelian, 44, 48; potentiality, xxii, 32, 33, 44–46, 74, 82–83, 84, 86, 139, 146, 161n16. *See also* classical theism; Hegel; modal collapse
modal collapse, 44–46, 54nn99–100
modalism, 5, 8, 75, 109n6
Molnar, Paul, 10–12, 17
Moltmann, Jürgen, 6; cry of dereliction, 58–59, 67n25, 89n53, 121; divine passibility, 34, 59, 84; immanent and economic Trinity, 45, 58, 91n92, 97; rejection of aseity, 58, 60
monotheism, 33, 41, 53n88, 61, 63, 94. *See also* God
mutability. *See* immutability.

narcissism, xxii, 9, 56, 58–62, 83
Nyssa, Gregory, 23nn16–17, 40, 131n15

panentheism, 17, 28n86, 44, 63
Pannenberg, Wolfhart, 93; eschatological Trinity, 97–98, 105–6; Reciprocal Self-Distinction, 7–8, 93–95, 107, 110n19; retroactive permanence, 105, 108. *See also* immanent and economic Trinity; Hegel; reign
pantheism, 17, 44, 63
passibility. *See* impassibility; Moltmann, Jürgen; suffering
paternal. *See* Father
Paul, Apostle, xvi, xxvin30–31, 65
Pelagian, xxiii, 140, 167
Pentecost, 168
perfection: as triune movement, xii, 65–66, 75, 78, 115; human participation in, 127, 170; of God, x, xii, xviii, xxii, 3, 10, 31–32, 38, 55–56; of hypostases, 40
perichoresis, xiv, xvii, 3–7, 8–9, 23n15, 23n17, 39, 40, 93; criticism of, xv, 6–7; kenosis and, 117. *See also* Divine-Dance
Personhood, 8, 126, 158. *See also* persons
persons: activity of, xvii, xxiii, 8–9; divine, 57, 81; hypostatic distinction 3, 5, 60–61; perfection of divine, 40; prosopon, xxvin30, 22n7; tri-hypostatic, 3, 8, 20, 73, 75, 79, 80, 86, 98, 100–101, 125, 149, 157; triune relations, 20, 60–61. *See also* equality; hypostases; personhood
pleroma, xx, 33, 47, 77, 141, 146. See also fullness.
pneumatology, 67n25, 89n53. *See also* the Holy Spirit
power: asymmetry of, 157–58, 163n42; dominance as, 19; intratrinitarian, 100, 103, 106, 112; in vulnerability, 29n101, 82; kenosis and, xxxn76, 29n101, 78, 165n79. *See also* reign
praise, xiii, xviii, 63, 64, 69n54, 108, 112n63, 154, 170
prayer, xiii, 84, 95, 126–28
process theology, 43, 54n110, 88n12, 98, 105, 113n82

Rahner's Rule, 25n41
Relations of Origin, xiv, xxiii, 20–21, 78–79, 94–97, 99–100, 107, 109n9, 109n11. *See also* generation and procession
resurrection, xiv, 62, 84, 96, 97, 116, 121–24
revelation: of divine nature, 29n100; of the Trinity, 21, 117. *See also* communication; Divine Self-Enrichment; Father; Jesus Christ; Karl Barth; Scripture
rule. *See* reign
reign: of God, 95–97, 108; in Pannenberg, 97, 106, 108, 114n85, 145. *See also* kingdom
redemption, 19, 29n100, 64, 65, 86, 120, 123, 127, 139, 140, 146, 147. *See also* salvation

sacrifice, xxxin80, 75, 78–79, 84–85, 86, 91n95, 126, 149
salvation: as communion with God, 63, 64; economy of, xv, 10, 11, 15, 16, 17, 19, 21, 60; for humanity, 107. *See also* redemption
Scripture: interpretation of, xv–xvi, 7, 18–21, 29n104, 97, 127–28; Old Testament and, 35, 128, 135n83, 154; as revelation, xii, 38, 96; Trinitarian hermeneutic, xii–xiv, xvii, xxvin31, xxviiin53, 7, 14, 20, 93–95, 116, 128. *See also* biblical
self-sufficiency. *See* aseity
semi-homoisian, 101, 109
sheol, 118

simplicity: contemporary views, 41–42; definition, 6, 32; incarnation and, xxi, 31, 39; Nicolas of Cusa, 41; Patristics and, 38–40; perichoresis and, 6; rejection of, 10, 34; theological purpose of, xxi, 36, 38, xxxn78; Trinity and, 31–32, 33, 37–38, 43, 52n57; tritheism and, 33, 38, 39. See also actus purus; Divine Self-Enrichment; metaphysics; perichoresis

sin, 80, 140, 146–48

Social Trinitarianism, xi, xv, 6, 145

the Son: kenosis of, 22, 30n115, 81, 83–84, 102, 112n68. See also Holy Spirit; Jesus Christ; subordination; Word

sonship, 59, 101

Sophia, 73–75, 77, 82, 84, 87n8, 137; Divine and Creaturely, 74, 76–77, 87n8, 88n12, 147–48

sophiology, 73, 78, 87n1, 88n12. See also Sophia

speech: human, 127, 155–56; intratrinitarian, 125–26, 128, 130, 142, 154; truth and, 155; verbal and non-verbal, 142, 154, 155–57. See also communication

spiration, 78, 94, 107. See also breathes; generation and procession; Holy Spirit

submission, 82, 99, 112n57, 159

subordination: evangelicals and, xv, 18; mutual, xxixn65, 20–21, 106, 112n57; problems of Trinitarian, xv–xvi, 18–21, 80, 99–101; reversed, 20, 29n105; of the Son, 99–102, 111n51, 111n56, 157, xv; as Trinitarian heresy, 5, 38–39, 109n6; of women, xxxin79, 18, 90n74, 164n67. See also Arian; Eternal Functional Subordination (EFS); hierarchy; semi-homoisian; submission

suffering. See kenosis; love; passibility; sacrifice

theodicy, 34, 47, 67n20,

Theotokos, 168, 170

Trinitarian: abundance, xxii, 9, 37, 38, 41–42, 48, 55–56, 65, 116, 123, 146; dynamic v static ontology, 8, 31–32, 36–38, 43, 55, 63, 69n48, 75; unity, xvii–xviii, 23n16, 75,79, 81, 86, 94, 96, 100, 108, 109n9, 117–19, 123–24. See also equality; Trinity

Trinity: broken Trinity view, 60, 89n53, 122; imitation of, xxiii, 14, 47, 48, 116, 139, 144–45, 155, 160n11, 160n12; oneness and threeness, 3–4, 23n16, 41, 46. See also biblical; the Church; Divine Self-Enrichment; Father; God; immanent and economic Trinity; inseparable operation; kenosis; love; monotheism; perfection; Simplicity; Trinitarian

tritheism, xvii, xxi, 3, 5–6, 8, 32, 75, 122

well-being: Church and the, 167; deficiency of, xi–xii, xviii, xxii, xxiii, xxxn78, 33, 55–56, 61, 63–64, 74, 76; difference of human and divine, 84, 105, 108, 143–48; distortion of, 33, 146–48; divine, x, 71, 76, 79, 86, 128, 130, 141; divine characteristics of, 125–28; general concepts, ix; goal of divine, xviii, 106; human actualization of, x, 14, 145, 147, 79–80, 127, 129, 137, 139–40, 148–60; human desire for, ix–x, 105; organizations for, 150–52, 155, 156–57; secular views, x, 152, 156; source of human, x–xii, 47, 55, 77, 107, 139. See also fullness; Trinitarian, abundance

Word: and act, 154–56; creation and salvation, 161n18; immortal, 85; incarnate, 64, 125–126; of God, xii, 78, 146, 154; the Son and 16n72, 78, 81. See also logos worship: as communion with God, xxii–xxiii, 63–65, 69n54, 139–40, 167, 168–71; intratrinitarian, 125–28, 112n63

About the Author

Jacqueline Service (PhD) is lecturer of systematic theology at St. Mark's National Theological Centre and associate head of school in the School of Theology at Charles Sturt University, Australia, where she lectures in Trinitarian theology, Christology, ecclesiology, and theological anthropology. With a background in international aid and development, she is also currently on the editorial board of *Religion & Development*, an open access journal at Humboldt-Universität zu Berlin.